An Indian Summer

An Indian Summer

The 1957 Milwaukee Braves, Champions of Baseball

THAD MUMAU

McFarland & Company, Inc., Publishers
Jefferson, North Carolina, and London

Unless otherwise credited, all of the photographs were provided by the National Baseball Hall of Fame Library, Cooperstown, New York.

LIBRARY OF CONGRESS CATALOGUING-IN-PUBLICATION DATA

Mumau, Thad.
    An Indian summer : the 1957 Milwaukee Braves, champions of baseball / Thad Mumau.
       p.   cm.
    Includes bibliographical references and index.

    ISBN-13: 978-0-7864-3011-6
    (softcover : 50# alkaline paper) ∞

    1. Milwaukee Braves (Baseball team) — History.   I. Title.
GV875.M5M85 2007
796.35709775'95 — dc22   2007002399

British Library cataloguing data are available

Cover photograph: Milwaukee Braves celebrate victory over the New York Yankees in game seven of the World Series, October 10, 1957 *(AP Photo)*

Manufactured in the United States of America

McFarland & Company, Inc., Publishers
  Box 611, Jefferson, North Carolina 28640
  www.mcfarlandpub.com

With much love to Dahlia
and to our girls, Erika and Laura

Acknowledgments

I have so many people to thank. My wife, Dahlia, is the best person I have ever known and certainly my best friend. I am grateful for her always being there for me and for being so calm and positive. Our daughters, Erika and Laura, are also wonderful people, and I am very proud of them for what they have accomplished and especially for the fine people they have become. These three fabulous ladies are my life.

I thank Laura so much for her enormous help in making this book a reality. She was my special editor and an extremely valuable one. Laura is my baseball buddy. We have attended games together and talked about baseball since she was a little girl. Like me, she has a warm feeling for baseball in the fifties and sixties, and she has an extensive knowledge of players from that era. She knows the game. Because of this, Laura was able to do much more than catch typographical and grammatical errors when reading the manuscript. She also strengthened the content with baseball-related observations and suggestions. Laura's contributions were enormous.

My parents loved sports and believed they played an important part in a boy's life. My dad bought me a baseball glove when I was eight years old and taught me about the game I would come to love. My mother was the fiercest competitor I have ever known. My parents were tremendously loving and supportive. They taught me about commitment and loyalty, and they did it through their examples. They were simply the best, the same phrase I use to describe my sister, Judy. Everyone would want her for a sister.

Above all, I thank God for good health, good opportunities, and good family. I am truly blessed.

Contents

Preface

This is the story of the 1957 Milwaukee Braves, arguably one of the all-time best baseball teams and certainly one of my favorites.

It was two days after my eleventh birthday, July 11, 1957, when my dad took me to old Forbes Field to see the Braves play the Pittsburgh Pirates. In the bottom of the first inning, the Pirates' leadoff batter, Bill Virdon, hit a pop-up to short center field. Braves center fielder Billy Bruton and shortstop Felix Mantilla had a terrible collision, and several minutes later, the two players were taken from the field through an exit right beside our seats. It was the only major league game I saw that summer.

My dad was a Pirates fan, but for some reason I had pulled hard for the Braves since I was eight. Seeing Spahn, Aaron, Mathews, and those guys in person was a treat. Following them through that '57 season was great, especially when they won the World Series.

This book takes readers through that exciting season, beginning with the Braves' near-miss of 1956. All of the key players are profiled, and the book is a day-to-day journey from the start to the end of the schedule. Transactions and injuries are an important part of every season, and they are also detailed. The seven-game World Series with the Yankees is chronicled nearly inning by inning.

Researching this project was fun, but tedious, too. I pored over scanned and microfilmed issues of *The New York Times*, scrutinizing game stories and box scores for forgotten and unknown facts about the club, their games, and their season. A number of reliable webpages — chief among them, Retrosheet. org and baseball-reference.com — proved helpful, too; they allowed me to quickly double-check information from print and electronic sources, fill in gaps in the stats and game logs, and confirm or disprove hunches before they developed into full-blown theories.

1

From Beaneaters to Braves

The feared New York Yankees appeared on the brink of working their fabled comeback magic once again as they loaded the bases with two outs in the ninth inning of Game Seven, with power-hitting Moose Skowron at the plate.

Skowron, a dangerous right-handed batter, pulled the ball sharply and ripped a hard ground ball between the bag and Milwaukee third baseman Eddie Mathews. The smash appeared headed for the left-field corner, a probable double, but Mathews speared the ball with a nice back-hand play, ran to the bag for the force out, and the game was over. So was the 1957 World Series, and the Braves were champions!

The Yankees were in their heyday, and it was a bit surprising whenever they did not win the World Series. But everyone knew they would have their hands full this time. In fact, it was apparent from the outset of the 1957 season that the Milwaukee Braves had what it took to be world champions. They realized that potential because their big-time players had big-time years and their complementary players put together outstanding seasons.

It was no fluke that the Braves dominated the National League and then won the World Series, where the New York Yankees showed up for their nearly annual appearance only to come up short. Milwaukee's three best starting pitchers combined for fifty-six wins, and the Braves' pitching staff led all of the major leagues in complete games. The Braves hit more home runs and scored more runs than all the other teams in both leagues, and Milwaukee's defense was second in the NL in fielding percentage and double plays.

The Braves' franchise figures quite prominently in the history of major league baseball, and the 1957 model is an exciting part of the story. Milwaukee had superb pitching, powerful hitting, and veteran leadership. All of the parts had gradually been put in place for a championship, and the Braves delivered.

The Braves are the only major league franchise to win World Series championships in three different cities. It happened twice while the team was based in Boston, once in Milwaukee, and there has been one world title in Atlanta.

The current Braves have become legendary for their long string of consecutive division championships. Without nearly as much fanfare, the Milwaukee Braves of the late 1950s also put together an impressive streak.

In fact, the Braves were the best team in the National League from 1956 through 1959. Their 365–251 record during that stretch was second-best in the major leagues only to the mighty New York Yankees, with the slim margin of just one game separating Milwaukee and the Pinstripes.

Aaron, Spahn, Mathews, and Burdette were household names for the Braves' fans in the latter half of the 1950s, when Milwaukee proudly flew two National League pennants and a World Series championship flag.

Divisional play had not yet materialized in those days. There were just eight teams in both the National and American League back then, and the team that finished in first place at the end of the regular season was the pennant winner. There were no playoffs, except when there was a tie for first place, and the two league champions met in the World Series, which was the only postseason.

Those who followed America's Pastime, and particularly folks who welcomed a major league team to Milwaukee and then bade it farewell within a span of thirteen years, could also reel off names like Schoendienst, Crandall, Logan, Adcock, and Buhl without batting an eye. Bruton, Covington, Torre, McMahon, Pafko, and many others did their part to make the Braves' four-year ride one to remember.

But 1957 was the year when the Milwaukee Braves won it all. The '57 season was a classic as the Braves started and finished the regular season with a bang, beat the storied Yankees in the World Series, and boasted the NL Most Valuable Player, baseball's Cy Young Award winner (there was only one back then), and the World Series MVP.

The year 1957 was special for a myriad of reasons. The United States Congress passed the Civil Rights Act and President Dwight Eisenhower ordered troops to Little Rock, Arkansas, to integrate the schools. Sputnik I and II were launched. The Cold War was under way. Mao Tse Tung was in power in China.

American Bandstand, Leave It to Beaver, and *Perry Mason* premiered on television, while *I Love Lucy* was in its last year of original episodes. Steve Allen was host of *The Tonight Show*. The Pulitzer Prize was awarded to John F. Kennedy for *Profiles in Courage*. Chevrolet turned out the Bel Air that is still considered one of the classic cars of all time. Ford introduced the Edsel.

Elizabeth Taylor had her second divorce and third marriage, and both of the men involved were named Michael. *The Music Man*, starring Robert Preston, opened on Broadway, and so did *West Side Story*. Humphrey Bogart died. Fred Astaire and Audrey Hepburn starred in the movie *Funny Face*. Dr. Seuss wrote *The Cat in the Hat*.[1]

In baseball, the Yankees played in their twenty-fifth World Series. Stan Musial of the St. Louis Cardinals won the National League batting title for the seventh time with an average of .351. Musial also set an NL record by playing in his 823rd consecutive game.

At the age of thirty-nine, the Boston Red Sox' Ted Williams led the American League with a batting average of .388, missing his second .400 season by five hits. In addition to winning his fifth batting title, The Splendid Splinter became the first AL player to hit three home runs in one game twice in a season. Williams lost the American League Most Valuable Player Award to Mickey Mantle of the Yankees by one vote.

The National League approved the move of the Dodgers and Giants to the West Coast. The Dodgers played and won their last game in Ebbets Field before moving to Los Angeles. The Giants played and lost their last game in the Polo Grounds before moving to San Francisco. The visiting team in both games was the Pittsburgh Pirates.

Jackie Robinson was no longer playing for the Dodgers. He announced his retirement from baseball. What most fans do not remember, or do not know, is that Robinson was traded before he quit. Brooklyn sent him to the rival New York Giants for journeyman pitcher Dick Littlefield and $30,000. Robinson said he would not report to the Giants, retiring instead, and the deal was voided on December 13, 1956, the same day it was made. The Cleveland Indians' brilliant left-handed pitcher, Herb Score, was hit in the face by a line drive off the bat of the Yankees' Gil McDougald and would never be the same again.[2]

The Braves franchise is the oldest in terms of consecutive years in the majors, having begun as the Boston Red Stockings in 1871, and like any club, it has had its share of ups and downs.

The modern-day Braves ran off an amazing string of fourteen consecutive division championships in Atlanta, but that city also saw its share of losing teams, with seven straight sub-.500 seasons prior to the 1991 division title that started the big ball rolling.

Losing was also a way of life in Boston where the Braves won eight National League titles in the nineteenth century, but also managed to finish above .500 only five times in a span of twenty-nine years. And from 1903 to 1912, the closest the Braves came to first place was when they ended thirty-two games behind the league champ. They finished fifty-one or more games out of the lead seven times and were buried sixty-six games back of the pennant winner in their worst effort.

Milwaukee was different. In a thirteen-year stay there, the Braves never had a losing season. The highlight came in 1957 when the Braves defeated the New York Yankees in seven games to win the World Series. Milwaukee just missed back-to-back world championships, losing to the Yanks in seven games in the 1958 Series.

Boston changed its nickname from the Red Stockings to the Beaneaters in 1883, to the Doves in 1907, and then to the Pilgrims in 1909. The club became the Braves in 1912 and kept that moniker until the owners of the team asked newspapermen to choose a new nickname from suggestions by the fans. The team was known as the Bees from 1936 to 1940 before changing back to the Braves for the 1941 season, and that name has stuck.[3]

Strangely enough, the Braves' nickname was originally selected because the team owner was a member of a northeastern Tammany Hall political organization that called itself the Braves.[4]

The 1914 Boston club is known as the Miracle Braves as a result of an unbelievable comeback, considered the greatest ever in big league baseball. On July nineteenth, Boston was 33–43, fifteen and one-half games behind the first-place New York Giants in the National League standings.[5]

The Braves went on a 34–10 tear, won sixty-one of their last seventy-seven games, and ran away with the NL pennant, passing seven teams in the standings along the way and finishing ten and a half games in front of the Giants. Boston then swept the Philadelphia Athletics in four games to win the World Series.

The Braves set a futility record by losing their 110th game of the season in September of 1935 and went on to drop 115, a National League record until the 1962 New York Mets lost 120 in a 162-game schedule. Boston's 1935 winning percentage of .248 is the worst in the NL since the start of the twentieth century.

It was during the 1935 season that Babe Ruth hit his last home run, and he did it as a Brave. After retiring from the Yankees, the Babe signed with the Braves as a player and first base coach in hopes of becoming the Boston manager the following season, something that did not happen. Ruth did manage a final blaze of glory when he blasted three home runs against the Pirates in Pittsburgh. On the third roundtripper, he tipped his cap to the Forbes Field crowd as he circled the bases for the 714th, and last, homer of his fantastic career.

Boston won the 1948 National League pennant behind the pitching duo of southpaw Warren Spahn and right-hander Johnny Sain. They carried the Braves and inspired this poem published by the *Boston Post*: "First we'll use Spahn, then we'll use Sain; then an off day, followed by rain; back will come Spahn, followed by Sain; and followed we hope, by two days of rain."

They combined for thirty-nine of the Braves' ninety-one victories, with Sain winning twenty-four games and Spahn fifteen. However, Boston ironically had a better record in games not started by Spahn or Sain than in the games they did start.[6]

Casey Stengel, who managed ten American League pennant winners and seven World Series champions with the New York Yankees, spent time as the Braves' manager before he became a genius. He was the Boston Braves' skipper from 1938–1943. Stengel's best season with the Braves was his first, when the team's record was 77–75, good for a fifth-place finish. The team never came close to .500 under Casey again.

His final year on the Braves' bench started with a bad omen as he was hit by a taxi. He suffered a broken leg and missed the first forty-seven games of the season. Stengel was fired after the 1943 season.

Dismissing Stengel was one of first things done by new owners Lou Perini, Guido Rugo, and Joseph Maney after purchasing the Braves' franchise in January of 1944. Boston won the 1948 National League pennant, sold more than one million tickets for three straight years, then saw attendance plummet by eighty percent by the end of the 1952 season. Rugo sold his share of the ball club to Perini and Maney in 1951. Perini, who owned a construction business, bought controlling interest of the Braves.[7]

Tired of losing fans and media attention to the Red Sox, Perini looked for another city. Browns owner Bill Veeck was experiencing the same frustrations trying to compete with the Cardinals in St. Louis, and he also sought a new home for his team. The city of Milwaukee caught the eye of both men.

Perini blocked the Browns' attempt to move to Milwaukee as he invoked his territorial privilege. That was in March of 1953. Just one month earlier, Braves players arrived at spring training in Bradenton, Florida, still wearing a B on their caps. They left with new caps and a new place to play.

The Braves' move to Milwaukee triggered several switches in franchise location. The Browns moved to Baltimore and became the Orioles in 1954. The Athletics moved from Philadelphia to Kansas City in 1955 and eventually moved to Oakland in 1968. The Dodgers and Giants both landed in California in 1958.

Although no one had known it at the time, the last game at Braves Field in Boston was on September 21, 1952, with the Brooklyn Dodgers winning, 8–2. The final win for the Boston Braves franchise came six days later in Brooklyn, when the Braves downed the Dodgers, 11–3. Eddie Mathews slammed three home runs for the Braves as they ended a ten-game losing streak.

The next day, September 28, 1952, marked the last game for the Boston Braves, a twelve-inning 5–5 tie with the Dodgers at Ebbets Field. The Braves' average home attendance was a pathetic 3,653 for the 1952 season.

The Braves left Boston after seventy-seven years with ten National League titles and two World Series championships. Their move to Milwaukee for the 1953 season was the first switch of a major league franchise in fifty years.[8]

Milwaukee was a city that had strongly supported a minor league team since 1902. The Brewers had played in tiny Borchert Field. County Stadium was built in 1950 in hopes of luring a major league team, and when it was announced that the Braves were coming, the city of Milwaukee went wild. Their enthusiasm was reflected at the turnstiles as the Braves passed their 1952 season attendance total in just their thirteenth home game and went on to set a major league attendance record of 1.8 million. That happened despite the fact that the Braves had made a frenzied move with no off-season promotion or ticket sales.

The Braves won their debut game as a Milwaukee franchise on April 13, 1953, shutting out the Reds, 2–0, in Cincinnati as Max Surkont pitched a three-hitter. The next day, Warren Spahn was on the mound for the Braves as they played for the first time in County Stadium. Billy Bruton hit a disputed home run in the tenth inning, the ball glancing off the glove of Cardinals outfielder Enos Slaughter, to give Milwaukee a 3–2 win.[9]

Milwaukee finished the 1953 season with a record of 92–62, thirty games over .500 and good for second place in the National League standings, but thirteen games behind the first-place Brooklyn Dodgers. Mathews led the league with forty-seven home runs and drove in 135 runs, second to Brooklyn catcher Roy Campanella, who had 142 RBI. Spahn posted the league's lowest earned run average of 2.10 and equaled the twenty-three wins of Philadelphia's Robin Roberts to lead the National League and all of baseball. Bruton, the speedy center fielder, had a league-leading twenty-six stolen bases.

Spahn and Mathews were selected for the All-Star Game, which was played in Cincinnati. Mathews walked and scored the first run for the National League and Spahn pitched two hitless innings to earn the win in a 5–1 victory.

The Braves set a record by slugging a dozen home runs in a doubleheader at Pittsburgh, with Jim Pendleton and Mathews hitting three homers apiece, Johnny Logan smacking a pair, and Joe Adcock, Del Crandall, Sid Gordon, and Jack Dittmer each hitting one.

It was a grand beginning. The team's success and the large fan turnouts inspired an immediate renovation to County Stadium, which had a seating capacity of 36,011. That was increased to 43,394 for 1954.[10]

The Braves would contend for the National League flag the rest of the decade, grabbing third place in 1954 and finishing second behind the Brooklyn Dodgers in 1955 and 1956 before winning the pennant in 1957 and 1958 and sharing first place with the Los Angeles Dodgers in 1959.

Milwaukee loved its Braves, and the Braves were an easy team to love. Their success was obviously a big part of the allure. Any team beating the New York Yankees in a World Series back then was considered quite the ticket, and the Braves did that, bringing the franchise its first world championship in forty-three years. The attraction was more than victories and titles, though.

The personalities that made up the club were interesting and entertaining. Spahn, the winningest lefty of all time, and right-hander Lew Burdette formed a rare pitching duo. Both men were superb hurlers who were also fine hitters and fielders, and both were fierce competitors and fun-loving pranksters.

Mathews, the slugging third baseman, and underrated shortstop Johnny Logan were scrappers who could hold their own in any brawl. They also more than held their own at the plate in clutch situations, while doing a better-than-average job of plugging the left side of the infield.

There was no shortage of talent on those Milwaukee Braves teams of the 1950s. The cast included four players whose plaques hang in Cooperstown. All-time major league home run leader Hank Aaron, Spahn, and Mathews are in the Hall of Fame for what they accomplished as Braves, while Red Schoendienst anchored infields in Milwaukee, New York, and St. Louis from his second base position before going on to an outstanding career as a manager.

Spahn and Burdette joined Bob Buhl to give Milwaukee three starting pitchers as good as any trio in the big leagues during that time. It was a staff that combined for sixty complete games and nine shutouts in 1957, during an era when "quality start" meant going the distance and winning. It was mighty hard to take the ball from those three guys, and there was seldom good reason to do so.

The Braves signed Aaron in June of 1952. He earned Rookie of the Year honors in the Northern League that year and debuted with the Milwaukee Braves less than two years later. He stepped into the starting lineup during spring training in 1954 when Bobby Thomson broke his ankle sliding into second base. Needless to say, Hammerin' Hank was there to stay.

Aaron and Mathews provided a devastating one-two power punch, teaming up to blast seventy-six of the Braves' 199 home runs in 1957, while the crafty Schoendienst and opportunistic Logan comprised a solid keystone combination and knocked in many a big run.

Slugger Joe Adcock and slick-fielding Frank Torre, Joe's older brother, platooned at first base. Del Crandall was like a manager on the field, a catcher who really hit when it counted. Billy Bruton, Wes Covington, and Andy Pafko were Aaron's most frequent outfield partners, with Bob "Hurricane" Hazle and even Bobby "The Giants Win The Pennant" Thomson seeing action.

The 1950s and 1960s formed what many believe to be the golden era of baseball. The Brooklyn Dodgers and New York Giants shared a fierce rivalry with each other in the National League and with the Yankees of the American League as New York was the hub of the American Pastime.

The 1950s were an especially wonderful time with all of the old ballparks tucked into the hearts of cities, frequent Sunday doubleheaders, and shirt-sleeved crowds in the outfield bleachers.

There were tremendous hitters like Teddy Ballgame, Stan the Man, the Mick, Big Klu, the Say Hey Kid, Campy, the Hammer, Yogi, the Duke, Frank Robinson, Gil Hodges, Ralph Kiner, Al Rosen, and Eddie Mathews.

Don Newcombe, Bob Lemon, Whitey Ford, Carl Erskine, Early Wynn, Virgil Trucks, Curt Simmons, Billy Pierce, Robin Roberts, and Spahn were among the best to toe the rubber.

It was a magical time for baseball, and nowhere was it more magical than Milwaukee, where the Braves were embraced, appreciated, and loved. The Green Bay Packers would become the most successful professional sports franchise ever in Wisconsin, but the Braves were that state's team in the fifties, and they were the first to make Milwaukee famous.

The 1956 season meant everything to the Milwaukee Braves' 1957 run to the National League pennant and World Series championship. The foundation had already been established in previous years in terms of key players being secured. But there were two very important things about the Braves' 1956 season.

First of all, the Braves learned that they could contend till the end; they could win a pennant. More importantly, however, they did not win the pennant—and this left both a bad and good taste in the players' mouths. Finishing one game behind the Dodgers in 1956 left them disappointed, but confident as they looked ahead to the '57 season.

Milwaukee had been a distant runner-up twice in the decade, finishing thirteen games back of Brooklyn in the National League in 1953 and thirteen and one-half games behind the Dodgers in the 1955 standings. In 1956, the Braves were honest-to-goodness contenders as they fought it out with the Dodgers and Cincinnati Redlegs in a hotly contested three-team pennant race.

Milwaukee, Brooklyn, and Cincinnati all won more than ninety games that season, while none of the other five NL teams even managed a .500 record over the 154-game schedule.

Brooklyn was obviously the team to beat. The Dodgers were defending World Series champs and had won three of the last four National League titles. Pee Wee Reese, Carl Furillo, Jackie Robinson, Duke Snider, Roy Campanella, and Gil Hodges fueled the offense.

The Dodgers' pitching was solid, led by veterans Don Newcombe, Carl Erskine, and Clem Labine, with second-year man Roger Craig joining manager Walter Alston's starting rotation. The staff included a couple of youngsters named Koufax and Drysdale, future Hall of Famers who would combine to win just seven games that year. Adding savvy and true grit to the mound corps was Sal Maglie, known as "The Barber," who was purchased by Brooklyn from the Cleveland Indians in the middle of May.

The Cincinnati Redlegs were surprise contenders in the National League race, having finished no higher than fifth place in the previous three years. They packed plenty of wallop in a lineup filled with power hitters, but the pitching was suspect. Skipper Birdie Tebbetts spent a long season trudging to the mound to change hurlers.

Rookie Frank Robinson joined Gus Bell and Wally Post to give the Redlegs one of the more potent offensive outfields in the league. Ted Kluszewski, whose arms were so large that he started a baseball fashion trend by cutting out the sleeves of his uniform, was a first baseman who hit the long ball and hit for average.

Ed Bailey and Smokey Burgess were both good-hitting catchers. Slick fielding shortstop Roy McMillan and second baseman Johnny Temple formed a fine double play combination.

Cincinnati tied a National League record by hitting 221 home runs in 1956, with five players belting twenty-eight or more. The power surge sparked an offense that led the league in runs scored with an average of five per game. However, the pitchers allowed over four runs a contest.

Post slugged thirty-six home runs for the Redlegs and Kluszewski hit thirty-five, Bell twenty-nine, and Bailey twenty-eight. Leading Cincinnati's home run parade was the new kid, Frank Robby, who hit thirty-eight to set what was then a major league rookie record (broken by Oakland's Mark McGwire, who hit forty-nine in 1987).

Brooklyn and Milwaukee placed second and third, respectively, in the NL home run race. The Dodgers got a league-leading forty-three from Snider, thirty-two from Hodges, twenty-one from Furillo, and twenty from Campanella for a total of 179 homers.

Adcock led the Braves in home runs with thirty-eight, Mathews hit thirty-seven, Aaron twenty-six, and Bobby Thomson twenty for a team total of 177 homers.

There was talk that the Dodgers and Giants were both thinking about building new stadiums. The Dodgers, who played fifteen games of the '56 season in Jersey City, were considering other locations in Brooklyn. The Giants were discussing a stadium in Manhattan that would seat more than 100,000 people at a cost of nearly seventy-five million dollars.[11]

Before the season started, on April 9, Milwaukee made a trade that appeared insignificant at the time, but would loom large more than a year later. The Braves dealt first baseman George Crowe to Cincinnati for virtually unknown outfielder Bob Hazle and a player to be named later. The player turned out to be Corky Valentine, who was sent to Milwaukee in May.

Milwaukee opened the season on April 17 with a 6–0 win over the Chicago Cubs as Lew Burdette pitched a five-hitter. Aaron and Adcock slammed home runs. A crowd of 39,760 watched the Braves win their fourth home opener in as many tries since moving into County Stadium. Fans braved thirty-nine-degree temperatures along with rain and snow that fell over the last four innings.

Two days later, Bob Buhl pitched seven strong innings as the Braves downed the Cubs again, 3–1. Buhl, a notoriously poor hitter, drove in a run with a double, and right fielder Hank Aaron threw a runner out at the plate. The following day, in St. Louis, Eddie Mathews blasted two home runs and went three for three, while rookie Wes Covington delivered a two-run pinch-hit homer. Bobby Thomson's long sacrifice fly drove in the winning run in Milwaukee's 5–4 win over the Cardinals.

The Braves won their first three games and used a five-game winning streak to take nine of their first twelve. Cincinnati started slowly, losing five of its first six games, then won six in a row. Brooklyn was victorious in seven of its first nine outings before dropping seven of eight.

Rain plagued Milwaukee's April schedule as the club played just seven games in the opening month. By the end of May, the Braves had a 19–10 record, putting them two games ahead of the Redlegs and three up on the Dodgers.

The month of May saw Carl Erskine of the Dodgers pitch a no-hitter against the Giants and Pittsburgh Pirates first baseman Dale Long hit home runs in eight consecutive games to set a major league record. Three Cincinnati pitchers combined to hold Milwaukee hitless for nine and two-thirds innings before the Braves went on to win, 2–1, in eleven innings.

June did not start well for the Braves. They lost their first three games and suffered through two more three-game slides in the opening twelve days of the month. When teams struggle, particularly if they are expected to contend for the pennant, managers often get fired. And that is what happened in Milwaukee.

Charlie Grimm began the 1956 season as the Braves' manager, having been on the job since he replaced Tommy Holmes early in the 1952 campaign. The Braves finished seventh in the National League standings that season.

The next year, the club's first in Milwaukee, the Braves had a 92–62 record and finished second behind Brooklyn. In 1954, Milwaukee dropped to third place, then returned to second in '55. Entering the 1956 season, Grimm's managerial record with the Braves was 317–263.

All that mattered was the current record. The Braves had lost twelve of the last seventeen games and were 24–22 in the middle of June. They were in fifth place, while the shocking Pittsburgh Pirates were in first. Roberto Clemente and Bill Mazeroski, both Hall of Famers, were in the early years of what would be long careers as Pirates. Brooklyn, St. Louis, and Cincinnati were also ahead of the Braves in the standings when the Milwaukee front office decided a change was needed.

Right in the middle of a four-game series in Brooklyn, Grimm was asked to resign. Fred Haney, one of the Braves' coaches, took over on June 17 as the team's manager. Milwaukee immediately became red-hot, winning its first eleven games under Haney, including two on his first day on the job. First baseman Joe Adcock ignited the win streak by smashing three of his thirteen career home runs at Ebbets Field in the Braves' doubleheader sweep.

Adcock belted a game-winning homer in the ninth inning of the first game, his shot off Ed Roebuck landing on the roof and making him the only player ever to hit a ball up there. The drive sailed over the 350-foot mark in left field and cleared an eighty-three-foot wall.

When the winning streak started, Milwaukee was three and a half games out of first place. When it ended, the Braves owned a two-game lead. At the end of June, they held a one-game edge over the Dodgers and Redlegs.

Cincinnati and Brooklyn had thirty-seven victories apiece, one more than Milwaukee, but the Braves had three fewer losses than both of those teams. Pittsburgh lost eight in a row and eleven of twelve games near the end of the month to tumble out of the National League lead, starting a downward spiral that would take it out of contention.

Griffith Stadium in Washington, D.C., hosted the July 10 All-Star Game. The National League won, 7–3, as future Hall of Famers Stan Musial, Willie Mays, Ted Williams, and Mickey Mantle hit home runs.

Four Braves were selected to the team by a vote of players. Hank Aaron and Warren Spahn both played in the game, while Eddie Mathews was not used. Del Crandall was replaced on the NL roster because of an injury.

At the break, Cincinnati was in first place in the National League standings, leading Milwaukee by one and a half games and Brooklyn by two.

The season resumed on July 12, with the Dodgers and Braves beginning a four-game series in Milwaukee. A crowd of over 41,000 jammed into County Stadium to watch the Braves' Bob Buhl shut out Brooklyn. It was his fifth victory of the season over the Dodgers. Joe Adcock belted his thirteenth home run of the year and the 100th of his career.

The Braves won a doubleheader the next day, with Adcock going deep in each game. His homer in the nightcap was a grand slam. The Braves' July 13 twin wins moved them past Cincinnati and into first place, one game ahead of the Redlegs. Milwaukee would remain there for almost two months.

Sal Maglie had a shutout in the seventh inning of the series finale until Adcock smacked a two-run roundtripper to tie the score. Aaron drove in the game-winner in the ninth as Milwaukee completed a sweep of Brooklyn.

Adcock had homered in five straight games, and half of his sixteen long balls had come off of Dodger pitching. His streak was stopped the next day by Pittsburgh as the Braves played their second twinbill in three days.

Milwaukee took two from the Pirates, as Warren Spahn went the distance in the first game, with Adcock hitting his sixth home run in seven games in the second contest. Aaron's eleventh homer of the season provided the difference as Buhl threw another complete game for his eleventh win.

The sweep of the Pirates made it seven wins in a row for the Braves. They lost to the Giants, won three straight, and then won two of three from the Phillies. Dating back before the All-Star Game, Milwaukee had played twenty successive games at home, winning fifteen of them.

A three-game sweep in the Polo Grounds gave the Braves a five-game win streak and fifteen victories in their last seventeen outings. On July 26, Milwaukee led the National League by five and a half games over Cincinnati.

It was the largest lead by any NL team in 1956. Brooklyn trailed by six full games before mounting an eight-game winning streak late in the month.

St. Louis, which began July only three games out of first place, won only nine of twenty-five outings during the month and plunged eleven games behind the league-leading Braves. The National League race was reduced to three teams with two months remaining on the schedule.

On August 18 at Cincinnati's Crosley Field, the Redlegs tied a major league record by slugging eight home runs in a 13–4 pounding of the Braves. Bob Thurman hit round trippers in three consecutive at-bats, with Frank Robinson and Ted Kluszewski leaving the park twice, and Wally Post adding a long ball.[12]

The Dodgers won six straight near the end of August and closed the gap between themselves and Milwaukee to two and one-half games, with the Redlegs another game back and in third place. The Braves were feeling the heat, and Brooklyn, a veteran club accustomed to winning pennants, was turning it up.

Milwaukee played .600 baseball in August, but lost ground to the Dodgers, who had a .667 winning percentage for the month. There was one month remaining in the season, and the Bums of Brooklyn were feeling confident. They had prevailed down the stretch in numerous pennant races. The Braves really had not experienced such pressure.

After the Braves won both games of a doubleheader from the Cubs at Chicago's Wrigley Field on September 9, Milwaukee held a one-game lead over the Dodgers, with the Redlegs trailing by three games.

The Braves paid a two-day visit to Ebbets Field, having beaten the Dodgers in eleven of twenty meetings so far in the season. Two important incidents took place before the first pitch was thrown.

Braves general manager John Quinn announced that Fred Haney would return to manage Milwaukee for the 1957 season. And Braves pitcher Lew Burdette took advantage of a chance meeting with Jackie Robinson under the stands to smooth a rocky situation.

When the Dodgers had played in Milwaukee in late August, Robinson took exception to Burdette's taunts of "watermelon stomach," resulting in the Brooklyn first baseman firing a baseball into the Braves' dugout during infield practice.

Beneath the bleachers, the Milwaukee pitcher apologized to Robinson, saying there was no place in baseball for racial insults and that his remark was in reference to Jackie having gained some weight around his middle. Robinson accepted the apology and said Burdette's remarks were gratifying.[13]

Facing perhaps the biggest game of the season for his club, Brooklyn manager Walter Alston sent Sal Maglie to the mound against Dodger killer Bob Buhl. The Barber out-pitched Buhl and drove in two runs, with Gil Hodges hitting a solo homer as Brooklyn won, 4–2, in front of more than 33,000 fans.

Milwaukee's runs came on Joe Adcock's thirty-sixth home run and Eddie Mathews' thirty-fifth. Brooklyn and Milwaukee were dead even atop the National League standings at 83–55, the first time since July 13 that the Braves had not been alone in first place.

The following day, the Braves jumped back in front by a game with an 8–7 win as Adcock smashed home run number thirty-seven, his thirteenth roundtripper against the Dodgers, tying the NL record for homers by a batter against one team in a season.

Buhl, the losing pitcher the previous day, pitched an inning of scoreless relief to pick up the win, his eighth of the season over Brooklyn. It was the first time since 1916, when Grover Cleveland Alexander recorded eight victories over the Phillies, that a National League pitcher had beaten a team that many times in one season.

A two-game sweep of the visiting Redlegs gave the Dodgers eight wins in a nine-game span and a one-game lead over the Braves, with Cincinnati falling four games behind with less than two weeks left in the season.

Milwaukee pulled even with Brooklyn with eight games to play, and the two teams matched each other win for win and loss for loss over the next four games, with Maglie throwing a no-hit shutout at Philadelphia.

Warren Spahn pitched and batted the Braves into the lead. He threw a six-hitter for his twentieth win and helped himself with a two-run double as Milwaukee downed the Redlegs. The Dodgers then lost to the Phillies.

With three games left for both teams, Milwaukee led Brooklyn by one game. Cincinnati, which had only two games to play, was two and a half games out of first place, but still had a chance to share the top spot in the standings.

The Braves played their final series against the fourth-place Cardinals at Sportsman's Park in St. Louis. The Dodgers stayed home at cozy Ebbets Field for three games with Pittsburgh, which was on its way to a seventh-place finish. The Redlegs visited Wrigley Field for a pair of meetings with the last-place Cubs.

The Cardinals nipped Milwaukee by a run twice, while Brooklyn took a doubleheader from the Pirates. The Braves and Dodgers switched places in the standings, and the last day of the season dawned with Milwaukee trailing Brooklyn by one game. The Braves had to win their finale, and they needed some help from Pittsburgh.

They didn't get it. Lew Burdette earned his nineteenth victory and Eddie

Mathews belted his thirty-seventh home run as Milwaukee did its part. But the Pirates couldn't, and the Braves saw the dismal news on the Sportsman's Park scoreboard in the sixth inning of their contest: Brooklyn 8, Pittsburgh 6.

The Dodgers finished one game in front of Milwaukee and two ahead of Cincinnati in the National League standings. It was the Dodgers' fourth pennant of the decade and it was to be their last as a Brooklyn franchise.

Hank Aaron was one of several Braves who enjoyed an outstanding season. At the age of twenty-two and in his third season in the big leagues, he led the National League with a .328 batting average and was the only major league player to get 200 hits.

Aaron also led the league with 340 total bases and with thirty-four doubles. His fourteen triples were one less than teammate Billy Bruton, the league leader.

Warren Spahn, who was thirty-five years old, was a twenty-game winner for the seventh time while starting a string of six straight years that he would win twenty or more. Spahnie smacked three home runs, giving him seven in two years. Lew Burdette won nineteen games and Bob Buhl won eighteen.

Milwaukee's pitching staff led the National League with a 3.11 earned run average. Burdette and Spahn, with 2.70 and 2.78, respectively, were one-two in ERA in the league. Burdette was the league leader in shutouts with six and Spahn had three. Spahn pitched twenty complete games, Burdette had sixteen, and Buhl thirteen as Braves pitchers went the distance a league-leading sixty four times.

Aaron finished third in the National League's most valuable player voting and Spahn was fourth. Brooklyn's Don Newcombe won the MVP award as well as the first Cy Young Award ever presented after posting a 27–7 record. Twenty-year-old Frank Robinson of Cincinnati was a unanimous pick as the NL Rookie of the Year after batting .290 and scoring 122 runs to go with his thirty-eight homers.

The Yankees defeated the Dodgers in seven games to win the World Series, which was highlighted by Don Larsen's perfect game.

October for Braves fans was filled with dreams of what might have been and what could possibly happen in 1957. When the '56 season ended in St. Louis, the Braves flew back to Milwaukee, where they were welcomed by nearly 20,000 appreciative fans.

All of those people, along with the ones getting off the plane after playing 154 games, could only borrow the infamous battle cry attributed to the Dodgers for so many seasons: "Wait till next year."

2

Getting a Fast Start

The Milwaukee Braves could not wait to start the 1957 season, and it was no surprise when they jumped to a fast start, winning their first five games and nine of the first ten. Along the way, a young slugger came of age, the Braves made a huge trade that provided some much needed glue, and a hurricane blew in from nowhere at just the right time. Those events and many more made for a very special summer. Indeed, it was a '57 classic.

Sportswriters and broadcasters polled during spring training predicted the Braves and New York Yankees would win their respective pennants and meet in the World Series. The predictions were based on Milwaukee's strong pitching backed by a hard-hitting lineup, and those qualities were showcased in the first week of the season.

Milwaukee's opening-day starting lineup looked like this:

Danny O'Connell	2B		Johnny Logan	SS
Hank Aaron	LF		Billy Bruton	CF
Eddie Mathews	3B		Del Crandall	C
Joe Adcock	1B		Warren Spahn	P
Bobby Thomson	RF			

Warren Spahn was the Braves' opening day pitcher, and he threw a four-hit complete game in a 4–1 victory over the Cubs at Chicago's Wrigley Field on April 16. Cubs hurler Bob Rush broke up a scoreless duel with a run-scoring double in the fifth inning. The Braves answered quickly with a four spot in the sixth. Hank Aaron singled and scored on Eddie Mathews' triple. Joe Adcock singled in Mathews and came around on Johnny Logan's home run.

The Braves played their home opener two days later, with more than 41,500 fans jamming County Stadium. Lew Burdette quieted the powerful Cincinnati Redlegs as the right-hander went the distance and allowed six hits in a 1–0 Milwaukee win. Aaron took care of the scoring with a home run in the sixth inning. An inspection of the box score revealed that Aaron played right field in the second game of the season after being in left for the opener. Right field would remain in Aaron's capable hands for most of the next eighteen years, while left field would be shared by no fewer than a dozen Braves in 1957.

The contest took only two hours and three minutes to play, but there was much more action after the last pitch had been thrown. Redlegs manager Birdie Tebbetts provided some fireworks by angrily referring to Burdette as a cheater.

"Before today, I have never said that Burdette threw a spitball," Tebbetts said, "but he went to his mouth before every pitch all day long. He's a cheating spitballer. Why should I complain, though? It hasn't done me any good for the last three years.

"I don't say he is the only man in the league who throws a spitball, but he is the only one who has utter disregard for the rules."

Burdette laughed when told of Tebbetts' comments and said, "It's a perfect day — I've got Birdie chirping. It's the best pitch I've got, and I don't throw it."

Back in Cincinnati, Redlegs general manager Gabe Paul said a protest would be sent to National League President Warren Giles, with a request for clarification of the rule that defines what a pitcher cannot do to a ball.

Reached in New York, Giles said he could not comment on the protest or the rule "at this time." But he added, "Until someone — the umpires or someone — presents evidence that he (Burdette) is using the spitter, I'll do nothing about it."[1]

Tebbetts, who would manage Burdette in Milwaukee at the end of the 1961 season and all of the '62 campaign, was understandably frustrated. The fidgety pitcher had just beaten Cincinnati for the eighth time in a row over a span of nearly two years.

The next day, the Braves scored three first-inning runs and held on to nip the Redlegs, with Tebbetts using seven pinch-hitters. Milwaukee completed a three-game sweep as Spahn scattered nine hits for his second route-going win. He repeatedly escaped early trouble before settling down to allow just one hit over the last five innings in the 3–1 victory. Catcher Del Crandall, who had homered in the previous game, singled in a pair of runs.

The Braves got some unusual fielding help. Cincinnati third baseman

Don Hoak was a baserunner at second base when Wally Post sent a bouncer between second and third. Hoak fielded the ball cleanly and tossed it to Milwaukee shortstop Johnny Logan. Hoak was automatically out for being hit with a batted ball, while Post was credited with a single.

Aaron doubled and homered, Adcock belted a home run that traveled 425 feet, and they joined Billy Bruton in driving in two runs apiece in a 9–4 victory over the visiting Cubs. Bob Buhl went seven innings to earn his first win as the Braves improved to 5–0.

The Braves received good news from the league office when Giles said neither he nor his umpires believed Burdette was guilty of throwing spitballs. In his announcement, the NL president said, "There is nothing in the rule that I can interpret as prohibiting a pitcher from moistening his fingers if he does not apply the moisture to the ball. If a pitcher, after appearing to moisten his fingers, wipes them off, that to me is sufficient evidence that the moisture (if any) that may have been on his fingers is not applied to the ball.

"As to the specific mention of Birdie Tebbetts' complaint about Burdette," Giles continued, "I personally have watched Burdette and studied his actions and inquired of all our umpires, including veterans such as Larry Goetz, Babe Pinelli, Lee Ballanfant, and others, and neither I nor they are of the opinion that he has, up to now, violated the intent or language of Rule 8.02."

Giles also issued a statement referring to instructions to umpires on April 18, 1955, about Rule 8.02. Those instructions said, in part: "There is nothing in this rule which prevents the pitcher from going to his mouth with his fingers, providing he does not apply moisture to the ball or expectorate on the ball or glove. Accordingly, umpires will not consider going to the mouth, or wiping the hands or fingers on neck or forehead as an infraction of the rule, if the pitcher wipes those same fingers off before touching the ball."[2]

Burdette, although he did not make a public response, was overjoyed. He knew every team and every batter in the league would be watching him closely, trying to determine if he was, indeed, wetting the baseball. That was exactly what he wanted. Anything to break the hitter's concentration was just one more weapon for the pitcher.

Chicago rookie Cal Neeman hit a game-winning home run off Burdette in the tenth inning to end Milwaukee's season-opening win streak, but the Braves started another one the next day. Crandall smacked a walk-off homer decades before the term was used to describe a roundtripper that ends a game. Home runs accounted for all of Milwaukee's runs as Aaron and Mathews both slammed three-run shots and Adcock added a solo blast in an 8–7 win over St. Louis.

The Braves made it four straight wins with their second three-game sweep of Cincinnati in less than two weeks. Adcock connected twice, and Crandall and Logan also left the park in support of Spahn, who pitched his third complete game in as many starts. One of Adcock's homers was a grand slam.

Burdette also went the distance, while Adcock and Aaron slugged homers, giving the Braves ten roundtrippers in their last three games. The Crosley Field crowd, aware of the controversy over Burdette allegedly throwing spitballs, booed the right-hander when he wiped his brow, touched his cap, moved his fingers to his mouth, and wiped his hands time after time.

The Braves made it six consecutive wins over the Redlegs despite a wild streak by both Taylor Phillips and Red Murff, who combined to issue ten bases on balls. Milwaukee's defense bailed out the two hurlers by turning four double plays. The Braves' four-game win streak gave them nine victories in their first ten games. Adcock had two hits, but had his homer streak stopped at three games.

Milwaukee obviously had the ingredients to win the National League pennant. Sportswriters, however, questioned the Braves' lack of activity on the trade market over the winter. Manager Fred Haney explained there was no burning need to make a deal; however, writers pointed out that the Braves had glaring weaknesses at second base and in left field. Haney also spent considerable time during the early part of 1957 looking over his shoulder at the 1956 season.

Much had been written about the Braves letting the league title slip away after being in first place for 122 days. Jackie Robinson, the Dodgers' star who retired following the '56 season, accused many of the Milwaukee players of keeping late hours that affected their performances on the field. Haney sensed that his discipline—or lack thereof—was being scrutinized. He seemed to feel a need to constantly remind people, particularly himself, that the Braves had what it took to outdistance the other eight NL teams to the finish line in 1957.

"The Dodgers are going to find it tougher to beat us this year," Haney said on the afternoon before his team would play the Giants in New York. "We are a better team because they will have to beat us. We're not going to beat ourselves. The little fundamentals we worked on all spring could pay off. That is probably why we are winning the one-run games.

"Just a couple of days ago, Hank Aaron rushed in from right field to back up a third-to-first overthrow and prevent an extra base. Last year, he never would have made that play. They are the plays that pay off. Stop an extra base here and there. They make the difference."[3]

Hours later, former Brave Johnny Antonelli pitched a seven-hitter and ripped a two-run homer in the Giants' 4–0 shutout of Milwaukee at the Polo Grounds, leaving the Braves with a 9–2 record for the month of April. The Braves' front office had been strongly criticized for getting rid of the young left-hander. Antonelli was twenty-three years old and coming off a 12–12 season with a 3.18 ERA when he was sent to the New York Giants with infielder Billy Klaus, southpaw pitcher Don Liddle, and catcher Ebba St. Claire, along with $50,000 for outfielder Bobby Thomson and catcher Sam Calderone.

The trade was made in February of 1954. In Antonelli's first season with the Giants, he won twenty-one games with a 2.30 earned run average, and he was again a twenty-game winner in 1956. People were wondering what it would be like if Milwaukee had him in the same rotation with Spahn, Burdette, and Buhl.

The Braves won three straight in Pittsburgh, all in extra innings, with Spahn getting a win and a save.

The ageless wonder — he had turned thirty-six a week earlier — pitched all ten innings and drove in a run, giving him four complete games in four starts. The score was 1–1 after nine innings. In the top of the tenth, Milwaukee second baseman Danny O'Connell tripled and scored on Aaron's single. After Mathews grounded into a force out, Frank Torre and Thomson belted back-to-back home runs for a 5–1 Braves victory. It was career victory number 207 for Spahn, who had allowed only five runs over thirty-seven innings in the young season.

Burdette squandered a three-run lead in the ninth, then watched as the Braves scored three times in the tenth to give him his third win. Milwaukee pounded out eighteen hits, five by Aaron, with O'Connell singling in the go-ahead run and later scoring in the tenth inning. Red Murff struck out the side to finish things.

The Braves wasted an even bigger lead the following day. They were ahead by six runs, but the Pirates scored three in the seventh and, just as they had the day before, three in the ninth. Thomson's single plated the winning run in the eleventh inning, making Pittsburgh relief ace Elroy Face the losing pitcher for the second straight day. Aaron drove in four runs with a single, a double, and a homer.

The Pirates threatened in their half of the eleventh with a double and a walk, and that sent Haney to the mound. He signaled for his ace, and Spahn came in to get the last out and nail down the win for Murff. Spahn had pitched ten innings two days earlier.

It is doubtful if today's fans would see such a move, especially just two weeks into the season. Sometimes, with post-season berths on the line or in the playoffs or World Series, a starter might be used in relief. But the fact that Haney called on his best pitcher, one who was thirty-six years of age and had gone ten innings just forty-eight hours earlier, said a lot about the times and about Spahn.

Vernon Law quieted the Milwaukee bats, throwing a two-hitter as the Pirates avoided a sweep with a 1–0 win. Juan Pizarro, the Braves' twenty-year-old rookie left-hander, allowed one run in seven innings. The Braves were 6–2 halfway through a long road trip, giving them a 12–3 overall record, with visits to Brooklyn, Philadelphia, and St. Louis coming up.

Every game at Ebbets Field was a big game for a team hoping to win the National League pennant. So, although it was only May 5, the Braves felt some extra adrenaline pumping as they opened a two-game series with the Dodgers. Nursing a one-game lead over Da Bums, Milwaukee sent Dodger nemesis Bob Buhl to the mound, while Brooklyn countered with Sal Maglie.

A crowd of nearly 27,000 showed up for an anticipated pitcher's duel, but were treated instead to an offensive show. Four pitches into the contest, Milwaukee had two runs after singles by O'Connell and Aaron. Dodger center fielder Duke Snider, normally an outstanding defensive player, let Aaron's hit get through him. It rolled all the way to the wall, and both Braves scored.

The Dodgers responded with five runs in the bottom of the first, three coming on Roy Campanella's drive into the left-field bleachers. Buhl's work day was a short one. He took an early shower after getting roughed up for five hits and five runs, while committing an error on a tap back to the box, in two-thirds of an inning.

Aaron singled and scored on Mathews' double in the third inning, but the Dodgers added two runs for a 7–3 lead. Maglie was gone by then, replaced by Don Bessent. He pitched the fourth and failed to get an out in the fifth as the Braves scored three runs in both innings, the last two off losing pitcher Rene Valdes. Aaron, who slammed a three-run home run in the fourth inning, had four hits in five at-bats and scored four times in raising his batting average to .417.

Ernie Johnson, a right-handed relief pitcher who would later gain tremendous popularity as an Atlanta Braves broadcaster, proved the man of the day for Milwaukee. He pitched the final six innings, allowing no runs and one hit, while striking out five Dodgers. Johnson also helped with his bat, getting an RBI single in the Braves' three-run sixth when they grabbed a 9–7 lead.

Milwaukee scored again in the eighth inning, and Johnson got out of trouble in the ninth. The Dodgers put two runners on base with one out and appeared to be in business when Carl Furillo hit a sinking line drive into

Ernie Johnson was reliable out of the bullpen, pitching long and short relief. The tall right-hander, an extremely popular Braves broadcaster in later years, won seven games and saved four more in 1957 while posting a 3.88 earned run average.

left-center field. Andy Pafko, who had replaced Braves left fielder Wes Covington for defensive purposes, made a spectacular catch from the seat of his pants.

That took the wind out of the Dodgers' sails, and the game ended moments later when Gil Hodges bounced to Logan at short. He flipped to

O'Connell to force Snider coming down from first for the final out of a game that had lasted more than three hours. The Braves owned a two-game lead over Brooklyn.

The thirty-two-year-old Johnson, who had not pitched since an April 7 exhibition game, retired sixteen Dodgers in a row before Gino Cimoli's pop-fly base hit in the ninth. Center fielder Billy Bruton and O'Connell each had three of the Braves' sixteen hits.

New York Times columnist Arthur Daley took advantage of the Braves being in town and made an appointment to meet with Milwaukee manager Fred Haney in his hotel room the morning after his club had defeated the Dodgers.

Haney was sipping coffee after a late breakfast and showing the effects of the beginning stages of a cold. He admitted the cold would bother him a lot more if the Braves had not won four of their last five games. Daley wanted to talk about Burdette and the accusations that he was throwing a spitball, and the skipper was accommodating.

"When I was managing Pittsburgh," Haney said, "I had heard about Burdette and the spitter. I even went in the runway with high-powered binoculars and studied him. I couldn't detect a spitter, but I was still curious when I first came to Milwaukee as a coach.

"When I was a young player, I hit against some real good spitball pitchers — Red Faber, Urban Shocker, Stan Coveleskie, and John Quinn. So I saw plenty of spitters, and I never saw one rotate on its way to the plate. They sort of float up like knucklers, which may be why they sometimes call the knuckler 'a dry spitter.' But every pitch that Burdette throws spins.

"I have been fortunate during my major league career in being close to the two soundest men ever on baseball theory, Ty Cobb and Branch Rickey," Haney continued. "They say that it's the friction of the air on a spinning ball that makes a curve. On a warm day with light atmosphere, a curve doesn't break well. Curves break sharper at night.

"I've played in Mexico City and Denver and Salt Lake, all cities with high altitudes. It's difficult to throw a good curve there, while a batted ball will travel farther. But let's get back to the spitter. All the old type spitball pitchers chewed slippery elm, and they'd put big gobs on the ball. I really doubt that one can be thrown with just a little moisture because it won't be enough to catch the air friction and make the pitch dip.

"Listen," Haney said to Daley, "there are roughly eighty pitchers in this league. I'll bet that not more than five would even know how to take a scuffed-up ball and make it do tricks the way the old-timers could. The others wouldn't know how to hold it or handle it or deliver it.

"When a fast ball, curve, sinker, or slider is thrown, the ball rolls off the pitcher's fingers and that makes it spin as it comes to the plate. A knuckler is pushed and doesn't rotate. A spitter slides off the pitcher's fingers and doesn't get that initial spinning impetus. That's why it doesn't rotate any more than a knuckler does. Every pitch thrown by Burdette rotates. He doesn't throw a spitter."

Daley finished his column by writing, "Mr. Haney thereupon dismissed the class on spitball pitching."[4]

That night, Burdette was on the mound for the Braves, matched against Brooklyn right-hander Don Drysdale. The Dodgers took a 3–1 lead on Furillo's three-run homer in the first inning. Eddie Mathews smashed a pair of home runs, one in the first inning and another in the sixth, the second blast landing deep in the center field seats.

Clem Labine relieved Drysdale and got out of a bases-loaded jam in the seventh, but Adcock hit a solo home run to tie it at 3–3 in the eighth. Burdette twice escaped big trouble, both times on double plays. Brooklyn loaded the bases with one out in the ninth inning, but pinch-hitter Elmer Valo grounded to second baseman O'Connell, who tossed to Logan, the shortstop firing to Adcock at first. In the tenth, Burdette issued two walks before Pee Wee Reese ended the threat by bouncing to third baseman Mathews, who started an around-the-horn double play.

Milwaukee took a 4–3 lead on Logan's sacrifice fly in the twelfth inning. The Dodgers tied the score when Gino Cimoli doubled off the screen in right field and came around on Furillo's bouncer that took a kangaroo hop over Logan's head for a single. Cimoli ended the game in the fourteenth. His fifth hit of the night was a home run off Murff that gave Sandy Koufax his first win of the season and sent the Ebbets Field crowd of almost 16,000 home at midnight after four hours of baseball. The Braves' lead over the Dodgers was again down to one game.

The Braves then came up empty in their two-game series in Philadelphia's Connie Mack Stadium, which was opened as Shibe Park in 1909 by the Athletics of the American League. The name was changed to Connie Mack Stadium in 1953 in honor of the Athletics' former owner and manager, who was known as The Grand Old Man of Baseball. The National League's Phillies moved out of the Baker Bowl in the middle of the 1938 season and into Shibe Park, which they shared with the Athletics. The Phils bought what was then Connie Mack Stadium in 1954, when the Athletics moved to Kansas City. The stadium was closed following the 1970 season, with the Phillies moving into Veterans Stadium. They moved into Citizens Bank Park in 2004.

Another great pitching matchup highlighted Milwaukee's first game in

Philadelphia, with Robin Roberts facing Warren Spahn. The Braves' left-hander was hit hard for the first time all season and suffered his first loss after four complete-game victories. He lasted just four innings, allowing seven hits and five runs, all of them earned.

Granville "Granny" Hamner, who was selected to the All-Star team as both a second baseman and shortstop during his stay in the major leagues and who ended his pro baseball career as a knuckleball pitcher, socked a home run for the Phils. Adcock's two-run double keyed a three-run sixth inning for the Braves, who sliced their deficit to 6–4. But the Phillies added a pair of runs in the seventh for an 8–4 win. Don Cardwell outdueled Gene Conley the next day in a 2–1 Philadelphia victory.

Milwaukee stopped a three-game slide to begin a four-game series in St. Louis. Juan Pizarro pitched a complete game and hit a home run, while Logan went four-for-four with a homer and five runs batted in. Mathews had a roundtripper among his three hits. It was the first major league win for Pizarro, a native of Puerto Rico.

The Braves made it four losses in five games when Spahn was hammered for the second straight time, giving up a dozen hits and seven earned runs to the Cardinals in six and two-thirds innings. Meanwhile, Cincinnati's win at Wrigley Field meant that the Redlegs had caught Milwaukee as both teams had 14–7 records. It was the first time since the fourth day of the season that the Braves had not been in first place by themselves.

The Cardinals played their home games in Sportsman's Park, which was also known as Busch Stadium after 1953. When Cardinals owner Gussie Busch purchased the stadium from the St. Louis Browns, he wanted to name it Budweiser Stadium to help promote his beer business, but pressure from the National League executives helped him change his mind. The Busch eagle, which sat atop the scoreboard in left-center field, flapped its wings every time a Cardinal player hit a home run. Following the last game at Busch Stadium on May 8, 1966, home plate was transported by helicopter to the Cardinals' new ballpark, Busch Memorial Stadium, which opened May 12 that year. The team moved into another brand new Busch Stadium for the 2006 season.

Hank Aaron homered in both games, and Milwaukee took a double-header from the Cards to win three out of four in St. Louis. The Redlegs also won twice, their sweep of the Cubs wrapping up a tremendous road trip in which Cincinnati won all twelve games.

Based on their dangerous lineup, the Redlegs had been picked by a few baseball prognosticators to win the National League pennant. Cincinnati had strengthened itself during the offseason by trading for Don Hoak and Jerry

Lynch. Hoak would provide a lift as much with his fiery spirit as with his play at third base. Lynch added a valuable left-handed bat off the bench.

But while they pointed to the booming bats swung by Frank Robinson, Gus Bell, Wally Post, and Ted Kluszewski, others close to the game questioned the arms of Brooks Lawrence, Hal Jeffcoat, and Joe Nuxhall, the heart of the Redlegs' starting rotation.

As always, Brooklyn was the team that most worried the Braves. The Dodgers visited Milwaukee for two games, and once more, there was a playoff atmosphere. Pitching dominated the mini series, with each team getting a 3–2 win.

Bob Buhl outdueled Don Newcombe in the first game, a crowd of nearly 35,000 watching the Braves' right-hander extend his magic spell over the Bums in spite of wildness that plagued him throughout the night. Buhl, who issued nine bases on balls, walked the bases full with no outs in the sixth inning. He escaped without allowing a run as the Braves pulled off one of their four double plays. Ernie Johnson pitched two and a third innings of scoreless relief to save it for Milwaukee, which closed the contest with a dazzling piece of defense. With Duke Snider on first with a single, shortstop Johnny Logan ranged deep into the hole to take away what looked like a hit by Carl Furillo, firing the ball to second sacker Danny O'Connell, who wheeled and completed the twin killing.

The second game was played in the afternoon. Don Drysdale got the start for Brooklyn in place of Sal Maglie, who had a stiff neck. Boston Celtic backup center Gene Conley was on the mound for the Braves. Milwaukee managed only two hits, one of them a two-run double by Frank Torre. The Dodgers got just five hits, but two of them left the park. Gil Hodges spoiled Conley's shutout with a seventh-inning blast. Don Zimmer won the game with a homer in the tenth off Lew Burdette, who had come on in relief two innings earlier. Clem Labine pitched three perfect innings to earn the win.

It was the middle of May, and the Braves shared first place with the Redlegs, both with 17–8 records. Brooklyn was two and a half games back at 14–10. Milwaukee sent pitcher Bob Trowbridge and outfielder Wes Covington to Wichita, the Braves' Triple-A farm team in the American Association. Covington told reporters he had not been given a fair shot at solving the Braves' problems in left field.

After having their winning streak stopped by Philadelphia in their first home game of the month, the Redlegs ripped off three more victories in a row, giving them fifteen in sixteen games. Their one-run win over the Giants came on a day the Braves were losing by a run to Pittsburgh. That shoved

Cincinnati into first place in the National League, and the Redlegs would stay there for almost a full month.

Fred Haney used Lew Burdette in relief four times during the 1957 season, including twice in five days. After working two and two-thirds innings and absorbing the loss to Brooklyn, Burdette pitched five innings out of the bullpen against Pittsburgh. He relieved his buddy, Spahn, who was roughed up for seven hits and four runs. Burdette allowed one run over five innings to get the victory, thanks to a pair of Hank Aaron home runs.

The Braves' right fielder launched a 420-foot shot over the center field fence and smacked a three-run homer to the opposite field. Aaron, the defending National League batting champ, lifted his batting average to .378 and held the major league lead in home runs with eleven after twenty-seven games.

Brooklyn's bats got hot, igniting a five-game winning streak that propelled the Dodgers into a second-place tie with Milwaukee. After a day off and a game that was stopped by rain before it became official, the Braves were 18–10. So were the Dodgers, who scored ten runs two straight days. Cincinnati was 21–10.

Chuck Tanner, who made more of a name for himself as a manager than as a player, hit his first home run of the season, and it was a big one. Tanner's drive in the bottom of the thirteenth inning came off the Phillies' Robin Roberts, who went the distance. Johnson continued his stellar relief work for the Braves, allowing one hit and striking out four in four scoreless innings. Tanner also made two sparkling catches in left field.

Warren Spahn's troubles continued. After beginning the season by pitching four complete games, the left-hander failed to finish for the fourth straight time. The Cubs handed him his second loss in six decisions. Frank Ernaga, an outfielder who had been brought up from the minors four days earlier, hit a home run in his first major league at-bat, and twenty-one-year-old Moe Drabowsky scattered nine hits for Chicago.

Drabowsky was one of two promising young right-handers who gave Cubs' fans reason to have high hopes for the future. The other was twenty-year-old Dick Drott. Both struck out 170 batters in 1957, with Drott winning fifteen games and Drabowsky winning thirteen. Drabowsky, who pitched in the majors for seventeen years, would only win as many as eleven games once the rest of his career. Drott never managed more than seven victories and was out of baseball in six years.

The day after getting shelled in Wrigley Field, Spahn came out of the bullpen to record the final out and the save in the Braves' 7–6 win over the Cubs. Milwaukee rapped out fourteen base hits, turned four double plays, and used twenty-one players.

The Braves fell to third place in the National League standings after dropping a doubleheader to the Cubs. Drott struck out fifteen hitters, Ernaga hit his second home run in as many games, and future Hall of Famer Ernie Banks drove in the winning run in both games. For the lowly Cubs, it was the first time all season they had won two in a row.

Cincinnati handed the Braves their third straight loss and their fourth in five games. The Redlegs took advantage of rare wildness on the part of Burdette, who walked five batters in eight innings. They batted around in the tenth, scoring five runs on four hits off Johnson to win, 11–6, in County Stadium. Cincinnati remained in first place, two games ahead of the Dodgers and three and one half in front of Milwaukee.

Tempers flared during the Redlegs' tenth-inning uprising, and, as usual, Braves shortstop Johnny Logan was right in the middle of things. Smoky Burgess, a rotund catcher who lengthened his career considerably with tremendous success as a pinch-hitter, came off the bench to single in the go-ahead run for Cincinnati. Pitcher Hal Jeffcoat ran for Burgess, and he slid into Logan on a play at second base. Logan and Jeffcoat swapped punches, both dugouts cleared, and when the dust settled, both players were thrown out of the game.

Del Crandall sent the game into extra innings with a two-run homer in the ninth as the Braves rallied from what had been a four-run deficit. The Milwaukee catcher was coming through with clutch hits and getting many of his RBI in the late innings of close games.

Aaron and Mathews were obviously the Braves' headliners, but Crandall was the glue. He played in an era when catchers did not look to the dugout before every pitch; they, along with the pitchers, decided what would be thrown. The Milwaukee staff was confident in Crandall and worked well with him. He was a fine receiver whose smooth way of catching a pitch made it look better for the umpires.

Crandall was always one of those guys referred to as "a coach on the field." He seemed mature beyond his years, and, like most catchers, he possessed an insight of baseball most players did not have. He played his first big league game at the age of nineteen and caught sixty-three games for the 1949 Boston Braves. He played a little more the next season, spent two years in the military service, and returned to his job behind the plate in 1953.

The Braves were in Milwaukee then, and Crandall was always a fan favorite because of the way he handled pitchers, his strong arm, and his ability to hit with runners on base. In 1953, his first season as the club's everyday catcher, the California native belted fifteen home runs. He would hit at least that many roundtrippers for eight consecutive years, with a high of twenty-six in 1955.

Del Crandall was a defensive whiz behind the plate. He caught and threw well, was a master at handling pitchers, and showed some power at bat by hitting fifteen home runs for the '57 pennant winners.

Ironically, although Crandall was a key player in the Braves' drive to the pennant and world championship in 1957, it was the only season in an eight-year stretch that he was not selected to the National League All-Star team. He batted .253 with fifteen home runs and forty-six RBI. His best offensive season was 1960 when he hit .294, while slamming nineteen homers and driving in seventy-seven runs. He won Gold Gloves as the National League's best fielding catcher four times, in 1958–60 and 1962.

Crandall caught an average of 125 games over an eight-year stretch before a shoulder injury caused him to miss all but a handful of games in 1961. He bounced back to catch ninety games in 1962, when he batted a career-best .297 and made his final All-Star appearance. He played four more years, and it was no surprise when he was named the Milwaukee Brewers' manager in 1972, just six years after his retirement as a player.

"Del was a hell of a defensive catcher," Hank Aaron said. "He couldn't hit with Campanella, but strictly as a catcher, he was the best," commented Joe Adcock.[5]

Every team needs a stopper, a pitcher who can turn in a brilliant performance when his club is struggling. Usually, what that pitcher is called upon to stop is a losing streak. When Spahn took the mound against the visiting Cincinnati Redlegs on May 28, he had been having as much trouble as the Braves. They had lost seven of ten games; he had not had a win since the first day of the month.

The stylish southpaw was equal to the task. He pitched an eight-hitter, did not walk a batter, and was helped by two double plays. Milwaukee scored the game's only run in the eighth inning when Bobby Thomson led off with a triple and scored on Frank Torre's single. Those were the only two hits the Braves got off of twenty-five-year-old lefty Don Gross.

Bob Buhl and Ray Crone followed Spahn's lead, both going the distance against the Cubs to give Milwaukee three straight complete-game victories. Buhl was particularly sharp in throwing a four-hitter. He displayed his best control in several weeks, striking out eight and issuing one base on balls. Utility infielder Felix Mantilla, who was filling in at third base for the injured Eddie Mathews, singled twice and doubled. Buhl, who had only six hits the whole season and who would strike out thirty-four times in seventy-three trips to the plate, got a pair of safeties and knocked in a run.

Del Rice was the Braves' catcher, just as he was each time Buhl started on the mound. Always known as a solid defensive catcher, Milwaukee obtained him from the St. Louis Cardinals in June of 1955 for outfielder Pete Whisenant. Thirty-two years old at the time of the trade, Rice had played ten and a half years with the Cardinals.

Steady Del Rice was Bob Buhl's personal catcher and provided pop as a hitter with nine home runs in only 144 at bats in 1957. He gave the Braves two outstanding defensive Dels behind the plate.

He played a career-high 147 games in 1952 when he batted .259 and drove in sixty-five runs, both also career highs. He hit eleven home runs that season and had twelve roundtrippers in 261 at-bats in 1947. Rice was selected to the National League All-Star team in 1953, when he batted .236 with six home runs and thirty-seven RBI while playing for the Cardinals.

Rice made his hits count for the Braves in 1957. Catching in just forty-eight games, he smacked nine homers and drove in twenty runs. One-third of his thirty-three hits were for extra bases.

One of Rice's home runs helped Milwaukee beat the Cubs in the first game of a May 30 doubleheader. He was behind the plate as a starter for a second straight game, and he responded with a single and two RBI to go with his homer. Billy Bruton also went deep, while Crone pitched one of his two complete games as a member of the Milwaukee staff.

Nearly 36,000 fans showed up at County Stadium, and they saw the Braves' win streak stopped in the second game. Turk Lown struck out Mantilla with the bases loaded in the ninth inning to nail down the Cubs' two-run victory.

Slugging third baseman Eddie Mathews, who had missed four days with a jammed thumb, was penciled into the Braves' starting lineup. But he was scratched after getting hit in the eye with a batted ball while playing pepper prior to the game. The swelling around Mathews' eye caused him to sit out the contest.

The Braves ended May with a record of 23–16 as they were nipped by the Cardinals. Milwaukee, in third place, trailed Brooklyn by a half-game and Cincinnati by two and a half. The surprising Philadelphia Phillies were in fourth place, a half-game behind the Braves. The Redlegs won twenty-one of twenty-eight games during the month, while the Braves were 14–14.

The Braves made some big news off the field by signing a high school hotshot to one of the largest rookie contracts on record. They out-bid six other major league teams to land Robert Dale "Hawk" Taylor, an eighteen-year-old catcher from Metropolis High School in Illinois.

A catcher who stood six-foot-two and weighed 190 pounds, Taylor signed a contract that was reported to be for more than $100,000. One family member said the Brooklyn Dodgers had offered $98,000. The official announcement from the Braves said Milwaukee scout Wid Matthews, a long-time friend of the Taylor family, offered the youngster "in excess of $4,000 dollars."

Matthews said every big league team with the exception of the Washington Senators and the Cincinnati Redlegs had shown interest in Taylor, a nephew of Ben Taylor, who played in ten games for the 1955 Braves.

Hawk Taylor, who belted thirty-four home runs in high school and American Legion ball, was to report straight to the Braves because of a rule regarding bonus babies. He spent the rest of the season on the bench, catching in one game, getting into six others, and going hitless in his only at-bat. He would never get more than 225 at-bats in a season, and he retired after eleven disappointing years in the majors. None of his sixteen career home runs came with Milwaukee as Taylor was traded to the New York Mets in 1963 and later played with California and Kansas City in the American League. He had a lifetime .218 batting average.

Taylor flopped as the Braves' hope for their next big-time catcher, and it wasn't until 1960 that they would sign the player who could fill the bill. That is when they landed Joe Torre, the kid brother of the Milwaukee first baseman, Frank Torre, and the man who would one day become a Hall of Fame-caliber manager with the New York Yankees.

First baseman Joe Adcock, who made an appearance as a pinch-hitter, still had not returned to the Braves' lineup. He had been out a few days because of a strained ligament in his right knee, and it would be another week before he was playing every day again.

Lew Burdette received a good doctor's report, but one tempered with caution. His sore pitching arm had responded well to treatment, an orthopedic specialist said the right-hander had a pulled tendon, and a calcium deposit was discovered. It was uncertain whether Burdette would be able to accompany his teammates on an upcoming fourteen-game road trip to New York and Pennsylvania.

And so it was, with one eye on the trainer's room and the other on the feared Brooklyn Dodgers, that Milwaukee manager Fred Haney started the month of June. He continued his steady banter of optimism for the press, but his thoughts were consumed with a two-week road trip and injuries that could prove costly.

3

The Big Three

Long before the 1957 season began, the Milwaukee Braves were feeling really good about their chances of winning the National League pennant. There were several reasons for their confidence, but three big ones towered over the rest.

Warren Spahn. Lew Burdette. Bob Buhl. The trio of starting pitchers was one of the main ingredients for the '57 edition of the Braves, who won the National League title and then beat the New York Yankees in the World Series.

Every team has an ace pitcher, someone the club can count on to stop losing streaks and prevent series sweeps by opponents. Milwaukee, in reality, had three aces. Spahn was the number one guy, but Burdette and Buhl would have filled that role on many other big league clubs.

In 1956, they combined for fifty-seven wins and forty-nine complete games as the Braves' staff went the distance a league-leading sixty times, while posting the National League's second-lowest earned run average.

Baseball has changed over the years, with today's game placing a big emphasis on the home run, which offers instant offense and puts fannies in the seats. People who attend games love to see the long ball, with most having little appreciation for the finer points of baseball.

Another difference is pitching. Pitchers who start games seldom finish them. Either the starters' durability has drastically decreased or their toughness has. Perhaps it is more a matter of expectations, or a lack of the same. Modern-day pitchers are specialists. In addition to the starters, there are middle-inning guys, set-up men, and closers. No longer are the pitchers in the bullpen known simply as relievers.

The save, and the generous requirements to earn one, has glorified and stuffed the pockets of men who make a career of pitching only the ninth inning. There is also a ludicrous statistic called a "hold" and the equally ludicrous opportunity for several pitchers to earn one in a single game. It is mainly a number to be used by agents in salary negotiations.

The term "quality start" has made starting pitchers somewhat of a pampered lot. There are exceptions, to be sure, but a surprising number of starters are content to pitch six innings and then grab a shower and a beer. The complete game has gone the way of the dinosaur.

There was a time when managers absolutely dreaded walking out to the mound and asking their pitcher for the ball. Crusty hurlers like Early Wynn, Bob Gibson, and Sal Maglie sometimes refused to hand it over, defying managers by declaring that there was no one in the bullpen more capable than they were.

Spahn and Burdette were much the same way, confident and competitive, believing there was no reason to turn the game over to a reliever because they honestly felt there was no one in the bullpen better than them. They wanted to pitch nine innings every time they took the mound. Many of today's pitchers are happy if they last long enough to qualify for a win. Some of them volunteer to leave games if they have a lead after five or six innings.

Through the 1960s and most of the '70s, pitchers who started games frequently finished them. Since then, there has been a steady decline in complete games. The sixteen National League teams combined for more than 100 complete games only twice in the first six years of this century.

In 2005, all of the NL pitchers together totaled 104 complete games, just forty-four more than the 1957 Milwaukee Braves. The most complete games any 2005 National League team had was fifteen, three less than Spahn himself pitched in the '57 season.

Only three 2005 National League pitchers logged as many as 240 innings. In 1957, at the age of thirty-six, Spahn pitched 271. Burdette worked 256.1 innings, and Buhl had 216.2. Buhl's total would have led five 2005 National League teams.

The three pitchers were fierce competitors, and they were very competitive with each other. When they played pepper, whichever one of them misplayed the most balls would buy drinks for the other two. Spahn and Burdette made little bets during batting practice. They would wager steak dinners on their hitting performances and also on who could catch the most balls while shagging flies in the outfield.

Sometimes the pitchers even orchestrated races to their hotel after games. Buhl and Eddie Mathews would hail a taxi, with Burdette and Spahn jumping into another cab, and the players in the car that arrived first at the Braves' hotel would be treated to dinner by the other pair. The players would pay cabbies an extra few dollars to drive faster than usual.

When the club was in New York, Buhl and Mathews would also team up against Spahn and Burdette in an expanded game of hide-and-seek. They marked off boundaries of certain blocks in the city and tried to find each other. The team that was found bought dinner for the other two.[1]

Those same four players had some fun a few years later when Charlie Dressen took over as the Braves' manager. Dressen loved to catch players who missed curfew, and everyone knew that. So, one night, Buhl, Burdette, Spahn, and Mathews played a prank on their skipper.

The Braves were in Los Angeles, the Dodgers' home beginning in 1958, and Milwaukee's players were staying in bungalows at Coconut Grove. One night, Buhl and Mathews, aware that Dressen was lurking in the bushes outside, ran from their room into the darkness.

Dressen chased them, but Buhl and Mathews ran back into their room. Dressen knocked on their door and asked if they had just been outside. They answered no. In the meantime, Burdette had turned on the sprinklers, and when Dressen went back outside, he was drenched.

Cursing while being showered with water, Dressen again saw two figures running through the shadows. It was Spahn and Burdette. While the Milwaukee manager ran after them, Mathews and Buhl turned the sprinklers on again, and Dressen was soaked a second time.

Dressen would later call Mathews, Buhl, Spahn, and Burdette "the four worst offenders" on the Milwaukee team. They joked about it and went on to have a picture taken with their caps turned sideways, with Spahn wearing what he called his manager's look. His mouth was open wide in the photo, which the quartet had enlarged. They signed the picture "the four worst offenders" and stuck it in Dressen's locker.

After he died, Dressen's wife told Burdette, Spahn, Buhl, and Mathews that her husband had the picture framed and put it on the wall at their home.[2]

Although they were known to be fun-loving, the three pitchers did not break curfew, and all three worked hard. They did a lot of running on days they were not scheduled to be on the mound and took advantage of batting practice to sharpen their skills at the plate.

Spahn and Burdette were both very good hitting pitchers who were sometimes used as pinch-hitters. Buhl was one of the worst hitters in all of baseball, but he was a good bunter.

Burdette and Spahn were baseball's version of Butch Cassidy and the Sundance Kid. This is not to say that they were outlaws, but their clubhouse antics were certainly well known. The Milwaukee mound duo had a good time on and off the baseball diamond. When pranks were played in the Braves' locker room, the two pitchers were the first suspects. They were leaders of the club in every way.

Spahn and Burdette were roommates the entire time both were with the Braves, and they spent a lot of time together. Back in the fifties, big league players were reputedly tough on youngsters breaking into the majors, but that was not always the case.

Claude Raymond, a pitcher, said that when he was a Milwaukee rookie, Spahn and Burdette were extremely nice to him. Both were always talking baseball, according to Raymond, and they helped young hurlers by offering suggestions about how they could improve.[3]

OLD SPAHNIE

There was something captivating about watching Warren Spahn pitch. His picturesque windup started with arms spread like an eagle's wings. Then came the trademark high leg kick that has been immortalized with a statue outside Turner Field in Atlanta. It all finished with a perfect follow-through.

Spahn made pitching an art form. Those who saw him on the mound must have known they were witnessing something special. Every time he pitched, it was like a foreboding snapshot of baseball history, a glimpse into a corner of the Hall of Fame where a reserved sign was posted. Anyone who saw Spahn pitch could easily have felt proud.

It was always quite obvious that Spahn loved baseball. He didn't just love the pitching; he was absorbed in being a part of the grand game. He liked taking his cuts in the batter's box, playing cat and mouse with a runner leading off first base, and using his expertise as a seasoned bench jockey to apply the needle to opponents. He was acknowledged as the Braves' leader and was also a frequent instigator of clubhouse high jinx.

He was known to fire a few expletives into the air when a young relief pitcher was brought in to replace him, then be the first to offer congratulations when the kid preserved a lead. It was nothing personal with Spahnie; he simply felt he should finish what he started and that no one was better equipped to get a big out than he was. He was as great a competitor as he was a pitcher.

Del Crandall, Spahn's longtime catcher with the Braves, has said he does not think his former batterymate receives the credit he deserves. And, although "winningest left-hander" accompanies any talk of Spahn, it does seem he is underrated.

The fact that he amassed 363 career victories — ironically, he had the same number of base hits — is only part of the story. He is sixth on the all-time wins list, with one less than Pud Galvin and ten less than Grover Cleveland Alexander and Christy Mathewson, who are tied for third place.

The fashionable southpaw completed 382 of his 665 starts, won twenty or more games thirteen times, and posted a sparkling lifetime earned run average of 3.09. Those rank at the top of his seemingly endless list of dazzling accomplishments.

Spahn pitched in three World Series, posting a 4–3 record and a 3.05 earned run average over fifty-six innings. At the plate, he had eight hits, batted .200 and drove in four runs.

As is the case with hitting, the media — and, as a result, most fans — are enamored with power when it comes to pitching. The guys who strike out the most batters and blow them away with fastballs clocked in the high nineties and faster are normally the ones listed at the top of the current "greatest ever" list.

And, while Roger Clemens, Randy Johnson, Nolan Ryan, and Sandy Koufax are all names that belong in any conversation regarding the all-time best hurlers, the objective of pitchers is to get hitters out and win games. Spahn did a lot of both.

A native of Buffalo, New York, he played first base and his father played third for the hometown Lake City Athletic Club. He wanted to be the first baseman for his high school, but the team had an all-city player at that position, so Spahn decided to try pitching.

Signed as an amateur free agent for a $150 bonus by the Boston Bees in 1940, he played that year in the Class D Pony League for eighty dollars a month. In his first professional season, he hurt his arm twice and had a 5–4 record with Bradford, Pennsylvania.

Spahn was healthy the next season when he pitched for Evansville in the Class B Three-I (Illinois-Indiana-Iowa) League. He led the league with nineteen wins and with a 1.83 earned run average, while striking out 193 batters in 212 innings.

Spahn did not get his first major league win until he was twenty-five years old. He was sent back to the minors in the spring of 1942 when he refused Boston Braves manager Casey Stengel's order to brush back Brooklyn's Pee Wee Reese in an exhibition game.

After being sent down, Spahn had another outstanding season, getting seventeen wins with a 1.96 ERA for Hartford of the Class A Eastern League.[4]

Warren Spahn's pitching form was a work of art, and his consistency was legendary. His 363 wins are the most ever in the major leagues by a left-hander, and his thirteen twenty-win seasons share the all-time top spot with Christy Mathewson.

He was recalled late in the season and pitched briefly for the Braves, appearing in two games to go with two others at the season's start, without a decision. Then he spent the next three years in a very different uniform and with much more on the line than the outcome of a ball game.

Before his big league career really got started, he entered the United States Army and served during World War II. Staff Sergeant Spahn saw action with the 276th Engineer Combat Battalion in the Ardennes, Alsace, the Rhineland, and in Central Europe. He was also at the Remagen bridgehead, where his unit worked feverishly for six days under constant fire to keep this key entrance into Germany under repair. Spahn fought in the Battle of the Bulge, was wounded in Europe, and was awarded the Purple Heart and the Bronze Star for bravery. He also earned a battlefield commission as a second lieutenant.[5]

"He was a war hero," fellow Hall of Fame pitcher Bob Feller said of Spahn. "Who knows how many games he would have won if it wasn't for World War II? In my mind, he was the greatest left-hander of all time."[6]

Considering his late arrival in the majors and the amount of time he missed when he was serving his country, Spahn could be projected to have easily won 400 games. But like Ted Williams, who also lost a sizeable chunk of time to the military service during the prime of his baseball career, Spahn never talked about what might have been, only of what he was glad to do for America. His wartime experience did, however, make him realize how fortunate he was to be able to play a game for a living.

"After what I went through overseas," he said, "I never thought of anything I was told to do in baseball as hard work. You get over feeling like that when you spend days on end sleeping in frozen tank tracks in enemy-threatened territory. The Army taught me about challenges and about what is important and what isn't."[7]

Spahn returned to baseball in 1946, when he pitched 125 innings and won eight games. He had twenty-one wins the next season and at least as many in three of the following four years after that. He was 14–19 for a 1952 Braves club that won just sixty-four games, but he still had a fine 2.98 earned run average.

In one particularly frustrating game that season, Spahn struck out eighteen batters in fifteen innings and smacked a home run, but the Cubs won, 2–1.

He was offered a contract which would have paid him a dime for every person who attended a Braves home game during the 1953 season. Spahn turned it down, and his decision proved costly. The Braves moved to Milwaukee and drew nearly two million fans. He would have made almost $200,000 had he agreed to the proposed deal. As it was, his salary for the year was $25,000.[8]

Spahn bounced back from his losingest season to go 23–7, finish twenty-four of thirty-two starts, save three games, and lead the league with a 2.10 earned run average.

He would be a twenty-game winner eight of the next nine seasons, including six in a row, and twelve times in a fifteen-year span. Twice pitching more than 300 innings, Spahn averaged twenty wins, 278 innings, and twenty-one complete games per season over a period of seventeen years.

He *averaged* twenty wins for seventeen seasons. It is so amazing that it bears repeating. Winning twenty games has always been a benchmark for a pitcher's production and consistency over the course of a season. To average twenty for so long is almost unbelievable.

At the age of thirty-seven, Spahn won twenty-two games in 1958, helping the Braves win their second straight National League pennant. He enjoyed his best season at the plate, pounding out thirty-six hits and knocking in fifteen runs on the way to a .333 batting average. Seven of his hits, including two homers, were for extra bases.

He earned two complete-game victories against the Yankees in the '58 World Series. In Game Four, he pitched a two-hit shutout in outdueling Whitey Ford. Spahn struck out seven in the game and had a run-scoring single in the Braves' 3–0 win.

Spahn pitched his first no-hitter when he was thirty-nine years old. The gem against the Phillies was his twentieth win of the 1960 season and was highlighted by a Milwaukee-record fifteen strikeouts.

When he was forty, he threw another no-hitter as he shut out the Giants. Later that season, on August 11, 1961, Spahn beat the Cubs, 2–1, making him the thirteenth pitcher to win 300 games. His catcher that day was Joe Torre. Spahn pitched a six-hitter and drove in a run with a sacrifice fly in becoming the first new member of the 300 club since Lefty Grove joined it twenty years earlier. There would be only one addition to the prestigious 300-win circle — Early Wynn in 1963 — over the next twenty-one years.

Following his monumental victory, Spahn found himself uncharacteristically on the receiving end of a practical joke. Aaron caught a fly ball in right field for the final out. While Torre ran out from behind the plate to congratulate Spahn, the pitcher glanced out to see Aaron throwing the prized baseball into the stands. At least, that's what Spahn thought he was seeing. Aaron, who had made a throwing motion and ended with an empty bare hand, had the baseball tucked in his glove. The normally reserved Aaron got a good laugh when he saw the left-hander come sprinting out to right field wild-eyed.[9]

In 1963, at the age of forty-two, Spahn equaled his career-best 23–7 record, with a sparkling 2.60 earned run average and seven shutouts. He threw twenty-two complete games, pitched 259.2 innings, and hit two home runs. He was the oldest pitcher in big league history to win twenty games and matched Christy Mathewson's major league record by doing it for the thirteenth time.

Perhaps the most notable performance of Spahn's career came during that 1963 season. He hooked up with future Hall of Fame member Juan Marichal, who was seventeen years younger, in a marathon pitchers' duel which was scoreless for fifteen innings. Willie Mays ended the game with a home run on Spahn's 201st pitch, giving the San Francisco Giants a 1–0 win over the Braves.

Looking back, 1963 would have been the perfect swan song for Spahn, who managed just thirteen victories while losing twenty-nine times as he struggled through two more seasons. He spent his final big league season of 1965 dividing time between the lowly New York Mets, as a player-coach, and the Giants. He was a winner in his final major league game, earning victory number 363 as San Francisco defeated the Chicago Cubs, 9–2, on September 12, 1965.

Even then, he did not quit as he pitched in 1966 with Mexico City in the Mexican League and in 1967 with Tulsa of the Pacific Coast League. Upon finally ending his playing days at the age of forty-six, he said, "I didn't quit; baseball retired me."[10] Criticized for hanging on too long, Spahn said, "I don't care what the public thinks. I'm pitching because I enjoy pitching."[11]

Spahn managed the Tulsa Oilers' minor league team from 1967–70 and was the Cleveland Indians' pitching coach in 1972 and '73. He was also a pitching instructor for the St. Louis Cardinals and California Angels.

"You know, after a certain period there are goals you'd like to reach," Spahn said. "And I think I'd like to reach for the moon and settle for whatever happens in the interim. And I feel that way about being the winningest left-hander. Number one, I worked cheap. God gave me a good arm. I loved playing baseball. I think I was afraid of that outside world, that I liked what I did for a living. And so, as a result, I happened to win 363 games. I'm proud of that."

The old southpaw talked about how he wanted to be remembered: "I'd like to think I was a role model for kids. I didn't have a drug addiction. I didn't dissipate in any way. I was able to go out on the mound whenever my time came up," Spahn said. "Good, bad, or indifferent, whatever I did in a game, and some of them weren't too good, it was my best that day. So that perseverance and stick-to-it-iveness are the type of things you'd like to be proud of. I think that I'd like to be remembered for that."[12]

Players cannot be considered for the Hall of Fame until they are out of baseball for five years. In January of 1973, Spahn's first year of eligibility, he was elected by the Baseball Writers Association of America to the Baseball Hall of Fame. He was inducted at Cooperstown in August along with Roberto Clemente, who had died tragically on New Year's Day.

A fourteen-time All-Star, Spahn holds the National League record for innings pitched with 5,243.2. He won 177 games after his thirty-fifth birthday.

Spahn helped himself with his bat as well as his glove. His thirty-five career home runs represent the record for a National League pitcher and are two less than Wes Ferrell's major league record for a pitcher. Spahn stayed in many games because of his bat as managers often let him hit for himself in situations where most pitchers would be removed for a pinch-hitter. And, when he was not on the mound, he was sometimes called upon to pinch-hit.

He featured a pickoff move that was one of the best in baseball. He fielded his position exquisitely and was what coaches tell young pitchers they are supposed to be defensively: a fifth infielder.

Former teammate Johnny Sain called Spahn one of the smartest men ever to play baseball, and one-time Braves pitching coach Whitlow Wyatt said every pitch the southpaw threw had an idea behind it.

"I pitched against Spahn in 1942," recounted Wyatt, "and fifteen years later he reminded me that the first time I faced him I threw him a fastball, then a curve, then another fastball that he hit to the shortstop. He not only remembered the hitters, but the pitchers, too."[13]

Early in his career, Spahn was a fastball pitcher who led the National League in strikeouts four consecutive seasons (1949–52). When his fastball lost some of its steam, he became a better pitcher, learning to change speeds and keep hitters off balance.

Dick Groat, who enjoyed a long and outstanding career as a shortstop for the Pirates, Cardinals, Phillies, and Giants, once explained the metamorphosis of Spahn as a pitcher. Groat said when he left baseball to enter the military service, Spahn was throwing fastballs and winning twenty games. He said when he returned to the majors, Spahn was still winning twenty games, but he seldom threw fastballs anymore.[14]

The screwball became his out pitch, and he also added a slider and sharpened his curveball. Rather than fading away when he could no longer overpower batters, Spahn learned to outsmart them. Instead of being stubborn, he adjusted. He once said pitching is a learning experience and that it comes down to smoke and mirrors.

Spahn was listed at six feet and 175 pounds. He did not have the leverage of a six-foot-ten Randy Johnson, and he didn't possess the tree-trunk thighs of a Roger Clemens or Tom Seaver, both of whom used tremendous leg drive to propel their pitches past hitters.

He also did not have the golden arm of Sandy Koufax, who is proclaimed by hordes of baseball experts as the greatest left-handed pitcher of all time. It is certainly hard to dispute that he was the most talented. And while a pitcher does not ring up 363 wins on luck, good fortune is involved. Spahn never experienced a serious arm problem, which was what prematurely ended Koufax's brilliant career. But Spahn also did not beg out of starting assignments when he felt soreness in his shoulder or elbow. He figured the best remedy was to throw; if throwing became too painful, then he would take a seat. That, however, did not happen. Spahn was good, and he was tough and durable.

It is interesting that Koufax himself may possess a deeper understanding and realization of just how great Spahn was than most of the people who research and chronicle baseball history.

A Team of the Century was selected in 1999, and at first it did not include Spahn. Koufax, who was selected, responded to the omission by saying that any such team without Warren Spahn was a joke. A special panel was convened, and it added Spahn, Christy Mathewson, Honus Wagner, and Stan Musial.

The thirty players selected to the legendary team were honored in pre-game ceremonies at the All-Star Game in Boston's Fenway Park. Those ceremonies are remembered for the emotional appearance of Ted Williams in a wheelchair, with current all-stars surrounding him in awe and tribute.

Plans for the old-time players' introductions called for each, when his name was announced, to climb steps and walk onto a stage. Spahn, who was seventy-eight years old at the time and was having some trouble walking, was to be announced right after Koufax.

Knowing Spahn would need some help, Koufax stayed back when his name was called. He waited until Spahn was announced, and the former Dodger took the old Brave by the arm, and they walked onto the stage together.[15]

The act of kindness might have been lost to most people at Fenway Park that night as well as the television audience, but it was a nice touch and, in a way, a salute from the man most people acknowledge as the greatest left-hander ever. Koufax, who has tremendous respect for Spahn, knows what was required to put up such impressive numbers for so long.

Spahn carried a burning desire to win; he expected to win, and he had every right to feel that way because he won nearly sixty percent of his decisions. He always thought he should win the crucial games for his team. When he did not, he felt he let his teammates down.

On the next-to-last day of the 1956 season, Milwaukee was playing in St. Louis, and the Braves needed a win to remain tied with Brooklyn for first place in the National League. Spahn hooked up in a pitching duel with Cardinals right-hander Herm Wehmeier, who had nothing to lose. The Braves' lefty, however, carried his team's pennant hopes on his shoulders.

Billy Bruton homered in the first inning for the Braves. Spahn pitched five shutout innings before giving up a two-out double and eventually surrendering the tying run in the sixth. It stayed that way, 1–1, until the twelfth inning.

Spahn, who had allowed only three hits until that point, became the losing pitcher when the Cards' Rip Repulski smashed a game-winning hit off the knee of Mathews at third base.

Stunned with disappointment and wrung out with fatigue, Spahn stood motionless on the field, then started walking to the dugout, a defeated warrior. As he walked, he began to cry, something he later recalled never having done on a ball field.

A photographer came running up and started taking pictures of the sobbing southpaw. Spahn, in a response so untypical of him, threw his glove at the man. The pitcher later apologized to the photographer in the locker room, but no one — not even the photographer — blamed the great hurler. Everybody knew he was hurting.

After the game, St. Louis outfielder Wally Moon called Spahn the greatest pitcher in baseball. Spahn said his only consolation was that he had proven he could still pitch at the age of thirty-five.

Bob Buhl had this to say about his friend and teammate: "I liked watching Spahn pitch because he was a master out there. You never saw the catcher run back to the screen. Everything was just like it was supposed to be.

"It's not that he wasn't an emotional pitcher. He would throw his glove or kick it if he lost a close game or got knocked out of a game early. And he would glare at umps and use his hands to ask where the pitch was, although he never did anything to show them up.

"It's just that when Spahn was on the mound, everything was under control. If he had a sore arm, you wouldn't know it because he always pitched."[16]

"How I loved to pitch," Spahn said. "Whenever they gave me the ball and it was my turn, I always had the same thought. This was my day in the sun."[17]

In August of 2003, a statue of Spahn was unveiled outside of Atlanta's Turner Field, joining likenesses of Hank Aaron, Ty Cobb, and Phil Niekro. The bronzed image of the left-hander portrayed him in the middle of his classic windup with his right leg high in the air.

Gary Caruso, a longtime fan of Spahn, spearheaded the effort to get the statue built and erected. Among the contributors to the project were Hall of Fame members Yogi Berra, Stan Musial, Nolan Ryan, Red Schoendienst, and Niekro; former Braves Ernie Johnson, Tom Glavine, and Greg Maddux; current Braves John Smoltz and Chipper Jones along with manager Bobby Cox; New York Yankees' pitcher Randy Johnson; former Boston Red Sox second baseman Bobby Doerr; pop music star Elton John; and Braves chairman Bill Bartholomay. Spahn, whose jersey number 21 has been retired by the Braves, attended the unveiling ceremony despite being confined to a wheelchair.

Noted baseball writer Thomas Boswell wrote this following the death of Spahn: "Line them up, all the best hurlers since Babe Ruth's home runs tempted baseball to juice its ball and shorten its fences in 1920. That's when the game we recognize today began. You can have Roger Clemens and Sandy Koufax, Lefty Grove and Nolan Ryan, Pedro Martinez and Randy Johnson, Tom Seaver and Steve Carlton, Bob Feller and Greg Maddux. With my one pick for total accomplishments and best entire career, just give me Warren Spahn.

"Not because he won more games than any southpaw ever because since 1900, only Christy Mathewson matched his thirteen seasons with twenty wins. The reason is simpler. No statistic is more basic, more bedrock, more full of indisputable truth than wins by a starting pitcher. Especially when, like Spahn, you loathe the sight of relievers and lead the league in complete games nine times."[18]

Teammates and opponents alike admired and respected the great left-hander. In his book, _I Had a Hammer_, Hank Aaron tells a heart-warming story that speaks volumes about his feelings for his former teammate. Aaron was recalling a 1965 game when the Braves played the Mets, with Spahn on the mound for the New York club.

"We found ourselves up against the man we'd been playing behind for more than a decade. For about as long as I had known them, Spahn and Eddie Mathews had argued back and forth about what would happen if they ever faced each other in a game. This was the time to find out.

"The bases were loaded, so there was no room to fool around. Eddie didn't. He walked up, dug in, and hit a grand slam. It was a big shot for the Braves, but there wasn't a lot of backslapping. We all felt for Spahn. He was forty-four years old, and he just didn't have it anymore.

"When I came up next, I couldn't bring myself to go after him. I won't say that I ever deliberately made an out, but I will say that I didn't have the heart to get a base hit that night against Warren Spahn. I just had too much respect for the man as a pitcher. I think I popped up."[19]

NITRO LEW

Lew Burdette had "the act" down before Gaylord Perry even thought about performing it.

The act consisted of incessant fidgeting that included touching the cap bill, the shirt, parts of the face and neck, and anything else to make the opposing team think the pitcher was throwing a spitball.

There was considerable speculation that both Burdette and Perry did more than go through the motions, that they actually loaded up the baseball. In fact, Perry was suspended in 1982 for doctoring the ball.

Any foreign substance on a baseball makes it move more, which is an obvious advantage for a pitcher. The notion that a pitcher might throw a spitball can also provide him with an edge. Putting that idea into hitters' heads was as vital to Burdette as his variety of pitches and his control. He shrewdly used the psychological ploy to great advantage.

Selva Lewis Burdette Junior, who started his baseball career in the New York Yankees organization, retired from the game in 1967, five years after Perry threw his first big league pitch. By that time, Burdette's antics on the mound were well chronicled.

A native of Nitro, West Virginia, he was dubbed "Nitro Lew" by Bob Prince, the famous and colorful Pittsburgh Pirates baseball broadcaster. Burdette played football and basketball for Nitro School, which included grades one through twelve, but there was no baseball team. He tried out for the American Legion team, but did not make it.

He recalled playing street baseball with tennis balls, and he played sandlot ball. Sometimes, his dad took Lew to see semi-pro baseball games in Charleston, which was fifteen miles from Nitro.

The Yankees signed Burdette as an amateur free agent in 1947 and sent him to their Norfolk Tars farm team in the Piedmont League. The same year, he pitched in the Class C Can-Am (Canadian-American) League. His record was only 9–10 with the Amsterdam Rugmakers, but he had a very good 2.82 ERA. Teammates said he spent much of his paycheck playing pinball. He went 16–11 with a 2.02 earned run average pitching for the Quincy Gems of the Three-I League in 1948 and was 6–7 the next year with a 5.26 ERA for the Kansas City Blues of the American Association. He was called up by New York late in the 1950 season after posting a 7–7 record with a 4.79 earned run average for the Blues. The Yanks sent him to San Francisco of the Pacific Coast League for the 1951 campaign, and he was 14–12 for the Seals.

The Yankees, wanting to strengthen their pitching for the stretch run of the 1951 pennant race, traded him to the Boston Braves in August for veteran Johnny Sain. The Braves also received 50,000 dollars.[20]

Burdette, whose career with the Yankees amounted to one and a third innings without a decision, got into three games with Boston in 1951. He pitched four and one-third innings and was roughed up for six hits and three earned runs.

The Braves put the right-hander to work the next season as he made forty-five appearances, including nine starts. He notched seven saves and got eight more in 1953, when he had a fine 15–5 record and 3.24 earned run average in 175 innings. He became a starter when Vern Bickford and Johnny Antonelli both suffered broken fingers.

Burdette joined Milwaukee's rotation on a regular basis in 1954, when he started thirty-two times, pitched 238 innings, had a 2.76 ERA, and again won fifteen games to go with fourteen losses.

After logging 230 innings the next season, he pitched at least 256 for six consecutive years, while averaging nineteen wins during that period. In 1956, he had nineteen wins, six shutouts, and a 2.70 earned run average, the latter two figures leading the National League. He became a twenty-game winner for the first time in 1958 and came back with twenty-one victories the following season.

In 1959, Burdette pitched a brilliant game and gained a win that was infamous in the sense that it came at the expense of the man who turned in the greatest all-time losing effort on the mound.

It was May 26, 1959, when Burdette and Pittsburgh left-hander Harvey Haddix hooked up in a tense pitching duel. The game was scoreless through twelve innings, and great drama was added by the fact that Haddix had a perfect game — thirty-six Braves had gone to the plate and thirty-six had been retired. Milwaukee scored a run in the bottom of the thirteenth to win, making the Pirates' little lefty the disappointed loser on a one-hitter. Burdette was the winner after scattering a dozen hits.

Burdette phoned Haddix in the Pirates' locker room after the game and told him it was a shame the way things turned out, even going so far as to say he would have given up the victory if Haddix could have gotten a perfect-game win.

Then, ever the jokester, Burdette said, "Harvey, I thought you knew better than to bunch your hits." Haddix hung up on Burdette, but the next day, he told a large group of sportswriters what the Braves' pitcher had said, and everyone enjoyed a big laugh.[21]

Burdette will always be remembered for winning three games in Milwaukee's 1957 World Series triumph over the Yankees. Another highlight was his 1960 no-hitter, when he scored the only run in a 1–0 win over the Phillies.

The only batter to reach base against him was Tony Gonzalez, who was hit by a pitch in the fifth inning and then was erased on a double play. So, Burdette faced the minimum of twenty-seven batters as he pitched the second of what would be three successive shutouts.

He won nineteen games in 1960 and had eighteen wins the following season. His record fell to 10–9 in 1962, when he was reduced to nineteen starts. The Braves traded Burdette to St. Louis in the middle of the 1963 season, and a year later, he was dealt by the Cardinals to the Chicago Cubs.

He also pitched for the Philadelphia Phillies before closing out his career with the California Angels in the American League, where he was used strictly in relief. He managed to reach double figures in victories just once in his last five years and did not start a game in either of his final two seasons.

Burdette notched his 200th win July 22, 1966, when he pitched two innings of scoreless relief for California. Ironically, the monumental victory came against the Yankees, the team with which he began his career and the team that helped him gain his greatest fame.

The Angels released Burdette in September of 1967, putting the wraps on an eighteen-year career that included a 203–144 record and two All-Star appearances. He had a .183 batting average and twelve home runs, smacking two in one game three times.

He had a 4–2 record in 49.1 innings in two World Series. His lone Fall Classic hit was a three-run homer.

Burdette did not throw all that hard and relied on moving the ball around and keeping it down, getting batters to hit into the dirt. He threw sidearm and three-quarters, so he had natural movement on his pitches. His best pitches were a slider, which broke down and away from a right-handed batter, and a sinker, which went down and in to righties.

Usually, when he threw the ball high, it was also inside, and he never minded coming in on hitters. Burdette said he was accused of throwing at hitters and noted that, "Early Wynn always said that he was the meanest pitcher in the American League, and I was the meanest in the National League."[22]

Burdette hit fifty-six batters in eighteen big league seasons, an average of just over three per year, with a high of eight. His control was very good as he averaged issuing 1.84 bases on balls per nine innings in a career that covered 3,067 innings. That is fourth behind Robin Roberts (1.73), Carl Hubbell, and Juan Marichal on the all-time list of modern-day pitchers with at least 3,000 innings.

But he was not always noted for possessing good control. Lefty O'Doul had been Burdette's manager when he played for the San Francisco Seals in the Pacific Coast League, and he told his right-hander to drill batters.

"He would stand on the dugout steps," Burdette recalled, "and tell me to hit the batter in the belly. So I had to do it. One Sunday morning, I read in the paper that I had tied O'Doul's league record for hit batsmen. The record had been set in 1922 or something like that.

"I didn't say anything about it, and I was pitching that day when O'Doul shouted, 'Hit him in the belly!' He didn't care if the batter heard him. And I shook my head no. He came out to the mound and questioned my refusal.

"I said, 'I read an interesting article in the paper this morning.' I told him I didn't want to beat him, just tie him. He said, 'Dammit, at least come close!' Lefty loved that story."[23]

Burdette, like Perry, enjoyed his reputation as a spitball pitcher. "Let them think I throw it," Burdette used to say. "That gives me an edge because it is another pitch they have to worry about. They are intimidated because I pitch inside, and I have an additional advantage because hitters worry that I throw a spitter."

Burleigh Grimes, who was the last pitcher to throw the spitter before it was banned, was a roving pitching coach with the New York Yankees minor league system when Burdette was in the Yankees' organization.

Burdette said he asked Grimes to teach him how to throw a spitter. Grimes told Burdette if he taught him the pitch and Burdette was caught, he would be thrown out of baseball. But, Grimes added, if Burdette made batters think he was throwing a spitball, they would be looking for it.

"Burleigh Grimes told me if my pitches moved, the hitters would complain because they were all egotistical," Burdette said. "I found that if I could get one of the first three hitters in the first inning to go back to the dugout and say I was cheating, by the fifth inning, everybody on the team would want to see the ball when they batted.

"If I made any motion to my mouth, they became suspicious. So I would go through my ritual, going to my hat and then crossing my chest. I got so many Catholic medals and sacred heart medals in the mail. I had a whole drawer of mementos which fans sent to me, 'from one good Catholic to another.' I was a Southern Baptist.

"Hitters were so funny," Burdette said, "that I just had a ball on the mound. I would almost bust out laughing when they would complain about a spitball after I had really thrown a bad change of pace, a screwball, or a slider.

"Even if they hit a hard liner straight at the center fielder, they went by the mound complaining like the dickens. I'd suck it all up. The umpires didn't believe them. They would come out and practically undress me. I would tell them they missed a certain place, and they'd get a little ticked."[24]

"Lew had ice water in his veins," teammate Gene Conley said. "Nothing bothered him, on or off the mound. He was a chatterbox out there ... he would talk to himself, to the batter, the umpire, and sometimes even to the ball."[25]

The Burdette prank that gained the most national attention involved baseball cards, the 1959 Topps set, to be specific. When posing for his picture to be used on the card, the right-handed Burdette picked up Spahn's glove, put it on and had his picture taken. The card gave the impression that he was a left-hander.

And, upon retiring from baseball, it was fitting that Burdette did so with a line that revived speculation about his having thrown a spitball. "They were starting to hit the dry side of the ball," he said, adding that was how he knew it was time to quit.[26]

THE DODGER KILLER

Bob Buhl never won twenty games in a season, he was chosen to just one All-Star team, and he lost his only World Series decision. But, although he was often lost in the shadows of Warren Spahn and Lew Burdette, he was a solid starting pitcher who won his share of big games.

Buhl was particularly tough on the Dodgers, and in 1956, he beat them eight times in nine decisions. He was very consistent, averaging eleven wins per year over fifteen seasons.

"The team I liked to face the most was Brooklyn," Buhl said. "I even looked forward to facing them in Ebbets Field, which was too small and had tough fans right on top of us.

"I wanted to beat the Dodgers because, ever since I was in the league, they went first-class and had the best. When we went on trains, they would be flying, and they would have Vero Beach for spring training, and we didn't have diddly. We were envious of them, especially since they kept winning pennants."[27]

Buhl, a right-hander, was always a fast worker. He was aggressive and pitched inside, staking a claim to his share of the plate. He knocked Brooklyn's Gil Hodges off the plate and then fed him curveballs on the outside corner. He tied up muscular catcher Roy Campanella with high, tight fastballs.

"I was mean on the mound," Buhl said. "I'd brush guys back; I didn't care who they were. And I was wild to begin with, so that helped me out. Right-handed batters didn't like to face me too much. The fellows I didn't have trouble with, I didn't have to bother with. I always figured they were looking for the brushback, so I would keep them waiting.

"I wouldn't let hitters dig in. They were thrown off stride because I had a herky-jerky motion and was quick. I was a short-armed pitcher, and instead of moving way back and way forward, I'd let loose tighter to my body.

"I never took a loss home," Buhl said. "If I was mad, I would get away from everybody because I didn't want to talk about it. After a little while, it was gone. Fortunately, I didn't always have to wait for my next start to pitch, but could relieve for a couple of innings to keep sharp."[28]

Originally signed by the Chicago White Sox, Buhl played with the Milwaukee Brewers, a Triple-A minor league team. His contract was bought by Dallas of the Double-A Texas League and then sold to the Boston Braves late in the 1950 season.

In December, he was drafted into the Army. He served two years in the military and was a paratrooper in Korea. He pitched his first game in the majors in 1953, and it was a start against the New York Giants.

"It was about twenty degrees in Milwaukee," Buhl said. "I knew it would sting the batters' hands if I threw inside fastballs. I believe I broke eight bats that night, and I got my first victory, 8–1.

"At one point, I had two outs, and Giants manager Leo Durocher had a guy try to steal home on me. He wanted to see if I was a rookie who would balk or if I knew what I was doing. I threw a hard pitch that knocked the hitter down, and the runner was out at home. Leo never tried that with me again."[29]

Buhl won thirteen games, pitched three shutouts, and had a 2.97 earned run average in his rookie season. The following winter, he played in Puerto Rico in order to improve his change-up and slider. Upon reporting to the Braves, he found he was worn out, and he was removed from the starting rotation. His record dropped to 2–7 in just 110.1 innings.

Buhl bounced back in 1955 to be a thirteen-game winner again. He had back-to-back seasons of winning eighteen games with 216.2 innings pitched each year. His 1957 earned run average was a career-best 2.74.

After winning forty-nine games in three years, Buhl experienced arm trouble in 1958. He started only ten games and pitched seventy-three innings, with five victories.

"I couldn't even lift my arm to put on a jacket," he recalled. "The Braves sent me to the Mayo Clinic, Johns Hopkins, and all over the country trying to find out what was wrong.

"I received shots in the back with cortisone and novocaine and was subjected to all kinds of tests. One doctor wanted to operate and take a tendon out of my shoulder, but another pitcher who had that done told me he couldn't use his arm afterward because he had lost control. One doctor said I would have to learn to pitch left-handed. These were professional doctors!

"I happened to be living in an apartment that was owned by a dentist, and he asked me to come to his office. He turned on an electrical device and went through every tooth, checking nerves. He found two teeth that had no

Bob Buhl, the old Dodger Killer, had outstanding stuff. Normally overshadowed by Spahn and Burdette, he was the Braves' stopper for the key stretch of 1957 when the other two aces were struggling.

nerves and said that the poison from those teeth could be settling in my arm at the spot I used the most.

"His brother, another dentist, pulled the teeth. He put two false teeth in and gave me medicine to take the poison out of my system. Two weeks later, I was pitching with no pain. I was very fortunate. A dentist saved my career."[30]

Buhl rebounded to win fifteen games and lead the National League with four shutouts, with a 2.86 earned run average in 1959. He had sixteen wins and a career-high 238.2 innings pitched in 1960 before dipping to a 9–10 record the next season. Then, after pitching just one game in 1962 with the Braves, they traded him to the Chicago Cubs for left-handed pitcher Jack Curtis.

Over four seasons, Buhl won twelve, eleven, fifteen, and thirteen games for the Cubs, earning his lone All-Star selection in 1964 when he pitched three shutouts.

He went to the Philadelphia Phillies in 1966 in the deal that sent eventual Hall of Famer Ferguson Jenkins to the Cubs. Buhl got six wins, then was released by the Phils after making only three relief appearances the following season.

Buhl was sometimes the target of jokes aimed at his batting, which was terrible, to say the least. Not only were his results ugly, so was his swing. It was not much better with a golf club, according to Burdette, who loved to tell the following story.

"Once, when we were playing golf on an afternoon off in San Francisco, we were playing with this guy who supplied meat to the best restaurants in the area. Buhl, who had an odd baseball stroke, swung at the ball on the first tee, and the guy told him he could get Bob a job for $50,000 a year in a slaughterhouse. He said, 'You've got the greatest steer-killing stroke I've ever seen in my life.'

"Buhl almost walked off the course," Burdette said. "We didn't really tease Bob about his hitting. We all knew he couldn't hit, but he was a good bunter. He could fake a bunt and chop down on the ball pretty good if he choked up on the bat."[31]

Buhl was a notoriously poor hitter who set a major league futility record by going hitless in seventy at-bats during the 1962 season. He extended the woeful streak to eighty-eight at-bats the following year before getting a single. He had a .089 lifetime batting average.

In fifteen seasons, Buhl compiled a record of 166–132 with a 3.55 ERA.

Despite all of the records Spahn set, he is not appreciated enough by modern-day fans. The fact that he pitched so well for so long, while piling up a huge number of innings and complete games as well as victories, is truly amazing.

Burdette's name will frequently come up in World Series conversations, but he should also be remembered for long-term consistency as well as his ability to win big games.

Buhl was underrated, mostly because he pitched in the same rotation as Spahn and Burdette. He had exceptional stuff and strung together some exceptional seasons. He was an ace in his own right.

There have not been many teams in baseball history that could throw pitchers like Spahn, Burdette, and Buhl against an opponent in the same series. The Milwaukee Braves were blessed in that respect.

4

Filling a Big Hole

During the winter months leading up to the 1957 season, the second base position was often the topic of discussion regarding the Milwaukee Braves and was constantly cited as their most glaring weakness. On a team that boasted three dangerous middle-of-the-lineup sluggers and three of the best starting pitchers in baseball, the second baseman was no better than mediocre, leaving something to be desired both offensively and defensively. Surely, thought sportswriters as well as the general managers of other National League teams, the Braves would go out and make a move. There were rumblings during the offseason that Milwaukee GM John Quinn was making overtures toward veteran Red Schoendienst of the New York Giants, but spring training came and went, the first two months of the season passed by, and, still, nothing had happened.

Danny O'Connell was therefore a man on the spot when he opened the season as the Braves' second sacker. He knew he was playing with one of the most talented teams in baseball, but he also knew he was considered its weakest link. And, while he was happy to not only be a member of a pennant contender, but a member of its starting lineup, he felt uncomfortable. Part of it was the position. He always felt more natural on the left side of the infield. He came up as a shortstop and would later play a lot of third base. He did not see the ball off the bat the same while playing on the right side, and he was not particularly good at making the pivot on the double play.

A native of New Jersey, O'Connell grew up hearing all about the Bums of Brooklyn and was thrilled to start his career in the Dodgers organization. He saw it as an opportunity, however, when he was traded to Pittsburgh, and he became an instant fan favorite there. Recalled from the minors in the middle of the 1950 season, O'Connell batted .292 while playing mostly shortstop for the Pirates. Following two years in the military, he hit .294 in 588 at-bats and played in 104 games at third base.

Branch Rickey, who had put together the St. Louis Cardinals' farm system and later signed Jackie Robinson for the Dodgers, was running things for the Pirates in the early fifties. He was known as a skinflint who often traded good players before they commanded high salaries. Rickey drew the ire of Pittsburgh followers when he dealt the popular O'Connell to Milwaukee on the day after Christmas in 1953. The Braves sent six players, including four pitchers, to the Pirates and also paid $100,000 to get O'Connell. Jack Dittmer had made twenty-three errors as the Braves' second baseman in the '53 season, and O'Connell was acquired, albeit at a costly price, to plug the hole.

He did the job offensively in his first season in Milwaukee, batting a solid .279, while committing a dozen errors in 103 games at second base. O'Connell fell off to .225 and .239 the next two years, and he was hitting .235 through the first third of the 1957 season. In the field, he was not getting to as many balls as other second basemen, and his limited range accentuated his limited defensive skills.

At the start of June, the Braves called up Bobby Malkmus from their Wichita farm club and inserted him into the lineup at second base when St. Louis visited County Stadium. Malkmus made a nice defensive play to help Warren Spahn get out of a bases-loaded mess in the sixth inning, but the roof caved in after that. The Cardinals scored two runs in the seventh and five in the eighth, when they knocked Spahn out of the box. He failed to get anybody out in the eighth inning and absorbed his third loss in four decisions. The only good news for the Braves was that third baseman Eddie Mathews returned to the lineup. They had lost their third straight to fall into fourth place, three and one-half games out of first.

Malkmus continued to start and lead off for Milwaukee over the next four games, but he managed just one hit, thus ending that experiment. Malkmus played in only two more games at second base and a total of thirteen games all season, an anemic .091 batting average punching his ticket out of Wisconsin. The next year, he was in the American League with the Washington Senators. He played in 121 games and hit .231 with the 1961 Philadelphia Phillies, his six-year major league career ending one year later.

Some of the Braves players thought Felix Mantilla might be the man to win the second base job. Hank Aaron's roommate in Milwaukee, he is the godfather of Aaron's daughter, Gaile. Mantilla did play second for thirteen games in 1957, and that was where he spent most of his time defensively when he had his two best years in the majors, both with the Boston Red Sox. He slammed thirty home runs and had sixty-four RBI in 1964, getting eighteen homers and ninety-two RBI the following season.

But Mantilla was young — twenty-two years old — and erratic, committing eleven errors in thirty-five games at shortstop, the position he played most frequently in 1957. At the plate, he showed flashes of power by hitting four home runs, but he batted .236 in 182 at-bats. He remained a capable utility infielder.

Ernie Johnson worked out of a ninth-inning mess to save Bob Buhl's fourth win as the Braves avoided being swept in the three-game series with the Cardinals. But after also losing two of three to the Giants in New York's Polo Grounds, Milwaukee was only six games over .500 and had fallen three games behind the league-leading Cincinnati Redlegs.

Schoendienst had Braves executives salivating in the third game as he belted his fourth home run of the three-game series and made a sparkling defensive play to rob Frank Torre of a base hit. In the lone Milwaukee win of the series, slow-footed Joe Adcock legged out an inside-the-park home run after hitting the ball 450 feet. Johnson was the winning pitcher in relief and slugged a three-run shot for the Braves.

O'Connell returned to second base, but in a new spot in the batting order. He was ill suited to be a leadoff guy and had been batting first because Milwaukee really did not have anyone else to do the job. Although he did not strike out much, his on-base percentage (OBP) was never very high. In a dozen big league seasons, his best OBP was .361, and it was barely over .300 in 1957. (In comparison, Richie Ashburn, the outstanding Phillies leadoff man who is in the Hall of Fame, had a career .396 OBP.)

O'Connell was batting in the seventh slot when the Braves opened a three-game series at Pittsburgh's Forbes Field. Haney moved speedy center fielder Billy Bruton from seventh into the leadoff spot, and Bruton responded with a single, a double, and a triple. Throughout his career, he did not have a high OBP, either, but Haney was hoping Bruton's speed might help produce more runs from the top of the lineup than from the bottom. The Braves' manager further shook up the batting order by moving Aaron from second to cleanup to take advantage of his ability to drive in runs, with Logan elevated from sixth to second.

On June 7, Spahn was back in form, shutting out the Pirates on seven hits for his sixth victory. His control was the key, as he walked only one batter and kept the ball out of the middle of the plate. The Milwaukee infield pulled off three slick double plays, and first baseman Joe Adcock lined a pair of doubles. Sitting at his locker and peeling off the gray shirt with the red number 21 on the back, Spahn felt a sense of relief. He had been struggling, going through a bad stretch — pitchers endure slumps just as hitters do — that seemed worse because of the circumstances. His roommate, Lew Burdette, was missing starts with arm troubles, and the ball club was not playing its best baseball. Spahn, as the Braves' elder statesman and leader, felt a responsibility to shoulder an additional load and pick up the slack. Although his teammates certainly did not feel the lefty was letting them down, he had felt that way, and it was good to pick his team up and pitch an outstanding game. Better yet, it was a complete game that gave Milwaukee's overworked bullpen a deserved rest.

The next day, right-hander Bob Trowbridge allowed one run and six hits over ten innings to earn his first win of the season, but the Pirates salvaged a double-header split with Milwaukee while the Redlegs were sweeping a pair from the Dodgers. Aaron homered in both games for the Braves, giving him fifteen in forty-seven outings.

Milwaukee began a four-game series with the Dodgers in fourth place as the Philadelphia Phillies had sneaked into third. The Braves were two and one-half games behind first-place Cincinnati, which was playing four games in Pittsburgh. The Pirates had a record of 16–32 and were fourteen games out of the National League lead, so it looked like the Redlegs had a golden chance to gain ground on both the Braves and the Dodgers. Bob Buhl and Don Newcombe were mound opponents in the Milwaukee-Brooklyn series opener. The game was played at Roosevelt Stadium in Jersey City, New Jersey, where the Dodgers occasionally scheduled home contests. The last three games of the series would be played at Ebbets Field.

Buhl, as he did so many times over his career, dazzled the Dodgers. He went the distance and gave up four hits in a 3–1 Braves win, with Gil Hodges getting three of the Dodgers' hits to raise his league-leading batting average to .371. Mathews homered and drove in two runs, and Logan, perhaps the most underrated shortstop in the NL, had three hits and took part in three double plays. The Pirates beat the Redlegs, and at the end of the day, Cincinnati, Milwaukee, Brooklyn, and Philadelphia were even in the loss column with twenty setbacks apiece, just one more than St. Louis. The race was tight, and it was crowded.

In the second game of the series, Bobby Thomson's grand slam highlighted a five-run fifth inning and Adcock also hit a home run as the Braves handed the Dodgers their fourth loss in a row, 7–2. Brooklyn's Roy Campanella smacked the 237th homer of his career, giving him the National League record for lifetime home runs by a catcher. Things were not going well for the Redlegs as they lost again in Pittsburgh. Their lead over Milwaukee had been trimmed to a half-game.

The Braves and Dodgers split the final two games of the series. Milwaukee starting pitcher Gene Conley did not last an inning and saw his record fall to 0–4 as Brooklyn scored nine runs in the first two innings and came out on top of an 11–9 slugfest. Burdette, seeing his first action in more than two weeks, relieved in the first inning and did not make it through the second. He was roughed up for five hits and six runs, three of them earned. The Dodgers scored six unearned runs as a result of errors by Conley and Logan.

Reserve catcher Carl Sawatski clouted a three-run homer and added a pair of doubles for the Braves in an 8–5 win. His homer came in the eighth inning off of Brooklyn relief ace Clem Labine, who had been almost perfect in recent weeks. With the score tied, Aaron and Frank Torre singled, and Thomson brought Aaron home with a double. Sawatski, who already had a pair of doubles, seemed a likely candidate to get an intentional walk since Bob Trowbridge, the Milwaukee pitcher, was the next scheduled hitter. But Brooklyn manager Walter Alston let Labine pitch to Sawatski, who delivered what would be the game-deciding blow. The Dodgers scored once in the ninth, but that was all. For the third time of the season, Ernie Johnson came out of the bullpen to stop a Brooklyn rally.

Sawatski, a twenty-nine-year-old third-string catcher whose bat was better than his glove, proved to be a valuable left-handed hitter off the bench for the Braves. Used mostly as a pinch-hitter, he popped six home runs and drove in seventeen runs in 105 at-bats in 1957, while appearing behind the plate in twenty-eight games.

Always known as a ready brawler, Sawatski was traded by the Braves to Philadelphia during the 1958 season and later enjoyed his best years with the St. Louis Cardinals. He caught in seventy games for them and hit thirteen home runs in 1962, a year after batting a career-high .299. He bounced around quite a bit and was twice a member of both the Phillies and the Braves. The journeyman catcher was involved in three mystery deals. The Philadelphia Phillies signed him in 1945 and sent him to the Boston Braves two years later in what was called an "unknown transaction." The same description was used for the deal that saw Sawatski go from the Braves to the Cubs in 1948. Five years later, he moved across town in Chicago when the White Sox claimed him on waivers from the Cubs. The ChiSox sent him to the Milwaukee Braves in another "unknown transaction" prior to the 1957 season, and Fred Haney was glad to have him on his bench.

Sawatski shared the offensive spotlight with center fielder Billy Bruton in the Braves' series-concluding win over the Dodgers. Milwaukee got a pair

Johnny Logan was from the old school, a hard-nosed scrapper who was solid at shortstop and at the plate. At different times, he batted near the top and bottom of the Milwaukee lineup, driving in big runs and advancing runners.

of home runs from Bruton and the crucial bomb from its reserve catcher in the 8–5 win. The game was spiced by a brawl, started when Don Drysdale hit Logan in the back with a fastball. The shortstop was the next batter following Bruton's second homer, a two-run blast into the upper deck in center field. When he reached first base, Logan shouted something to Drysdale and then charged the mound. Dodger first baseman Gil Hodges attempted to grab Logan, but was tackled by Milwaukee first base coach John Riddle.

Alston, who was on his way to the mound to remove Drysdale, found himself in the middle of the action. Drysdale landed a crisp right cross to the head of Logan, opening a gash above the shortstop's left eye. Alston and others pulled Logan away, while Mathews sprinted from the on-deck circle to smack Drysdale with a right-hand punch and throw him to the ground, with players from both teams streaming onto the field and piling on. Hodges pulled Mathews out of the mass of bodies and dragged him halfway to third base. Finally, after five minutes of mayhem, the game resumed with Logan and Drysdale both getting thrown out by the umpires. The Dodgers' pitcher was going to be sent to the showers anyway; he just had his billfold lightened in the process.

Throughout his career, Drysdale was known as a tough customer who not only pitched inside, but would plunk hitters who dug in or who had the misfortune of following batters who had hit home runs off him. Like Early Wynn, who won 300 games pitching in the American League, he was said to be the kind of hurler who would brush back his own mother. Drysdale admitted being angry after Bruton's homer, but said he did not mean to hit Logan, that the pitch was simply a fastball that got away. Logan, too proud to say Drysdale may have gotten the better of him in the fight, laughed about his cut and said it was the result of a fight with Cincinnati's Hal Jeffcoat nearly three weeks earlier.[1]

Logan was no stranger to fisticuffs, and, in fact, he always seemed to enjoy a good fight. It was not that he went looking for trouble; trouble just seemed to find him. For his part, Logan did not go out of his way to avoid confrontations. He took offense even when none was intended, and his ears were like antennae, tuned in to possible insults that he felt called for retaliation. The shortstop was something of a sergeant of arms for the Braves; he was always quick to defend his teammates when one of them was hit by a pitch or was barreled into extra hard by a baserunner. Some of the Milwaukee players liked to tease Logan, saying he started fights and Eddie Mathews saved his neck by finishing them.

On a team that had four future Hall of Famers, Logan was often overlooked. But not by his teammates, who recognized him as a clutch hitter and hard-nosed leader. Logan played hard, and he expected others to do the same, and he never hesitated to say something to anyone — star or part-timer — whom he felt was giving less than his best.

Logan did not have outstanding range, but he studied hitters and positioned himself well, thereby enabling him to make plays because of his experience and savvy. He did not possess an exceptionally strong arm, but made up for it with a quick release. His release and smart positioning helped him lead National League shortstops in assists in 1954 (489), '55 (511), '57 (440), and '58 (481). He led the league in fielding percentage by a shortstop for three straight years (1952–54), with a high of .975 in 1954. Logan was one of those players about whom it was said that he got everything he could out of what he had.

He had some pop in his bat and hit ninety-three career home runs, with a high of fifteen in 1956 and six seasons with ten or more. His best year at the plate was 1955, when he batted .297 with thirteen homers and eighty-three runs batted in. That was one of back-to-back seasons in which he played all 154 games. He never struck out more than fifty-eight times in a season, averaging just one K for every eleven at-bats during his thirteen-year big league career. Logan did make quite a few errors, committing thirty or more three times. He also did many of those little things that do not show up on a stat sheet, but help win ballgames.

Logan was signed by the Boston Braves in 1947 following a year of college and a stint in the military. He was twenty years old when he began his pro baseball career at Evansville of the Three-I League. In 1948, he played with Dallas in the Texas League and with Pawtucket in the New England League, and two years later, he joined the Milwaukee Brewers of the American Association. His big league debut was April 17, 1951, but he was sent back to Milwaukee, where he played until late in the 1952 season. He returned to Milwaukee again the next spring, but it was with the Braves.

Somewhat of a character, Logan is credited with some quotes that would later be known as Yogi-isms because of the penchant of the Yankee catcher for making everyday conversations extremely funny. Here are a few expressions attributed to the Milwaukee shortstop:

• "Rome wasn't born in a day."

• "I'll have pie a la mode with ice cream."

• "I heard his footprints coming down the hall."

• "I will perish this trophy forever."

- "I know the name but I can't replace the face."

- "Tonight, we're honoring one of the all-time greats in baseball, Stan Musial. He's immoral." — Logan introducing Musial at a banquet.

- Informed that a box score depriving him of a hit was a typographical error, Logan responded, "The Hell it was. That was a clean base hit."[2]

Logan was one of those guys who might boot a routine grounder in a game that was hopelessly lost or in which the Braves had a big lead. Then, the next day, with the game on the line, he would come up with a sensational stop, going into the hole and throwing out the runner at first or diving for a ball behind second and tossing to the second baseman for a force out. In other words, he was a much better shortstop than his fielding percentage would indicate. The rest of the Milwaukee players knew he was a winner.

Taking three out of four games from the Dodgers was always a big deal; doing it in Ebbets Field (and Jersey's Roosevelt Stadium) was extra sweet. Meanwhile, the Redlegs were swept in their four-game stay in Pittsburgh. The result was a three-game change in the standings that left the Braves one-half game ahead of Cincinnati. The Redlegs stopped their four-game skid with a win in the Polo Grounds, then continued their tailspin by losing four more in a row.

Milwaukee won the first three of a four-game series in Philadelphia. Spahn threw a three-hitter, and the Braves broke open a close game with a six-run explosion in the ninth inning of the opener against the Phillies. Hank Aaron's seventeenth home run was an opposite-field blast that came in the sixth with two runners on base and wiped out the Phils' one-run lead. Logan had three hits and two RBI. Spahn helped himself by knocking in a run and starting two double plays on bouncers to the mound.

Buhl gave up four hits and went nine innings, and Milwaukee again pulled away in the late innings by scoring four runs over the last three frames. Aaron hit another home run and Thomson had four hits and two runs batted in, but the batting star of the day was Del Rice, Buhl's "personal" catcher. Rice slammed a two-run homer and also had a single and a triple. Halfway through June, the Braves were eleven games above .500 and two games in front of the second-place Dodgers.

The trading deadline was June fifteenth at midnight, and six hours before the clock struck twelve, Milwaukee finally made the long-anticipated deal for Red Schoendienst. The transaction was, in the minds of all of the Braves' players, one of the keys to their 1957 season. Surely, it was important that Lew Burdette's arm injury was not serious and that neither Hank Aaron nor Eddie

Mathews missed many games. Acquiring Schoendienst, though, meant so much in so many ways. He was a fine player who produced with his bat and glove, he was a leader, and he had played on a World Series winner with the Cardinals in 1946.

Schoendienst, who was thirty-four years old at the time and in his thirteenth major league season, went to Milwaukee from New York. The Giants got Bobby Thomson, who remains the most heroic figure of all time for fans of the team when it was in New York, along with Danny O'Connell and right-handed pitcher Ray Crone.

The Giants, and particularly their fans, were excited to see Thomson back in the Polo Grounds. He had swatted thirty-two home runs in his magical 1951 season, the high of six years in which he hit at least twenty-four roundtrippers for the New York team. He also drove in more than 100 runs four times. In Milwaukee, he connected for twenty home runs just once in two seasons and parts of two others, and he never knocked in more than seventy-four runs. His 1954 season with the Braves was shortened to forty-one games by a broken ankle in spring training. Thomson was batting .236 with four home runs when he left the Braves.

He would not enjoy another premium season. Playing in eighty-one games for the Giants in 1957, Thomson hit eight home runs and batted .242. When the team moved to San Francisco, it traded Thomson to the Cubs for outfielder Bob Speake and cash just days before the 1958 season began. Thomson hit .283, slugged twenty-one home runs, and had eighty-two RBI for the Cubs, but it was downhill after that, and he finished out his career in 1960 in the American League.

The key to the trade, as far as the Giants were concerned, was Crone. Only twenty-five, he already had two double-figure win seasons, with ten victories in 1955 and eleven in '56, and his earned run average was under 4.00 both years. His record at the time of the trade was 3–1 for the Braves. His future was bright, and the New York front office could see Crone as a solid member of the club's starting rotation for years to come. That it did not work out that way was a bitter disappointment. Crone went 4–8 for the Giants over the last three and a half months of the 1957 season. The next year, he made only one start and pitched just fourteen innings before his career came to an end.

O'Connell hit thirty points higher for New York than he had for Milwaukee and also smacked seven home runs, but he did very little for the Giants or anybody else after 1957. In analyzing the trade today, it was very one-sided in favor of the Braves. In fact, many people believe it was a deal that handed the pennant to Milwaukee. Schoendienst was that much of a factor.

Albert "Red" Schoendienst always wanted to be a big league baseball player, and he always wanted to be a St. Louis Cardinal. Growing up in Germantown, Illinois, he had listened to Cardinals games on the radio, and he dreamed of some day having his exploits broadcast as well. He quit school at the age of sixteen and joined the Civilian Conservation Corps. While working with the government-sponsored CCC, he was building fences when a staple ricocheted off of a hedge post into his left eye. The injury not only dimmed his chances of following his brother into professional baseball, it also threatened the loss of the eye. Doctors said the eye would have to be removed, but one physician felt it could be saved. It was. Schoendienst, who had 20/200 vision in his left eye after the injury, did exercises every day to strengthen the eye. But he had difficulty picking up a pitched ball, especially on cloudy days.

Elmer Schoendienst had signed a pro baseball contract, and that is what Red wanted to do. He attended a St. Louis Cardinals tryout and was signed for seventy-five dollars a month. While playing for Union City (Tennessee) in the Class D Kitty League, Schoendienst began his professional career by getting hits in his first eight at-bats. Then he surprisingly asked his manager for permission to bat left-handed against right-handed pitchers. A natural right-handed batter, Schoendienst explained that he could not follow a curve ball from a right-handed pitcher without turning his head because of the problems with his left eye. Fate dealt him a sweet hand as he would become one of the best switch-hitters in major league history, finishing with 2,449 hits and a .289 lifetime batting average in a nineteen-year career that would land him in the Hall of Fame in 1989.[3]

After signing a minor league contract with the Cardinals in 1942, he played for Rochester and was the International League Most Valuable Player the next year. Schoendienst was in the Army and was discharged in 1944 because of his eye problems and a shoulder injury. A few months later, he earned the St. Louis left fielder's job, vacant because Stan Musial was serving in the Army, and led the National League with twenty-six stolen bases. In 1946, with Musial back in left, Schoendienst played some shortstop and third base, but when Lou Klein left the Cards to play in the Mexican League, Red became the everyday second baseman, a job he was already on the way to winning before Klein departed. He led National League second basemen in fielding that season and six more times throughout his career. In 1950, he handled 320 consecutive chances without committing an error, and his 1956 fielding percentage of .9934 was an NL record until broken by the Cubs' Ryan Sandberg thirty years later.

Schoendienst always looked very relaxed at the plate, with tremendous hand-eye coordination that allowed him to frequently spoil pitches by fouling them off until he eventually got a ball he could line for a single or double. But he had good power and hit eighty-four home runs in the majors, including a high of fifteen in 1953 and 1957. His most acclaimed homer came in the fourteenth inning of the 1950 All-Star Game and was a game-winner for the National League. He hit .342 in 1953 and finished second behind Brooklyn's Carl Furillo in the NL batting race, rapping out 193 base hits on the way to a career-high .405 on-base percentage. Schoendienst seldom struck out, fanning an average of just once in every twenty-five at-bats over the course of his career. The most strikeouts he had in a season were thirty-two in 1950 when he amassed 642 official trips to the plate.

To say Schoendienst was disappointed when his beloved Cardinals traded him away was an understatement; he was heart-broken. On June 14, 1956, he went to the New York Giants as part of a nine-player deal. It was mighty hard for him to clean out his locker at Sportsman's Park after spending eleven years with the Redbirds and helping them win two World Series championships.

One year and one day later, the Giants sent him packing again. At the time of the trade, Schoendienst was batting .307 for the New York club, which was in sixth place in the National League, trailing first-place Milwaukee by nine games. The veteran second baseman made up a lot of ground in the standings when he joined the league-leading Braves.

Without Red Schoendienst, the Milwaukee Braves were an outstanding baseball club, one that might have won the 1957 pennant. Any team that has two sluggers the caliber of Hank Aaron and Eddie Mathews in its lineup is certainly dangerous. And any pitching rotation that includes Warren Spahn, Lew Burdette, and Bob Buhl, all in their prime, is capable of stacking victories in bunches. Something was missing, however, until The Trade.

With Schoendienst, the Braves were one of the best ball clubs of all time. While there would still be times when left field was a bit of a problem area, the redhead was a three-fold blessing. First, he solidified Milwaukee's defense with the same kind of steady, if not spectacular, play at second base. Next, he gave the Braves a productive bat at the top of the lineup. And, perhaps most importantly, he gave them leadership.

Almost every Brave would have pointed to Spahn as the team leader. He had years of experience, had pitched for a pennant winner in 1948, and he produced, throwing some of his best games in some of his biggest games. But it is nice to have an everyday player who can lead. Aaron was too young and was not the kind of player a club rallied behind. Ditto for Mathews. The closest thing to an on-field leader before Schoendienst's arrival was shortstop Johnny Logan. He had neither Schoendienst's individual track record nor his good fortune of having played for a pennant-winning team.

The Braves traded for Red Schoendienst, and the veteran second baseman gave the club great leadership along with a good glove and bat. The switch-hitter batted .310 in ninety-three games for Milwaukee in 1957.

"We all look up to Red," Mathews would say as the season progressed. "He's the old pro who has held us together."[4]

Aaron put it this way: "Red came in to the clubhouse and put on the Braves' uniform, and it made us all feel like Superman. We knew he was going to mean so much to our club that wouldn't show up in the box score. He provided the leadership in the clubhouse and on the field. He was never a rah-rah kind of guy, but he definitely became the leader of that ball club."[5]

Milwaukee manager Fred Haney said, "Red's biggest value to the club is the way he has taken charge on the field. That was the big reason we wanted him in the first place. And when he first reported to us, I asked him to take over that role. The boys listen to Schoendienst, where they and players on other clubs wouldn't listen to others, because he is a likeable, modest fellow. He's not a pop-off. By his very experience and personality, he commands respect."[6]

It should be noted, despite all the fanfare about the trade — before and after it was made — Danny O'Connell was not having a miserable season. He simply was not able to provide, offensively or defensively, the kind of every-day play the Braves needed.

"We had other good second basemen on the Braves," pitcher Bob Buhl noted, "but they couldn't turn a double play or hit .300 like Red. He was an established ballplayer, and he got along with everybody. With Red at second, Johnny Logan at short, and Mathews at third, we had a tremendous infield defense."[7]

Batting in the number two slot, Schoendienst added spice to an already potent Milwaukee lineup as he moved runners along the bases and set the table for the Mathews-Aaron home run derby. Haney knew the good thing about putting Schoendienst in the two spot in the batting order was that the veteran second baseman was not concerned about individual statistics. He cared only about winning. Therefore, he did not think twice about giving up an at-bat to advance a base runner or laying down a bunt rather than having the chance to drive in a run. (He laid down seven sacrifice bunts after joining the Braves.) He usually got his bat on the ball, he could hit behind the runner, and he was a clutch hitter. Many of the same attributes helped make Schoendienst an ideal choice to bat leadoff when Billy Bruton later left the team with an injury.

"Schoendienst was a switch hitter with a 'mirror' swing; it was said of him that you could take a picture of him batting right-handed, reverse the negative, and he looked exactly the same as he did batting left."[8]

For the Braves, Schoendienst would rap out 122 hits in ninety-three games and bat .310. Milwaukee went 63–38 after he joined the team. He finished the season with 200 hits and an overall .309 batting average.

In his first game with the Braves, Schoendienst had a single and a triple and scored a run in a 3–2 win in Philadelphia. Juan Pizarro pitched a complete-game five-hitter and Eddie Mathews had two singles and a double. The Phillies took the second game of the doubleheader, 1–0, even though Burdette threw a one-hitter. Lefty Curt Simmons held Milwaukee to six hits and allowed only one runner to reach third base. Both hurlers went the distance in scorching heat that set a Philadelphia record of ninety-nine degrees for June 16. The only hit off Burdette resulted in the game's only run. Joe Lonnett doubled in the sixth, moved to third on an infield out, and scored on Richie Ashburn's sacrifice fly. The combined time of the two games was just four hours and eleven minutes.

The Pirates stopped off at County Stadium for one game and rallied for four runs in the ninth to beat the Braves, who got four hits from Schoendienst and seventeen in all. Milwaukee recalled outfielder Wes Covington from Wichita to fill the outfield vacancy left by Thomson's trade to the Giants. Covington had spent a month in the Triple-A American Association where he had been hitting the ball with authority. He would become the everyday left fielder for the Braves, who had used Thomson and Andy Pafko at the position, with neither able to produce consistently at the plate.

The Giants began a three-game series in Milwaukee on June 18 by extending the Braves' losing streak to three games. New York scored three runs in the sixth inning in rallying for a 5–4 victory that made a winning pitcher out of Ray Crone, who was making his first appearance against his former teammates. Crone replaced Johnny Antonelli during the Braves' three-run fourth inning with nobody out and pitched six innings of three-hit shutout relief. Both Thomson and Schoendienst were hitless in their first meeting since the big trade, while O'Connell had two singles. Spahn, the losing pitcher, was victimized by three Milwaukee errors that led to three unearned runs. Coach Connie Ryan managed the Braves as Fred Haney was hospitalized with acute gastritis.

Buhl stopped the Braves' skid by pitching a four-hitter and shutting out New York. The right-hander's second straight complete game and seventh victory in nine decisions would be Milwaukee's lone win sandwiched between two three-game slides. Hank Aaron blasted his nineteenth home run of the season and would have had his twentieth if Willie Mays had not robbed him with a magnificent leaping catch at the 402-foot mark in center field at County Stadium. Covington hit a three-run homer. It was his first of the season and came in the Braves' fifty-ninth game, a fact worth noting when looking at the powerful left-handed hitter's numbers at the end of the schedule.

The Braves dropped their next three games, giving them a disappointing 1–5 start to a sixteen-game homestand. Bruton and Mathews homered in the first inning against the Giants, who bounced back to win in twelve innings. The Phillies beat Milwaukee twice as Curt Simmons scattered eight hits and gave up one run, with Jack Sanford allowing six hits and two runs. Sanford stopped Aaron's hitting streak at fifteen games. There was a logjam at the top of the National League standings, which took on a new look. The St. Louis

Cardinals were in first place, Milwaukee sharing second with Philadelphia and Cincinnati. Those three teams trailed St. Louis by one and a half games, with Brooklyn in fifth place, two and a half back.

The Cardinals were red-hot. They won eight games in a row, all on the road, and fifteen of nineteen after being a sub-.500 club most of the time since opening day. At thirty-six years of age, Stan "The Man" Musial was still going strong. He was on his way to a seventh — and what would be his last — batting title as he would hit .351 with twenty-nine home runs and 102 runs batted in. Musial, who had moved from left field to first base, got plenty of hitting support from the Cardinals' outfield, which was comprised of Wally Moon, Ken Boyer, and former Phillie slugger Del Ennis. Moon and Ennis hit twenty-four homers each, with Ennis driving in 105 runs. Boyer, the future All-Star third baseman, played a solid center field and clouted nineteen home runs. Lindy McDaniel, Larry Jackson, Sad Sam Jones, Herm Wehmeier, and Willard Schmidt headed a balanced pitching staff, with each of them winning at least ten games. Hoyt Wilhelm, who would knuckleball himself into the Hall of Fame, anchored the bullpen. The Cards had not posted a winning record in four years and were coming off a fourth-place finish in 1956, their first season under manager Fred Hutchinson. The Cardinals' last pennant had come in 1946, the year they won the World Series.

The Philadelphia Phillies of 1957 were a mere shadow of their 1950 Whiz Kids outfit, who, with an average age of twenty-six, was the youngest team ever to win the National League pennant. Such success at such a young age painted a bright future for the Phillies, but it did not materialize as they could finish no higher than third place the rest of the decade. In fact, by the end of it, Philadelphia had taken up what would be a four-year residence in last place. Still on the Phils from the 1950 club were Granny Hamner, who had switched from shortstop to second base; Richie Ashburn, the swift center fielder and excellent leadoff hitter; third baseman Willie Jones, who possessed one of baseball's all-time best nicknames of "Puddinhead;" and the righty-lefty pitching pair of Robin Roberts and Simmons. Sanford, however, was the new ace of the Philadelphia staff, winning nineteen games in his first full season in the majors, while Roberts lost twenty-two times and won ten.

More than 36,000 County Stadium fans watched the Braves score seven runs in both games of a doubleheader and down the Phillies twice. Milwaukee pushed across the winning run in the bottom of the ninth inning in the opener and did it with two outs. Schoendienst, Mathews, and Aaron singled, with Aaron's hit driving in the deciding run. Bob Buhl pitched his fourth consecutive complete game victory despite giving up ten hits and walking six. Bruton had four hits — a single, double, triple, and home run — in the twinbill, scored four runs, stole a base, and batted in four runs, three in the night-cap. Bruton's homer tied the score in the first game and his two-run triple put the Braves ahead to stay in the second contest. Southpaw reliever Taylor Phillips made a rare start in the second game and was rewarded with the win after pitching six innings. Bob Trowbridge closed out the victory with three shutout innings of relief. Eddie Mathews crushed a long home run, and Schoendienst rapped out three hits and knocked in a pair of runs.

What should have been a joyous night for the Braves was not. Their two wins inched them within a half game of front-running St. Louis, but Milwaukee also suffered a huge loss. First baseman Joe Adcock broke a small bone in his lower right leg, just above the ankle, and also tore ligaments while sliding into second base in the second inning of the second game. He was carried off the field on a stretcher and taken to Milwaukee Hospital where doctors' prognosis was that he would likely miss from six to eight weeks. The target date for Adcock's return was sometime in August.

Adcock's injury triggered a parade of Braves to the trainer's room. The next day, Red Schoendienst fell down the dugout steps, hurt his back, and had to leave Milwaukee's loss to Philadelphia after five innings. Reliever Dave Jolly was hit by a line drive in the eighth, but continued to pitch. The Phillies slugged three home runs in handing Spahn his fifth loss against seven wins. Del Crandall moved from behind the plate and played first base after Frank Torre left the game for a pinch-hitter.

On June 25, Lew Burdette was once again a tough-luck loser. He allowed the visiting Dodgers just four hits and did not walk a batter, but saw his record fall to 5–5. Duke Snider's first-inning home run was all Brooklyn would need, and the Bums added an insurance run in the ninth for a 2–0 victory. Rookie left-hander Danny McDevitt also gave up four hits — all singles — and walked six, but Milwaukee left eight runners on base and hit into two double plays. McDevitt, who had been called up from the minors two weeks earlier, was making his third big league start. The Braves' injury list continued to grow. Backup infielder Dick Cole, playing second base in place of Red Schoendienst, jammed his right thumb when a hard bouncer off the bat of Snider took a bad hop and hit him in the bare hand. Cole was replaced by Felix Mantilla. Schoendienst's ailing back kept him out of the game, the first of seven that he would miss with the injury.

The Braves stopped their two-game slide and started a six-game winning streak by winning a slugfest from the Dodgers, 13–9. Milwaukee treated a County Stadium crowd of almost 40,000 to a fifteen-hit attack that included five home runs, two from Mathews. All five of the Braves' homers came off of Brooklyn ace Don Newcombe. Mathews started the long ball show with a two-run shot in the third inning. Then, in the fifth, Hank Aaron, Mathews, and Wes Covington connected in succession. Aaron, who was temporarily moved back to the second slot in the batting order during Schoendienst's absence, blasted his twentieth home run of the season. Carl Sawatski also went deep for the Braves, but they trailed by two runs going into the bottom of the eighth inning. That is when they exploded for six runs, all of them charged to Clem Labine, the Dodgers' main man out of the bullpen. Strangely enough, the uprising came without benefit of a long ball as Felix Mantilla, Billy Bruton, and Frank Torre each smacked a double, with Torre's two-bagger plating a pair of runs. Mathews' evening was quite productive as he had three hits and five RBI.

It was the end of a bad day all around for the Dodgers, who were not happy about the hospitality they had received at their Milwaukee hotel. It seemed a civic organization was holding a convention at the same hotel, and the large contingent partied into the wee hours of the morning, with the noise keeping many of the Brooklyn players awake. To make matters worse, a tear gas canister was dropped into the hotel's ventilation system, requiring the fire department to make a visit that took a long time to get rid of the fumes. Topping things off, Duke Snider was ejected from the game for arguing too long and too loudly after being called out when trying to stretch a single into a double. Brooklyn first base coach Jake Pitler came to Snider's rescue and also got the heave-ho for his trouble.[9]

Bob Buhl was looking more like the ace of the Milwaukee staff instead of the number three man. The right-hander with the herky-jerky motion and a knack for beating the Dodgers did it again. He defeated Brooklyn and hurled his fifth complete game in a row, out-pitching Don Drysdale as the Braves nipped the Dodgers, 2–1. The victory was Buhl's ninth, the most of any Milwaukee pitcher. Buhl, who tossed a four-hitter, matched zeroes with Drysdale for seven innings before the weirdest thing happened. With one out, Drysdale walked his mound opponent. It was his only base on balls of the afternoon and was issued to perhaps the worst hitter in the major leagues. Bruton hit what looked like an inning-ending double-play ground ball right at Dodger second baseman Jim Gilliam. But shortstop Charlie Neal muffed the throw from Gilliam. Both runners were safe, and they scored when Aaron lashed a triple into the right-centerfield gap. Brooklyn put its first two batters on base in the top of the ninth as Gil Hodges and Gino Cimoli both singled. Hodges scored on a groundout by Carl Furillo, but that was all the Dodgers could manage. Buhl jammed pinch-hitter Elmer Valo, who fouled out, walked Roy Campanella, then struck out Sandy Amoros to strand two runners and end the game.

Warren Spahn could not get enough. He averaged 250 innings over a big league career that lasted twenty-one years. One of his few complaints during the month of June was not about being used too much, but the opposite. He loathed the five-man rotation, wanting the ball every fourth day and saying three days between starts was plenty. Spahn grew impatient waiting so long to take his next turn, and he was especially antsy following a loss; he was eager to get on the mound and make amends, get a victory. Burdette was the same way; he was another advocate of the four-man rotation. He, like his roomie, was a workhorse. If it had not been for Burdette's short bout with arm trouble, he would have been right with Spahn in terms of innings pitched in 1957. The left-hander made thirty-five starts and worked 271 innings, fourteen and two-thirds more than Burdette, who started thirty-three games. Buhl had thirty-one starts, Gene Conley and Bob Trowbridge starting eighteen and sixteen games, respectively.

Early in the 1957 season, Fred Haney went with a five-man rotation once his club was playing every day. Until then, he used off days to get extra starts for Spahn, Burdette, and Buhl. Then, Conley, Trowbridge, and Ray Crone alternately joined the big three in the rotation, with lefties Taylor Phillips and Juan Pizarro given spot starts, especially in double-headers. By the middle of June, Haney saw that he needed to send his three aces to the mound as often as possible. All three were strong, and all three wanted the ball. So the Braves used a four-man rotation, with Burdette, Buhl, and Spahn all happily taking the mound every fourth day. Three days of rest suited them all just fine. If there was a rainout or a day off, they did not take an extra day of rest; they just moved up in the rotation and the fourth man would be skipped. The fourth man was Trowbridge most of the time, with Conley and Pizarro plugged in at certain times. When the season concluded, Spahn and Burdette had both worked over 250 innings, Buhl pitched more than 200, Conley had 148, and Trowbridge 126. No other Milwaukee hurler pitched 100 innings.

On June 28, Spahn threw a five-hitter at the Pittsburgh Pirates and slammed a solo home run over the right-field fence. The homer was his first of the season and the eighteenth of his career. His battery mate, Crandall, lined a three-run double. The 4–2 win lifted the Braves into first place in the National League as they swapped places with St. Louis. The Cardinals' loss to the Giants left St. Louis a half-game behind Milwaukee and second in the standings, four percentage points ahead of the Redlegs, who were also one-half game out of the top spot.

Crandall, Mantilla, Aaron, and Mathews all ripped home runs in the Braves' 13–6 pounding of the Pirates, but Burdette could not cash in for the win. Instead, Juan Pizarro got the victory with three and two-thirds innings

Don McMahon, a hard-throwing right-hander, did not reach the majors until he was twenty-seven years old. Upon his arrival in 1957, he immediately became the Braves' closer. (©Brace Photo. Used by permission.)

of shutout relief. The homer for Aaron, who had again been batting in the second spot in the order since Schoendienst went to the bench with a back injury, was a three-run job. Frank Torre, playing first base every day for Milwaukee in Joe Adcock's absence, continued his fine hitting with a pair of singles and an RBI.

The Braves closed the month of June by sweeping a doubleheader from Pittsburgh as their winning streak grew to six games. Aaron hit a home run in both games, giving him roundtrippers in his last three outings and twenty-three for the season. Felix Mantilla, playing every day at second base while Schoendienst healed, keyed both victories with his bat. In the first game, his two-run single sparked a five-run rally in the eighth inning. Carl Sawatski, who had homered earlier, contributed an RBI single to the cause. In the second contest, Mantilla blasted a dramatic two-run, two-out homer in the ninth inning. The Pirates scored a run in the top of the thirteenth before the Braves finally won it on a two-run clout by Mathews.

Cincinnati won both ends of a doubleheader with Philadelphia to remain a half-game behind Milwaukee. St. Louis was two and a half back, fourth-place Brooklyn trailed by four games, and the Phillies were five and a half games behind and in fifth place. The Braves' winning streak gave them a 9–7 record for their sixteen-game homestand.

The Sunday doubleheader, or twinbill, was a staple of major league baseball for many years. It was a special attraction for families and fans who could only attend games on weekends, and seeing two for the price of one was a great deal. Seldom are doubleheaders played in the majors anymore. Players hate playing two games in one day, and so do managers because of what it does to pitching staffs and starting rotations. Doubleheaders usually occur nowadays, not as a treat for fans, but to make up rained-out games. In 1957, the Braves played eleven twinbills. They won both games four times, were swept twice, and had five splits.

Don McMahon made his big league debut in the nightcap for the Braves, and he was impressive. The hard-throwing right-hander pitched four shutout innings of relief, giving up two hits and striking out seven Pirates. And, so it was that Milwaukee found its bullpen ace on the final day of June.

A native of Brooklyn where he attended the same high school as eventual Oakland Raiders owner Al Davis, McMahon was beginning his major league career at the age of twenty-seven. Following the 1955 season, in which McMahon had a record of 2–13 with a 5.01 earned run average as a starting pitcher for Toledo in the American Association, he was converted to a reliever by Mud Hens' manager Whitlow Wyatt. McMahon would appear in thirty-two games over the last three months of the season and became the Braves' closer, although that was not in the baseball vocabulary back in the fifties. He earned nine saves, had a sparkling 1.54 earned run average, and had a 2–3 record, while giving the team a power pitcher to call on in the late innings. No other Milwaukee reliever had more than four saves or an earned run average under 3.50. McMahon could get the big strikeout with a runner on third base, and he frequently did just that. He averaged almost a strikeout per inning, registering forty-six in 46.2 innings, while giving up thirty-three hits.

The go-to guy in the bullpen was used much differently in those days. He might be brought in to pitch in the seventh or eighth inning with the idea of finishing the game. Today, the closer normally pitches the ninth inning of games in which his team has a lead of three runs or less. McMahon averaged an inning and a half per appearance in 1957 and throughout his eighteen-year big league career. Fred Haney often called on his big right-hander in the eighth inning, with the plan of having him pitch through the ninth.

McMahon put up some amazing numbers as he pitched more than 1,300 innings in 874 games, all but two in relief. In 1959, he appeared in sixty games for Milwaukee and finished forty-nine of them, while working over eighty innings and recording a National League-leading fifteen saves. He was traded to Houston in 1962 and then to Cleveland after a year and a half. In 1964, with the Indians, McMahon came out of the bullpen seventy times, pitched 101 innings, finished thirty-nine games, won six, saved sixteen and had a 2.41 earned run average. Five years later, splitting the season between the Boston Red Sox and the Chicago White Sox, he pitched a career-high 109.1 innings with a 1.98 ERA. At the age of forty, he worked in sixty-one games for the San Francisco Giants, finishing forty-four times, winning nine games, and saving a career-best nineteen.

In 1974, McMahon was the Giants' pitching coach when the club needed an arm or two. So he returned to the active roster, appeared in nine games and had a 3.09 ERA. Following that season, he quit pitching for good, leaving with a 90–68 record, 2.96 earned run average, and 153 saves.[10]

The rest of the bullpen was kind of a mixed bag of middle-inning guys and part-time starters, including five pitchers who saved at least one game apiece. Ernie Johnson had been the Braves' top reliever until the arrival of McMahon. Johnson concluded the season with thirty appearances, a 7–3 record, four saves, and a 3.88 ERA in sixty-five innings of work. The number one left-hander out of the pen was Taylor Phillips, who was in his second year in the major leagues. He started six games, relieved in twenty-one, won three games and saved two in seventy-three innings. Another southpaw, Juan Pizarro, got ten starts among his twenty-four games, and went 5–6 in 99.1 innings. Six-foot-eight Gene Conley came out of the bullpen for seventeen of his thirty-five games. He had a 3.16 earned run average and a 9–9 record in 148 innings. Bob Trowbridge, a starter in half of his thirty-two outings, was 7–5 with a 3.64 ERA in 126 innings. Dave Jolly pitched 37.2 innings in his twenty-three games, all in relief. The big three of Spahn, Burdette, and Buhl combined for eleven relief appearances, with four each for Spahn and Burdette. Milwaukee's pitching staff was young, with the exception of the thirty-six-year-old Spahn. Johnson was thirty-three years old, Burdette thirty, Buhl twenty-eight, Trowbridge twenty-seven, Conley twenty-six, Phillips twenty-four, and Pizarro twenty.

Milwaukee's pitchers helped themselves at the plate. Spahn and Burdette had thirteen hits and two home runs apiece, with Burdette driving in nine runs and Spahn eight. Pizarro batted .250 with a homer. Johnson had seven RBI in only seventeen at-bats, getting a home run and five other hits for a .353 batting average. The staff combined to get sixty-nine hits and knock in thirty-eight runs. Braves pitchers also fielded well, committing only nine errors as a group. Spahn handled sixty-five chances flawlessly.

5

Catching the Cardinals

The Brooklyn Dodgers were expected to win ... year after year. At least, that was the case in the fifties. The first seven years of the decade saw the Dodgers win four National League pennants. They finished second the other three seasons, twice by the slimmest of margins. The Philadelphia Phillies edged Brooklyn by one game in 1950, and the next year was when Bobby Thomson's dramatic home run made broadcaster Russ Hodges famous with his cries of, "The Giants Win the Pennant! The Giants Win the Pennant!" Thomson's blast gave New York the NL flag and took it from the Bums on the last day of the 1951 season. Brooklyn stormed back to win league championships the next two years before being beaten out again by their hated rivals, the Giants, in 1954. The Dodgers won two more pennants in a row, giving them four in five years, and also managed their first World Series triumph when they defeated the New York Yankees in 1955.

And so it was that no matter how good the Braves were — and they were extremely good in 1957 — the Dodgers were always in their rear-view mirror. Sportswriters warned readers that the boys from Brooklyn would be making their move. Contenders in the National League did not need to be warned; they were already looking over their shoulders. Especially the Braves, who had witnessed first-hand the Dodgers' ability to overcome a late-season deficit to win a pennant. Milwaukee had been victimized the previous season.

But in 1957, the Boys of Summer, as Roger Kahn so eloquently described the Dodgers in his book by that title, were becoming the boys of autumn. They were getting old and injured. Figuring up their average age would be misleading; the numbers to look at were the ones next to the names of the everyday players, the ones Walter Alston penciled onto his lineup card game after game. And some of those numbers were getting up there. Catcher Roy Campanella was thirty-five years old, and so was right fielder Carl Furillo. The years took a toll more on Campy because of all the squatting and getting up and down. After catching an average of nearly 130 games over the past eight seasons, he was behind the plate for just 100 in 1957. Sadly, it would turn out to be the final season for the Hall of Famer and three-time Most Valuable Player as an automobile accident after the season relegated him to a wheelchair for the rest of his life. The oldest Dodger was Pee Wee Reese, the team captain. At thirty-eight, the wear and tear of having base runners bang into his shins was beginning to show. After starting the 1957 season on the bench with injuries, the Hall of Fame shortstop managed to play only 103 games, and most of them were at third base. Pitcher Carl Erskine, who was thirty, pitched in only fifteen games during the season because of arm problems.

As July began, the Dodgers won twice in the Polo Grounds, while the Braves lost a pair in St. Louis. As a result, Milwaukee fell out of first place and would not regain the National League lead for quite some time. Shoddy fielding cost the Braves five unearned runs in a 9–5 loss to the Cardinals. The left side of Milwaukee's infield caved in as third baseman Eddie Mathews and shortstop Johnny Logan committed two errors apiece. The Braves wasted home runs by Hank Aaron and Wes Covington, who also had a single and a triple. Bob Buhl, who had pitched masterfully in recent weeks, did not last three innings as his winning streak was stopped at five games. Red Schoendienst, who was not able to play for a week because of a back injury, made a pinch-hitting appearance and returned to the lineup at second base the following day. Two more errors resulted in an unearned run, and Warren Spahn's record dropped to 8–6 as the Cards won again. Milwaukee's skid reached three games when the Redlegs beat Lew Burdette for the first time in ten tries covering a period of two years. In successive days, Spahn, Buhl, and Burdette absorbed losses.

Milwaukee snapped out of it with a win in Cincinnati before losing twice to the Cubs, with the Braves' pitchers giving up six or more runs seven times in an eight-game stretch. The big bats of Aaron and Mathews helped the Braves rally for four runs in the eighth inning and outscore the Redlegs, 10–7. Milwaukee overcame a seventeen-hit Cincinnati attack led by former Braves first baseman George Crowe, who had five hits that included a pair of home runs. Aaron blasted his twenty-sixth homer, a two-run job, to go with two run-scoring doubles. Mathews hit his seventeenth roundtripper.

Aaron remained on fire. He doubled in a run and belted a solo home run in the ninth inning of a loss to the Cubs. It was his seventh homer in eight games and his twenty-seventh of the season, matching his previous big league high which came in 1955. Buhl, who took his second straight loss, did not last two full innings. Spahn also was a loser, Milwaukee dropping a 3–2 decision to the Cubbies despite getting only seven hits off the left-hander. The Braves left a dozen runners on base.

Burdette pitched a six-hitter to beat Chicago, and Wes Covington drove in two runs with a pair of hits, including his third triple in seven games. Aaron had three singles in four trips to the plate. Frank Torre, though he was not the long ball threat of injured Joe Adcock, continued to provide steady play at first base. He turned in a nifty unassisted double play, laid down a sacrifice bunt, tripled, and had an RBI. Burdette struck out seven, did not walk a batter, and set down the last fifteen Cubs in a row in throwing a complete game. A crowd of 33,616 showed up at County Stadium to shove Milwaukee over the one million figure in attendance and make the Braves the first team in the majors to reach that plateau for the fifth consecutive year.

The twenty-fourth All-Star Game was a fiasco before players even gathered for the July 9 contest at Sportsman's Park, also known as Busch Stadium, in St. Louis. Managers and fans had chosen the players the first two years for the mid-season game, which began in 1933. Managers alone picked the players the next twelve years. The fans' votes determined the starting eight position players from 1947–57, and managers filled out the roster with pitchers and reserves. The confusion and controversy caused in 1957 by a landslide of votes in Cincinnati brought about a change in 1958, with players voting on the starting eight. That procedure continued until the vote was returned to the fans in 1970.

What happened in 1957 was that fans in Cincinnati stuffed the ballot box. They voted, voted, and voted some more, with most of their ballot marks made beside the hometown Redlegs' names. There was a promotion by the Cincinnati Enquirer newspaper, which printed pre-marked ballots and distributed them in the Sunday paper. When votes were counted, all eight National League position starters were Cincinnati players. Top vote-getters included catcher Ed Bailey, first baseman George Crowe, second baseman Johnny Temple, shortstop Roy McMillan, third baseman Don Hoak, left fielder Frank Robinson, center fielder Gus Bell, and right fielder Wally Post.

Baseball Commissioner Ford Frick was on the spot. He did not want his game's mid-season spectacle to become a farce, but, after all, no stipulations had ever been made as to how many players from one team could be in a league's starting All-Star lineup. So Frick used his judgment in naming first baseman Stan Musial of the St. Louis Cardinals, New York Giants center fielder Willie Mays, and Milwaukee right fielder Hank Aaron as starters. All three players were second at their positions in the official balloting. The Commissioner looked at voting totals before a flood of ballots came in from Cincinnati, and he determined that Bailey, Temple, McMillan, Hoak, and Robinson were either leading or strongly challenging for the lead at their positions. Prior to the outpouring of more than a half-million votes from Cincinnati, Crowe was not listed among the leaders at first base, Bell had been third among center fielders, with Mays the leader, and Post was second among right fielders, trailing Aaron.

Frick, after meeting with National League president Warren Giles and American League president Will Harridge, said, "The rules set up provide that the eight men receiving the largest number of ballots would constitute the starting lineup and remain in the All-Star Game for three innings. The National League, while recognizing this rule, feels that the overbalance of Cincinnati ballots has resulted in the selection of a team which would not be typical of the league."[1]

Redlegs manager Birdie Tebbetts said Crowe, Bell, and Post should be named honorary members of the National League All-Star team, at the very least. Cincinnati general manager Gabe Paul said the trio should be included on the actual NL squad.[2]

The American League won the game, 6–5, as Detroit's Al Kaline had two hits and two RBI. Aaron had one hit in four at-bats, while Mathews went hitless in three tries. Burdette pitched four shutout innings in relief of the Cardinals' Curt Simmons, who started for the National League. Logan and Spahn were on the NL team, but did not play. At the All-Star break, St. Louis led Milwaukee by two and one-half games, with Cincinnati in third place, three and a half back. Philadelphia trailed the Cardinals by four games, while Brooklyn was five behind and in fifth place.

When the regular season resumed, Pittsburgh handed the Braves their sixth loss in eight games, dropping them three games behind league-leading St. Louis and leaving them just a half-game in front of third-place Cincinnati. Milwaukee scored twice in the first inning on a one-out single by Red Schoendienst followed by Eddie Mathews' eighteenth home run. Bob Purkey of the Pirates then pitched four-hit baseball over eight and two-thirds shutout innings, sending Buhl to yet another setback, his third straight. Ernie Johnson's arm seemed sound again as he pitched two scoreless innings of relief.

The next game saw the Braves begin a stretch in which they would win eight of ten games, but the July 11 victory over the Pirates proved extremely costly. In the bottom of the first inning, with dusk settling over storied Forbes Field, center fielder Bill Virdon led off for the Pirates. A right-handed thrower

Milwaukee was without Billy Bruton's speed and outstanding defense in center field after he injured his knee in a July 11 collision with teammate Felix Mantilla.

who batted from the left side, Virdon was an excellent outfielder who got an outstanding jump on the ball and ran very well. Three years later, when the Pirates won the pennant and the 1960 World Series by beating the Yankees, Virdon and number two hitter Dick Groat made the hit-and-run a dangerous weapon. The center fielder would get on base and take off, with the shortstop hitting behind him. On this evening, Virdon settled into the box, took a couple of pitches from Braves right-hander Bob Trowbridge, and then lifted a pop fly into short center field.

It was trouble from the start for the Braves. Felix Mantilla, playing shortstop to give Johnny Logan a night off, did not get a good start running into the outfield grass. Milwaukee center fielder Billy Bruton ran hard as he came in on the ball. It was not hit high into the air, and because it was not one of those towering flies that allow infielders and outfielders to communicate, neither Mantilla nor Bruton had a chance to take charge and call the other player off the ball. The result was a terrible, bone-shattering collision that resembled two special-teams players in football crashing into each other at full speed on a kickoff. The ball could not be caught, and Virdon hustled into second base with a double. As he did so, he looked into center field anxiously, hoping what he heard was not as bad as it sounded. Fans sitting in the boxes close to the field could also hear the gruesome crunch of flesh and bones hitting head-on. The crowd of 17,000 or so grew immediately quiet. After what seemed an eternity while medical personnel attended to the two fallen Braves, Bruton was carried off the field on a stretcher and Mantilla was helped off with his arms slung over the shoulders of two teammates.

The early prognosis did not sound all that serious. Mantilla had cuts on his face and a bruised chest. Bruton required eight stitches to close a cut on his lip, and his knee injury was diagnosed as a bad bruise. The Milwaukee players, coaches, and manager Fred Haney all hoped for the best, but they did so with trepidation as they awaited the results of X-rays to be taken the next day. The collision would turn out to be much more damaging than originally believed.[3]

Andy Pafko replaced Bruton in center field for the Braves and Logan went in at shortstop, his day off lasting just a half-inning. Logan clouted a two-run homer in the fourth inning, when Milwaukee scored four times on the way to a 7–2 victory. He also had a run-scoring single. Trowbridge pitched nine innings and survived twelve Pittsburgh hits and three bases on balls as the Pirates stranded eleven runners.

The next day, Spahn was cruising with a six-hitter and a three-run lead going into the ninth inning, but he seemed to run out of gas. A double and two singles plated one Pirate run before Don McMahon got the call from the bullpen. He induced a ground ball that produced a run and the second out of the inning, then got a foul out to catcher Del Crandall. The Braves had a one-run triumph and Spahn had his ninth win of the season. Aaron smacked a two-run home run and Torre came up with another big hit, a two-run single. Spahn doubled and Covington tripled, while joining Mathews, Aaron, Pafko, and Crandall with two hits apiece in Milwaukee's fourteen-hit offensive show.

The Braves received more good news in the form of a medical report on the conditions of Mantilla and Bruton. They each had bruised right knees, but X-rays were negative for both players. Doctors gave no timetable for their return. An update on Joe Adcock's broken right leg was promising. He could stop using crutches in a week, and X-rays showed the leg was healing properly.[4]

Bruton and Mantilla were examined by doctors again the following day, and both were told they would miss at least another week of action. The report from Milwaukee Hospital was that both Braves had the same kind of injury, including a hemorrhage and sprained ligaments around the right knee. Doctors said they did not think there was cartilage damage.[5]

Left fielder Wes Covington continued his hot hitting in Milwaukee's second straight one-run win at Pittsburgh. Covington ripped an inside-the-park home run, Del Crandall hit a two-run homer, and Torre had an RBI single. Aaron's fourth-inning single gave him a fourteen-game hitting streak and kept him on top of the National League batting race. Burdette pitched his second straight complete game, improving his career record against the Pirates to 12–2. The Braves pulled within one and a half games of the Cardinals, who did not play. The Phillies were three games back, the Dodgers were four behind, and the Redlegs had fallen to fifth place, four and a half games out of first.

Red Schoendienst, who was so perfectly equipped to bat second in the lineup, became the Braves' leadoff hitter after Bruton was injured. Logan was back in the number two slot, where he had batted earlier in the season, with Aaron returning to the cleanup spot. The injury to Bruton not only brought a switch for Aaron in the batting order, but in the outfield as well. Knowing he was the team's fastest and best all-around outfielder, Haney shifted Aaron from right to center. Schoendienst led off Milwaukee's game at Ebbets Field with a home run. Brooklyn's Gil Hodges ended it with a homer. It was the middle of July, and the Dodgers were looking to make a move. Where better to start than against the team picked by many to win the National League pennant?

After Schoendienst's roundtripper, the Dodgers scored a run in the bottom of the first, and it stayed 1–1 until the ninth. Bob Buhl threw seven innings of zeroes for the Braves. Sal Maglie and Johnny Podres, the Bums' left-handed starter who relieved in the eighth, did likewise for the Dodgers. In the ninth, Frank Torre lined his third double of the game. Burdette ran for him and scored the go-ahead run on a double by Andy Pafko. Brooklyn tied the score in the bottom of the inning on a Charlie Neal double, a fly ball, and a pop foul caught by Mathews with his back to the plate so that he was unable to throw home. Hodges then cracked his game-winning blow into the left field stands. Buhl, who had beaten the Dodgers three times during the season, saw apparent victory turn into his fourth straight loss.

The following day, July 15, things tightened considerably in the NL standings. The Phillies downed the Cardinals. The Redlegs did not play. The Dodgers defeated the Braves. That left St. Louis and Philadelphia in a tie for first place, one game ahead of Milwaukee, one and a half ahead of Cincinnati, and two in front of Brooklyn. But the Dodgers did not just defeat the Braves; they annihilated them. The final score was 20–4. The Bums pounded out sixteen hits off of five Milwaukee pitchers who contributed to the massacre by issuing ten bases on balls. Neal belted two of five Dodger home runs and winning pitcher Don Drysdale went deep. He also teamed with Ed Roebuck to stop Aaron's sixteen-game hitting streak.

The Braves could have been licking their wounds and hanging their heads as they opened a three-game visit to Philadelphia. Instead, they swept the series en route to a five-game winning streak. Spahn pitched a complete-game six-hitter and knocked in a run with a triple in the first game against the Phillies. Aaron belted a two-run homer in the first inning and Crandall reached the seats for his tenth time of the season. The Phillies loaded the bases in the ninth with two outs. Richie Ashburn smashed a line drive toward the gap in right-center field. Pafko raced over from right, speared the ball, and rolled to the grass, holding on to end the Phils' threat and their four-game win streak. At the end of the day, the National League standings were even tighter. Milwaukee joined St. Louis and Philadelphia in a three-way tie for first place, with Brooklyn trailing by one-half game and Cincinnati by two games.

Nearly 25,000 fans were at Connie Mack Stadium for the second game of the series, and they were excited over the prospect of seeing their Phillies in sole possession of first place. They felt good about their chances of moving ahead of Milwaukee in the standings because Robin Roberts, a future Hall of Fame member, was the Phils' starting pitcher. It did not take long before their excitement turned into frenzy as Roberts was thrown out of the game after a heated argument in the first inning. Beer cans rained onto the field, and there was a delay of almost twenty minutes before the contest resumed. When it did, the Braves used a thirteen-hit attack to get a 10–3 win. Lew Burdette batted in a run and pitched into the sixth inning before McMahon finished up. Torre had a perfect day with three singles, a double, and two RBI. Schoendienst and Aaron added three hits apiece. The Braves got a scare when Aaron left the game in the seventh inning after twisting his ankle while making a play in center field.

Aaron was not in the lineup the next day; in fact, he would miss five games. Playing center field in his place was rookie John DeMerit, a twenty-one-year old bonus baby signed out of the University of Wisconsin in May. Schoendienst had two hits and started three double plays to complete the Braves' sweep of the Phillies, who fell into fourth place. Buhl ended a personal four-game skid and earned his tenth victory. Del Rice, who always caught for Buhl, drove in three runs, two with a home run following a DeMerit single in the second inning. The victory gave Milwaukee sole possession of first place, a game in front of St. Louis.

Andy Pafko, at thirty-six, was the oldest player on the Braves' roster. He was the club's fifth outfielder when the season started, before Bobby Thomson was traded to the Giants and before Billy Bruton collided with Felix Mantilla. Bruton's injury forced Fred Haney, who was running out of outfielders, to plug Pafko into the everyday lineup in right field. He batted seventh until Aaron was hurt and then was moved to the cleanup spot. In his second game there, Pafko re-lived days of old by slamming two home runs, one a two-run blast, that accounted for all of Milwaukee's scoring in a win over the Giants in the Polo Grounds. The homers were his second and third of the season, all coming in July. Gene Conley pitched nine innings for the Braves. Schoendienst singled in the eighth to extend his hitting streak to sixteen games. Milwaukee pulled off three double plays for the second straight game. All three started with grounders to Conley, the last one coming in the ninth when former Brave Danny O'Connell bounced back to the mound to squelch a potential New York rally.

Whether it was being pounded by teammates congratulating him on his big night or just soreness that set in, Pafko's back stiffened and he was unable to play the second of the four-game series in New York. Catcher Del Crandall was pressed into service in right field, and he dropped a fly ball that resulted in five unearned eighth-inning runs and cost Bob Trowbridge a win. Wes Covington made a winner out of reliever Ernie Johnson by crushing a two-run homer with two outs in the ninth, his second roundtripper of the game. Crandall also homered, while Schoendienst kept his hitting streak alive. Barely 7,000 fans showed up in the Polo Grounds, the Giants' 1957 attendance hurt by their fans' displeasure over the decision to move the team to the West Coast after the season.

Good pitching, hitting, and defense are normally the reasons for a winning streak, but a stroke of good luck every now and then does not hurt either. The Braves got a dose of it in their 7–5 win at New York. In the second inning, Giants' right fielder Don Mueller legged out an infield hit to the right of Red Schoendienst. When the second baseman's throw was wide of Milwaukee first baseman Frank Torre, Mueller, who had run across the bag, headed for second. The ball bounced off of Giants first base coach Tommy Henrich, with Torre picking it up and throwing Mueller out at second base. The Braves placed center fielder Billy Bruton on the thirty-day disabled list with sprained ligaments in his right knee. He had injured the knee nine days earlier.

The Giants snapped Milwaukee's five-game win streak in the opener of a doubleheader before the Braves mounted a sixteen-hit attack to take the nightcap. Johnny Logan had five of the hits, and Del Crandall had three, including a two-run homer. Schoendienst also had three hits, giving him at least one safety in nineteen consecutive games. Nippy Jones, the club's backup first baseman, saw action in the outfield. The Braves, who came back from a four-run deficit to win, stayed a game ahead of the Cardinals and Dodgers, with the Redlegs trailing by two.

Following a 9–4 road trip, Milwaukee returned to County Stadium for sixteen games. The home stand did not start well, however, as the Phillies won two out of three from the Braves. Bob Buhl was dazzling in the first game, pitching a two-hitter for his eleventh victory. Logan tripled in Crandall in the second inning for the game's only run. An eighth-inning single by Schoendienst extended his hitting streak to twenty games. Hank Aaron was back in the lineup playing center field and batting cleanup. Right-handers Jack Sanford and Robin Roberts stifled Milwaukee on back-to-back nights. Aaron belted his thirtieth home run against Roberts, who was surrendering his twenty-ninth roundtripper of the season. Warren Spahn saw his record dip to 10–8 as he lasted only five innings and gave up three runs, all earned. Schoendienst got a hit in both contests, running his hitting streak to twenty-two games. Philadelphia was back within three games of the league-leading Braves, with Brooklyn, St. Louis, and Cincinnati all just one game off the pace.

The Braves said Ernie Johnson would be unable to pitch for at least a week because of elbow problems. It was a recurrence of a previous injury. Johnson had fluid drained from his right elbow. He became the thirteenth Milwaukee player to miss time during the season because of an injury. Three of them, including regulars Billy Bruton and Joe Adcock, still were not available.

When Adcock broke his leg, Nippy Jones' contract was purchased by Milwaukee from Sacramento of the Pacific Coast League. He had not been in the major leagues since the 1952 season, when he played in eight games for the Philadelphia Phillies. Jones, who had one hit in twelve trips to the plate since his recall, paid big dividends for the Braves in the opener of a four-game series with the Giants. He slugged a three-run game-winning home run in the eleventh inning. The shot came off New York reliever Stu Miller, the soft-tossing right-hander who threw slow, slower, and slowest. Using a fastball as his "changeup," Miller kept hitters off balance with his array of slow curves and tantalizing off-speed pitches. The winning pitcher was Gene Conley, the six-foot-eight part-time center and forward for the Boston Celtics. Conley was superb in relief of Lew Burdette, pitching three perfect innings without allowing a ball to be hit out of the infield. Crandall, leading off the eleventh, caught everyone by surprise by dropping a bunt down the third-base line and beating it out. Logan sacrificed the catcher to second, and Andy Pafko was intentionally walked. Then Jones delivered. Eddie Mathews walloped his nineteenth home run. Schoendienst had an RBI double, giving him at least one hit in twenty-three games in a row.

The Redhead's hitting streak came to an end the next day as he was silenced by Ray Crone, who went to New York when Schoendienst went to Milwaukee, and Ramon Monzant. Schoendienst fell well short of the Braves' franchise-record thirty-seven-game streak by Tommy Holmes in 1945. Buhl blanked the Giants for eight innings, pushing his scoreless-inning streak to twenty-one, to get his twelfth win, tops on the Braves' pitching staff. Mathews, continuing to show his steady improvement in the field, had three hits and staged a clinic at the hot corner with three defensive gems. His stab of a smash off the bat of Ray Jablonski in the sixth inning turned what looked like a double into a double play. More than 68,000 fans attended the first two games of the series in County Stadium.

Listed under Transactions in July 27 editions of newspapers was the report that the Braves had called up two players from the minors. Mel Roach, a second baseman, was elevated from Jacksonville in the Class A South Atlantic League. His addition was not counted on Milwaukee's roster because he had recently left the military. The Braves also purchased the contract of Bob Hazle from Wichita in the Triple-A American Association. The twenty-seven-year-old outfielder was hitting .279. Utility infielder Dick Cole, who batted .071 in fifteen games for the Braves, was sent to Wichita to make room for Hazle. The small newspaper item did not appear significant, but the call-up of Hazle was to be reflected upon as a huge turning point in the 1957 National League season.

Listed at six feet tall and 190 pounds, he was not an imposing physical specimen. A three-sport high school standout in South Carolina, Hazle signed a bonus deal with the Cincinnati Redlegs in 1949. Playing for Cincinnati farm team Nashville, he led the Southern Association in home runs with twenty-nine and in runs scored with 114 in 1955. He was rewarded with a late-season promotion to the Redlegs and had three hits in thirteen at-bats. Headed back to the minors for the 1956 season, he was traded to Milwaukee on May 10 along with a player to be named later for first baseman George Crowe.

Hazle was playing for the Braves' Triple-A farm team in Wichita, and he was playing well. He was starting to hit the ball with some power and consistency, and then he hurt his knee when he banged into a fence trying to catch a fly ball. It was a recurrence of an old injury, and it pretty much ended his season. He sat in whirlpools and he rested, but nothing seemed to help. Hazle was on the brink of retiring from baseball, but decided to give himself one more chance to make the big leagues. If he did not, he would call it quits. However, when spring training started, so did his knee problem. He thought about catching a bus back to South Carolina. But as time went on, the knee felt stronger, and the pain decreased. Back in Wichita, his hitting progressed right along with his knee. Hazle was batting around .220 early in the 1957 season when he started to hit. His average was continuing its gradual climb when he was summoned by the Braves.

Hazle did not stop hitting upon his arrival in Milwaukee. In fact, he assaulted National League pitchers at such a torrid pace that he was nicknamed Hurricane Hazle. That was in reference to the 1954 hurricane, Hazel, that is still considered the worst in North Carolina history. The outfielder did not just play hero for a day or a week; he was on fire for the rest of the season. Playing in forty-one games, he batted a lusty .403, with fifty-four hits in 134 trips to the plate. Nineteen of those hits went for extra bases as he belted a dozen doubles and seven home runs. Hazle drove in twenty-seven runs, and his eighty-seven total bases produced a .649 slugging percentage. For comparison purposes, Hank Aaron finished the season with a .600 slugging percentage, while Eddie Mathews slugged .540. Of course, both had hundreds of more at-bats than Hazle. Drawing eighteen walks, Hazle posted a .477 on-base percentage.

Years later, in looking back on the rookie's impact on the Braves, Mathews said, "Hazle is the guy who won the 1957 pennant for us." Frank Torre said, "He looked like the best hitter in the world. He never got fooled." In the early weeks of Hazle's tear, Red Schoendienst said, "I suppose he will cool

With the memory of 1954's Hurricane Hazel still fresh in the popular culture, Bob Hazle was nicknamed "Hurricane" after taking the National League by storm over the latter weeks of the 1957 season. His .403 batting average and twenty-seven RBI in forty-one games were valuable additions down the stretch.

off, but right now, he's like Musial, Mantle, and Williams all wrapped into one."

Time after time in the remaining nine weeks of the season, Bob Hazle came through with big hits and knocked in big runs. And, yet, when the Braves assembled to decide on how they would divide World Series money, his teammates voted him only a three-fourths share. While that seems reasonable considering the short time Hazle spent with the club, it was hardly in direct proportion with what he contributed down the stretch as Milwaukee won the National League flag.[6]

A crowd of more than 40,000 packed County Stadium for a Sunday doubleheader, hoping to see the Braves sweep the Giants and possibly put some distance between Milwaukee and St. Louis in the NL standings. As it turned out, they were lucky to see a split. Johnny Antonelli came back to haunt the Braves again as he threw a seven-hit shutout to out-duel Bob Trowbridge, 2–0. New York grabbed a 2–1 lead in the second game before Milwaukee rallied with four runs in the fourth inning, keyed by Mathews' two-run single, and won by a 5–3 count. The sometimes eccentric Conley pitched a complete game to earn the win in the nightcap, then told sportswriters afterward that he had come up with a new mystery pitch, but he would not tell what it was. The victory triggered a tremendous stretch by the Braves. They were blazing hot for two and one-half weeks and would lose just once in sixteen games.

An unusual Monday series-ender culminated an equally rare five-game stand with the Giants, and it was a thriller. Warren Spahn's troubles continued. The great southpaw was visibly frustrated as his normal pinpoint control abandoned him. He issued four bases on balls, consistently left pitches up and in the middle of the plate, and was totally ineffective. Spahn, who was more successful at the plate with an RBI double and a walk, gave up six hits and four runs, all earned, in four and two-thirds innings. Fred Haney, wanting to leave his ace pitcher on the mound in hopes that he would work through his recent problems, finally signaled to the bullpen. Dave Jolly, Juan Pizarro, Don McMahon, and Trowbridge followed Spahn to the hill, and the Giants kept scoring. Their three-run ninth inning built a four-run lead, but Milwaukee stormed back.

When Wes Covington struck out to start the bottom of the ninth, most of the County Stadium faithful headed for their cars in disappointment. Some of them stopped in their tracks and grew hopeful when Del Crandall lifted a fly ball that cleared the left-field fence. Johnny Logan's single made more fans turn around, and many of them scurried back to their seats when Andy Pafko greeted New York ace reliever Marv Grissom with another single. Pinch-hitter Carl Sawatski lined a base hit to right to score Logan, and suddenly, the Braves had the potential tying runs on base with just one out. Rookie outfielder John DeMerit ran for the plodding Sawatski. Milwaukee fans became louder and more excited with Schoendienst at the plate, but the ball park grew silent again when he fouled out to Giants first baseman Whitey Lockman.

Normally, Frank Torre would have been the hitter as the first baseman had been batting in the number two slot for the past week. Before the game, though, it was learned that he was the latest to join the growing list of Braves who missed 1957 games because they were either injured or ill. Torre's ailment was an eye inflammation that would keep him out of action for four games. So, instead of having the left-handed batting Torre at the plate to face Grissom, a right-hander, Milwaukee was counting on the right-handed hitting Nippy Jones. He did not let the crowd or his teammates down. Jones singled to right field, plating Pafko with the third run of the rally and pulling the Braves within one run of the Giants. On the play, Ozzie Virgil, used for defensive insurance by New York manager Bill Rigney, had an odd thing happen. When he reached back to throw into second base, the ball slipped out of his right hand and rolled behind him. By the time Virgil recovered, DeMerit had scampered home to tie the score, 8–8.

Milwaukee won the game in the tenth when Felix Mantilla coaxed a bases-loaded walk from Al Worthington. Mantilla was pinch-hitting for Trowbridge, who pitched a scoreless inning to get credit for the victory. Covington singled, homered, and drove in three runs. The Braves used an old Little League trick in the third inning and were successful. They victimized Willie Mays, who was on third base. Ray Jablonski was on first, and when he took off to steal second, Crandall faked as if throwing the ball to second. Mays bolted for the plate and was caught in a rundown.

The Braves concluded the month of July by sweeping two games from the visiting Pittsburgh Pirates as Burdette and Buhl both pitched complete games. Burdette allowed five hits and fanned six in notching his ninth win. Logan supported the right-hander with his glove and bat. The shortstop ranged into the hole and far to his left in robbing the Bucs of a couple of hits, while rapping a pair of RBI singles. Buhl carried a shutout into the ninth inning for the third straight game and was denied for the second time in a row when Pittsburgh scored twice. Only one of the runs was earned, and Buhl scattered eight hits for his fourth straight triumph and his team-high thirteenth win. Despite his mound mastery of recent weeks, what Buhl wanted to talk about in the locker room was his hitting. He had two singles, accounting for one-third of his base hits in the 1957 season. Bob Hazle played right field for the Braves and had one hit, an RBI double, in four trips to the plate. Schoendienst enjoyed a perfect night, with a single, double, walk, and home run. Logan also homered.

Entering August, Milwaukee and St. Louis were tied for first place in the National League. Brooklyn trailed by two games, with Cincinnati and Philadelphia sharing fourth place, four games out of the lead.

6

A Powerful Pair

Hank Aaron and Eddie Mathews comprised the most potent one-two punch in major league baseball history. They combined to slug 1,267 home runs, sixty more than the fabled New York Yankees duo of Babe Ruth and Lou Gehrig.

Aaron and Mathews smashed a total of 1,226 homers as members of the Boston, Milwaukee, and Atlanta Braves. Ruth and Gehrig hit 1,152 of their home runs while playing for the Yankees. While they were actually teammates, from 1954–1966, Aaron and Mathews combined to hit 863 home runs. Ruth and Gehrig combined for 859 homers in their years together with the Yankees.

Aaron and Mathews shared the Braves' franchise single-season home run record of forty-seven until 2005, when Andruw Jones clouted fifty-one homers.

Mathews and Aaron made each other better, not just by hitting back-to-back in the batting order, but through competing with each other. Wholesome competition between teammates can be good for the individuals and the team as long as jealousy is not a by-product. It was not with these two sluggers. If one of them hit a home run, the other was eager to knock the ball out of the park his next time at bat.

Braves pitcher Bob Buhl once observed that he felt the competition between the two stiffened when Aaron became an established power hitter.

"They never criticized each other," Buhl said, "but you could see it. Each one felt he could do better than the other, and they tried to prove it. Henry was a better hitter than Eddie, but Eddie could hit the ball farther. I don't think there was jealousy between the two. They were friends, although they didn't chum together off the field."[1]

In Aaron's book, *I Had A Hammer*, Milwaukee catcher Del Crandall, Braves outfielder Wes Covington, and Mathews all were quoted on the competition between Aaron and Mathews.

"To me, Henry was the best ballplayer I ever saw," Crandall said. "I think Willie Mays was his only rival. If there was a competition with Henry, I think it was with Eddie Mathews. It was a good competition. Mathews had a way of bringing Henry into the real world of kidding, understanding the value of humor, maybe a little sarcasm. It seemed to me that Eddie Mathews was a very important person in Henry's life."[2]

"Hank and Mathews got along very well," Covington said, "because there was something that was similar about the way they both approached their careers. They had the same drive to get to the top. Hank would hurt inside when he couldn't drive in the winning run, and Mathews was the same way. I believe they respected each other more than any two people on the team. They had a rivalry going, but it was out of respect for the other's ability. Henry would hit a home run, and where somebody else would say he got lucky, Mathews would say, 'What a shot.' Mathews would hit a home run, and Hank would say, 'Helluva shot.' Their relationship was like fourteen-karat gold."[3]

"Hank and I had a friendly rivalry," Mathews said. "He pushed me and I pushed him. He'd win the home run title one year, I might win it the next. Rivalries were important to us. We always looked for rivalries to keep us going. If we were in St. Louis, for instance, I might say to myself that I want to beat Ken Boyer this series in every department.

"Maybe we felt that way because guys like Hank and I didn't get the publicity we should have due to the fact that we were playing in Milwaukee. Willie Mays, in my opinion, wasn't as good a player as Hank Aaron, but whenever Willie did something, the New York press and the skies lit up. I just felt that Hank was a touch better than Willie. Hank was a complete ballplayer. He never threw to the wrong base, never missed the cutoff man. Willie never hit the cutoff man. Henry didn't steal bases like Willie, but he could steal bases. He could run like hell, and he didn't even look like he was running. I'll bet you in a footrace, Hank would have beaten Willie. But he didn't run like Willie. It was hard to explain with Henry, but he could hit full speed in three steps and look like he wasn't even running."[4]

"Eddie and I had a friendly competition," Aaron said, "but we weren't jealous of each other. That's one reason we were so successful."[5]

THE HAMMER

Aaron was one of the greatest all-around big league players of all time. There are other factors to consider, of course, than the numbers. But being the all-time home run king is certainly an impressive start. Babe Ruth, Willie Mays, Ted Williams, and Barry Bonds are other names to be considered in the greatest ever equation.

Williams, many baseball historians agree, was the best hitter. Pete Rose amassed more hits, Ty Cobb compiled a higher lifetime batting average, and several players hit more home runs. But in measuring with the yardsticks of batting, Williams is the best all-around hitter. His lifetime average of .344, 521 home runs, .634 slugging percentage, and .482 on-base percentage over the course of nineteen big league seasons back that up. And, of course, when talking about the Splendid Splinter, what he did not do — or did not get the chance to do — is always a part of the conversation. A big part. The fact that Williams had two chunks of his prime taken away by military duty leaves fans to wonder just what his already illustrious numbers would have been.

It is hard to argue against Ruth as the greatest player of all time. His offensive feats include 714 home runs, a lifetime batting average of .342, a .474 on-base percentage, and a .690 slugging percentage. He drove in 2,062 runs and scored 2,175. In addition, he was a dominating pitcher who had back-to-back seasons of twenty-three and twenty-four wins to go with a career 2.28 earned run average. In World Series play, Ruth had a 3–0 pitching record and an 0.89 ERA, while hitting fifteen home runs and knocking in thirty-three runs.

Mays certainly ranks high for his all-around skills. The Say Hey Kid could run down just about any ball that stayed in the park, he swiped 338 bases, hit 660 home runs, and batted .302 over twenty-two major league seasons.

And, yet, as good as Mays was, Aaron is right there with him in almost every category and ahead in some. He is the all-time home run leader with 755 and also owns the records for most RBI with 2,297, total bases with 6,856, and extra-base hits with 1,477. Aaron is tied with Ruth for second in runs scored with 2,174 and he is third on the all-time hits list with 3,771. He is the only player to hit thirty or more home runs in fifteen seasons and at least twenty homers in twenty seasons. He is the first player to get 3,000 hits and 500 home runs.

Mays, who spent much of his career batting in the leadoff spot, has an on-base percentage of .384, while Aaron's is .374. Mays' stolen base success

Hank Aaron put together an MVP season in helping the Braves win the 1957 National League pennant and the World Series. He led the team in games played with 151, hit forty-four home runs, and drove in 132 runs.

rate is 76.6 percent. Aaron's percentage is 76.7, with 240 steals. Mays ran more, yet Aaron still managed to average more than ten stolen bases per season.

Mays has a couple of things on his side when it comes to being remembered. He was very flashy. This is not to say he was a show-off; he simply did everything with a flair. Those who saw him play will recall his cap flying off when he chased balls in center field and when he dashed around the bases. He played the first six years of his big league career in New York City, and the vast newspaper coverage he received in those early years painted a sensational picture for a huge audience.

Aaron, on the other hand, played the first half of his big league career in Milwaukee, which is a wonderful baseball town, but far from a big city heavy with media influence. The Hammer is a fitting nickname for Aaron because of the manner in which he drove the baseball for twenty-two years. It does not, however, suggest the pizzazz of Say Hey. There was not much flash and dash to Aaron's performance.

As a result, he was sometimes criticized for not playing hard. It was written from time to time that Aaron did not get everything he could have from the ability he had, that he could have given a greater effort. The assumption that he gave less than 100 percent effort is unfair; he simply made a very difficult game look easy because he was so gifted. So, it seems Hank Aaron's greatest sin as a baseball player was that he had little, if any, theatrics. Anybody who ever watched him play will recall how he kind of strolled up to the plate, adjusted his batting helmet, and settled into the batter's box as if he was sitting in a rocker on the front porch. It did not matter if it was the third inning of a blowout or the ninth inning with two outs, the Braves trailing by a run, and a runner on base. Aaron was the same. Nonchalant was the word most frequently used to describe him and the way he approached baseball. But that word is ill chosen. The definition of nonchalant is "marked by or exhibiting a lack of interest or excitement; casually indifferent." While it is true Aaron never looked excited, he was very interested and he was anything but indifferent. One does not clobber hundreds of balls over fences, chase down flies on a daily basis, and play nine innings day after day despite being hurt if he is indifferent or not interested.

Hank Aaron, for all of his records, loved playing baseball and he wanted his team to win. He went about his business in a professional manner and left the Hollywood stuff to the folks in Hollywood. He was such a natural talent, whipping those magnificent wrists and rifling line drives all over ball parks and often over the fence. Aaron glided through his career.

Bonds was always a fine player. In fact, long before his home run totals soared, he was considered to be the best all-around player in the game. When he could still run, no one in baseball at the time could do all the things he did as well as he did them. He could go get the ball in left field, steal bases, hit for average, and hit for power. Then, for whatever reason, his head and body swelled to enormous proportions, and so did his home run figures. Bonds' name will forever be linked to steroids because of the monstrous home run numbers he put up at a time in his career when most players would be heading downhill. After adopting what he called a strict body-building regimen in his mid-30s, Bonds resembled someone who had been blown up like a balloon rather than pumped up with weights.

Because of the strong suspicion that Bonds' home run production in his late thirties was enhanced by steroids, it may be difficult for some baseball purists to count him among the greatest all-time players. And, if Bonds' feats prior to his home run explosion are separated and measured against Aaron's, they do not stack up. But, then, neither do anyone else's.

Aaron, lithe and slender at six feet tall and 175 or 180 pounds for most of his career, came along before the emphasis on weight-lifting. He was in great shape, but he did not have sleeve-popping muscles. He took care of his body, but he never went out and created a new one. Therefore, it seems an injustice that his home run record may be broken by anyone gaining an unfair edge by using body-building substances.

· Aaron's longtime teammate, Warren Spahn, had this to say about Aaron: "Hank was built — you know, the amazing thing about him: I think he had a waist of, like, twenty-eight inches. And, you know, Hank weighed about 175 pounds. But big hands, big wrists, big forearms, and I see all these people that are lifting weights in baseball today. You don't need those things. All you need is forearms and wrists. I think Ted Williams proved that. Musial proved that. And Hank.

"And I thought, 'This guy is special.' Then we were playing St. Louis and it had rained before the game so that the ground was wet. And Hank was playing right field. And I think it was Marty Marion that hit the ball and hit it over Hank's head. And when he turned to run back, he slipped. And when he did, his glove hand went down to the ground and, you know, now his back is to the infield. And he threw up his right hand to catch his balance and the ball hit in it and he caught it.

"And I thought, 'God gave this guy the kind of ability that he's going to do great things in baseball.' And he proved that right. I think Hank could have been a twenty-game winner if he wanted to pitch. That's how good he was. And his endurance, his physique, he was a perfect ballplayer. If you had to clone a ballplayer, he might be the one to clone."[6]

Henry Louis Aaron was born in Mobile, Alabama, one of eight children. His life was changed when his father took Hank to see the Brooklyn Dodgers play an exhibition game in Mobile and to hear Jackie Robinson speak. From that day, Aaron knew what he wanted to be. A skinny kid, who batted cross-handed (his left hand on top, although he was a right-handed hitter), he never cared much for school; he had his sights set on being a professional baseball player. He played semi-pro ball for the Pritchett Athletics for three dollars a game, then made ten dollars a game with the Mobile Black Bears. Aaron astounded onlookers with the way he could hit. One day in 1951, the Bears were playing the Indianapolis Clowns of the Negro American League, and he turned the heads of the Clowns' management. The Clowns sent him a contract during the winter, offering him $200 a month, and he signed it. The shy youngster who had never been away from home took a paper bag packed with two sandwiches his mother had made and boarded a train bound for Winston-Salem, North Carolina, where he would join the Clowns for their 1952 spring training.

Aaron showed up wearing spikes that had long before been worn out and carrying a glove that made the old guys on the team laugh. He was not welcomed warmly and only got a chance to play because injuries depleted the Indianapolis team of infielders. Nobody noticed him much until he stepped into the batter's box, and then everybody's eyes stayed on him. His batting style was different from the other players. Aaron hit off his front foot, and he had the uncanny knack of waiting until the last instant before whipping his bat into the ball and hitting it much farther than seemed possible for someone so thin. It was the wrists, people said. The skinny kid had wrists that were astonishingly quick. The ball jumped off his bat, and it traveled far distances. Aaron sent line drives whistling past and over opposing fielders with regularity, and he appeared to be so relaxed while doing it, as if he had been born to hit a baseball.

Word traveled rapidly about the Clowns' shortstop and the way he could swing a bat. A Braves scout, after watching Aaron bat and seeing those wrists in action, quickly filed a succinct report to the Braves' management. "I don't know if he can field," the scout wired, "but he's worth $10,000 just for that swing." Aaron's contract was purchased by the Boston Braves for $10,000 in June of 1952. After that, it was a fast track to the major leagues. Playing for Eau Claire, Wisconsin, he was voted Rookie of the Year in the Northern League. The next year, playing second base for Jacksonville, he led the South Atlantic League with a .362 batting average, with 208 hits, and with 125 runs batted in and was named the league's Most Valuable Player. After the season, he played winter ball in Puerto Rico, where he learned to play the outfield.

Aaron's first year in the majors was 1954. In spring training, it did not look as if he would stick with the Braves' big club. Then, Bobby Thomson broke a leg sliding into second base, and Aaron landed a spot on the Braves' roster for their second season in Milwaukee. In a March exhibition game, he got his first start and celebrated by hitting a home run.[7] At the age of twenty, playing left field, he batted a solid .280 with thirteen home runs. His season came to an early end when he broke his ankle at the start of September.

Aaron's production really took off in 1955, his second big league season, when he batted .314 with twenty-seven home runs, 106 RBI, and 189 hits. It was the first of thirteen consecutive seasons in which he scored more than 100 runs. He played in his first All-Star Game that season and had two hits in two trips to the plate.

Aaron, in addition to being a prodigious power hitter, consistently hit for a high average. He had 200 hits in 1956 on the way to winning his first National League batting title with a .328 average and smacked twenty-six home runs to go with thirty-four doubles and fourteen triples. He finished third in the NL Most Valuable Player voting behind Brooklyn pitchers Don Newcombe and Sal Maglie. The selection of Newcombe was understandable since he won twenty-seven games for the pennant-winning Dodgers. Maglie posted a modest 13–5 record, not exactly MVP-type credentials. Aaron was named *The Sporting News* National League Player of the Year.

The Braves' slugger, who moved to right field in 1955, had at least 191 hits six times in a seven-year stretch. His high mark in hits was 223 in 1959, when he again led the league in hitting with a career-high .355 average.

He made a run at the triple crown in 1957, winning his first home run title, leading the National League in RBI, and finishing fourth with a .322 batting average. He clouted forty-four roundtrippers, the first of four times that his season homer total would match his uniform number. Aaron led the league three of those years and won a fourth home run crown, finishing second four times, including 1971 when he blasted a career-high forty-seven. He was a three-time league leader in RBI, with a high of 132 in 1957.

Two things happened that season that helped Aaron's offensive production. He was moved from second in the batting order to fourth when the Braves obtained Red Schoendienst from the New York Giants in the middle of June. Aaron was ideal for the cleanup slot, where he had a greater opportunity to drive in runs, his power making him better suited for the middle of the lineup than the second spot. He also changed bats, going to a thirty-four-ouncer instead of the thirty-six-ounce model he had been using. The lighter bat made his wrists even more lethal.

The Braves signed Aaron as an infielder, but moved him to the outfield to take advantage of his speed. He played twenty-seven games at second base in his second year with Milwaukee, and he made some cameo appearances at second and third over the years. Late in his career, he saw quite a bit of action at first base, but he was an outfielder for more than 2,700 games, and he was a very good one. A three-time Gold Glove winner, Aaron was a steady defensive player who got a good jump on the ball, thereby making many difficult catches appear to be routine. Possessing a strong and accurate arm, he had a career-high seventeen outfield assists in 1956, with a dozen or more in eight other seasons.

Aaron slammed three home runs in a game for the only time in his career on June 21, 1959, as all three roundtrippers against the Giants were two-run shots. On June 8, 1961, he joined Mathews, Joe Adcock, and Frank Thomas in becoming the first four players to hit successive homers in a game. Later that summer, he was paid $30,000 to compete in the Home Run Derby television program. That was nearly as much as his salary with the Braves. Aaron came closest to winning a triple crown in 1963, when he led the National League with forty-four home runs and 130 runs batted in, while finishing seven points behind batting leader Tommy Davis of the Los Angeles Dodgers (.326 to .319). Fittingly, Aaron hit the last home run by a Milwaukee Brave in County Stadium when he connected off Philadelphia's Ray Culp on September 20, 1965.

Beginning in 1955, Aaron was selected to the All-Star team a record twenty-one consecutive years. He shares the record with Stan Musial and Willie Mays of playing in twenty-four All-Star Games (there were two All-Star Games from 1959–62). He made the most of his post-season opportunities. In the 1957 World Series, he belted three home runs, drove in seven runs, and had eleven hits in the seven games for a .393 batting average. He likely would have been the Series MVP except for the amazing pitching performance by teammate Lew Burdette. Aaron hit .333 in the 1958 Fall Classic. The New York Mets swept Atlanta in three straight games in the 1969 National League Championship Series, but Aaron did his part. He homered in each game and added two doubles and seven RBI with a .357 batting average.

It was a thrill for those at Fulton County Stadium the night of April 8, 1974, when Aaron blasted a fastball from Al Downing of the Los Angeles Dodgers over the left-centerfield fence for home run number 715, breaking Ruth's record. After the game, hundreds of reporters, jammed like sardines in a can into the Braves' locker room, crowded around Aaron. "I'm glad it came here," he said, "and I'm very glad that this is over." He did not comment on the absence of Major League Baseball Commissioner Bowie Kuhn, although it was more than curious that Kuhn did not make it a priority to be on hand for the historic occasion.

"Tonight changes a lot of things," Aaron said, smiling. "To break a record held by Mr. Ruth for thirty-nine years has given me some of the recognition I have been slighted while working hard for years."[8]

Although he did not spend a lot of time talking about them, the hate letters that flooded the Braves' mailbox took a toll on the slugger. After ending the 1973 season with 713 home runs, Aaron spent a nerve-racking winter that brought an onslaught of death threats and letters dripping with hatred.

Here is a sample: "Dear Nigger Henry, It has come to my attention that you are going to break Babe Ruth's record. I don't think you are going to break this record established by the great Babe Ruth if I can help it. I don't think that any coon should ever play baseball. Whites are far more superior than jungle bunnies. I will be going to the rest of your games and if you hit one more home run it will be your last. My gun is watching your every black move. This is no joke."[9]

The letters, thousands and thousands of them, were sent from all over the United States. People even had the audacity to suggest that Aaron stop trying to hit home runs; in fact, many letters "advised" him to simply retire from baseball and, thus, leave the record intact. It was estimated that Aaron received about 3,000 letters per day. A large number of them reeked of ugliness and hate. It would be easy to discount the threats as empty and to say such mail was coming from a bunch of nuts who would never do any more than write letters, usually without even having the nerve to sign their names. It is easy to do that if you are not the one receiving the letters. It would have been quite another matter to have been Hank Aaron and have felt the hatred directed at him because of the color of his skin and because he was talented enough to be on the brink of breaking baseball's most glamorous record, one set by the game's most enamored star.

The late Lewis Grizzard, the noted Southern comedian and author of several humorous books, was the sports editor of *The Atlanta Journal* at the time. Grizzard said he had an Aaron obituary prepared just in case. Later, there was substantial public support, with Babe Ruth's widow denouncing the racism and saying that The Babe would have been cheering Aaron's run at his home run record.[10]

Aaron, for his part, never changed. He kept his emotions, anxieties, and possibly his fears bottled inside and did what he had always done: played terrific baseball. Day in and day out, he was steady; that is the kind of man and athlete Aaron was. Only he can know what kind of torture he suffered inside.

Paul Casanova, a catcher who was Aaron's teammate in 1974, said this: "He (Aaron) almost never mentioned Babe Ruth ... one time he said to me, 'Cassy, I'm not trying to break any record of Babe Ruth. I'm just trying to make one of my own.' It was terrible the way people hated him for trying to break the record. The whole thing must have been eating him up. One day in Philadelphia we walked across the street from the hotel to eat breakfast and that was the first time he told me about the letters he had been getting.

I couldn't believe what he was telling me. I said, 'What?' He said, 'Cassy, these people are crazy. I don't know what's going on, I really don't.' But he was worried. As hard as he was to read, you could tell he was worried."[11]

Imagine Aaron standing at home plate and trying to concentrate on hitting baseballs whizzing in at ninety-plus miles per hour, while pondering whether that last crazy letter may just be from someone who really might follow through and harm his wife and children.

Roger Maris lost hair as a result of stress while chasing Ruth's single-season home run record in 1961. Bonds talked of the pressure he felt when trying to catch the home run kings, Aaron and Ruth. Hank Aaron experienced bewilderment in the early years of his major league career when he had to eat on the team bus or stay in a shabby dwelling while the rest of the team was in a nice hotel. He went through the turmoil of being bombarded with a daily avalanche of hate mail while approaching Ruth's 714 home run total.

Aaron hit his first home run off Vic Raschi of the Cardinals on April 23, 1954; his 100th came off the Redlegs' Don Gross on August 15, 1957; number 200 came off the Cardinals' Ron Kline on July 3, 1960; he hit his 300th off the Mets' Jay Hook on April 19, 1963; number 400 was off Bob Priddy of the Giants on April 20, 1966; he hit his 500th off the Giants' Mike McCormick on July 14, 1968; number 600 came off Gaylord Perry of the Giants on April 27, 1971; and he hit his 700th off the Phillies' Ken Brett on July 21, 1973. The pitcher he victimized most during his career was the Dodgers' Don Drysdale, who gave up seventeen of Aaron's home runs.

Aaron hit home runs off a Brewer, a Boozer, and a Barr. He hit one off a Mabe and a Rabe. Other victims included a Morehead and a Moorhead, R. Miller and R.L. Miller, a Veale and a Lamb, and three different pitchers named Jackson. He went deep off of Hall of Famers Sandy Koufax and Don Sutton as well as Joe Trimble, who never won a major league game. Whammy Douglas, Thornton Kipper, and Art Caccerelli were hammered by the Hammer. So were Johnny O'Brien, an infielder who took the mound one night, and Wilmer "Vinegar Bend" Mizell, the southpaw who went on to become a North Carolina congressman.

Aaron's final home run in a Braves uniform came on October 2, 1974. Following that season, Atlanta traded him to the Milwaukee Brewers for outfielder Dave May and a player to be named later. Playing only four games in the outfield in two seasons with the Brewers, Aaron was the club's designated hitter and totaled thirty-two home runs in the American League.

In July of 1975, Aaron made his debut as an American League All-Star in Milwaukee after twenty-three appearances as a National League All-Star. When he was introduced to the fans, many of whom had watched him break in as a rookie in 1954, they cheered him with a standing ovation that lasted two full minutes. The crowd clapped in thunderous unison as County Stadium seemed to quiver with the collective weight of 51,480 people on their feet. On the field, the players were lined up along the first- and third-base foul lines. As Aaron trotted onto the field to his introduction, the players joined the crowd in applauding one of baseball's all-time giants.

His jersey number 44 was retired, strangely enough, first by the Brewers in 1976 and then by the Braves in '77. A street running past Atlanta's Turner Field is named Hank Aaron Drive, and there is a statue of the slugger outside the stadium, which became the new Braves' home in April of 1997 (after being built for the 1996 Summer Olympics). Turner Field's home address is 755 Hank Aaron Drive SE. And, while that is nice, it would have been a fitting tribute to name the Braves' new home for Aaron instead of the multimillionaire who owned the team at the time the stadium was built. Far more people associate the franchise with Aaron than they do Ted Turner.

Aaron was inducted into the Baseball Hall of Fame on August 1, 1982. Major League Baseball announced a new award in his honor in February of 1999. Since then, the Hank Aaron Award is presented every year to the top overall hitter in the National League and the American League.[12]

He ended his career as the most underappreciated star in team sports history. On the night that Aaron ended his great chase and passed Babe Ruth to become the leading home run hitter in baseball history, the baseball commissioner (Bowie Kuhn) was missing, pleading that a "previous commitment" required his presence in Cleveland. In the final week of the 1973 season, when Aaron was at 712 home runs — two short of the Babe — he played before 40,000 empty seats in his home stadium in Atlanta.[13]

BIG EDDIE

Mathews averaged thirty home runs per season over a major league career that spanned seventeen years, and he was the number one homer-hitting third baseman of all time until he was passed by the Philadelphia Phillies' Mike Schmidt, who finished with 548. Mathews hit at least twenty home runs in a season fourteen of his seventeen big league seasons, had thirty or more ten times, and he slugged forty or more homers four times. His career got off to a tremendous start as he hit 190 home runs in his first five seasons in the majors, and he had not yet turned twenty-five years old.

When he hit his 500th career home run in 1967 while playing for the Houston Astros, Mathews became just the seventh player in major league history to get that many. There are now twenty members of the 500-homer club, with Mathews and Ernie Banks sharing seventeenth place with 512 apiece.

Johnny Logan once called Eddie Mathews one of the most underrated players in the major leagues, and that is saying something considering the Braves' third baseman is in the Hall of Fame.

Logan played beside Mathews as the Boston and then Milwaukee short-stop for nine years until being traded to the Pittsburgh Pirates during the 1961 season. They worked hard to plug up the left side of the Braves' infield, and their defense was solid. They also did their share of fighting, battling opposing players as well as barroom hecklers.

Mathews did not start out his major league career as a smooth fielder. His technique often amounted to playing balls off his chest and then throwing them to first base. He was not content, though, to be known as a muscleman who could hit balls into outer space and not hold his own with the glove. He did not want to be remembered as a good-hit, no-field guy. So he put in extra time on his defense.

"Eddie would work hard," Logan said. "He was a below-average fielder when he came up, but he made himself into a good third baseman. Connie Ryan, one of our coaches, would hit fifty to 100 ground balls to Eddie every day in spring training. He would knock them down and pick them up. He broke his nose three times fielding balls."[14]

Ty Cobb praised Eddie Mathews' swing, and the Milwaukee third baseman used it to rip thirty-two home runs during the pennant-winning '57 season. He worked hard to improve his defense and turned in numerous outstanding plays at the hot corner.

Edwin Lee Mathews Junior was born in Texarkana, Texas, and was raised in Santa Barbara, California. He was offered college football scholarships, and he could have received more money to sign with other major league teams. Instead, he signed on his high school graduation day, at the age of seventeen, with the Boston Braves in 1949. He played in the minor leagues for three years, making stops in Atlanta and Milwaukee, two cities in which he would later be a big leaguer. He became the Braves' full-time third baseman in 1952, blasting twenty-five home runs as a twenty-year-old rookie, including three in one game. In his second season, 1953, the Braves were making a big splash in Milwaukee, and so was he.[15]

He bashed a National League-leading forty-seven home runs and drove in 135 runs, both career highs, while batting .302 and scoring 110 runs. His performance earned him a second-place finish in the NL Most Valuable Player voting as Brooklyn catcher Roy Campanella won the award. Mathews was the cover boy for the very first issue of *Sports Illustrated* magazine. The issue was dated August 16, 1954.

Mathews was again the MVP runner-up in 1959, when Chicago shortstop Ernie Banks won it. That season, Mathews recorded career highs with a .306 batting average, 182 hits, and 118 runs scored, while slamming forty-six home runs and driving in 114 runs. He led the National League in homers in 1953 and 1959. His last really big season was 1960, when he had thirty-nine home runs and a career-high 124 RBI, the latter figure second-best in the league.

From 1953–61, Mathews hit no fewer than thirty-one home runs in a season, while averaging thirty-eight homers per year during that period. He scored more than 100 runs eight times, all in a ten-year stretch, and had ninety-six and ninety-seven the other two seasons. His slugging percentage was over .600 three straight years (1953–55), and he drew ninety or more bases on balls nine times, with a high of 124 in 1963. His 1,376 walks remain the record for the Braves' franchise, and he totaled 1,444 walks for his career. He only hit one World Series home run, but it was a dramatic shot, coming with a runner on in the bottom of the tenth inning of Game Four in 1957, and it was a game-winner for Milwaukee. His only two All-Star Game hits were homers.

Mathews was the perfect player for the Braves. He was the star, the building block that owner Lou Perini had when he moved his franchise from Boston to Milwaukee.[16]

A strong left-handed hitter and a nine-time All-Star, Mathews was given a supreme compliment by Ty Cobb, who said, "I have known three or four perfect swings in my time, and this lad (Mathews) has one of them."[17] Brooklyn Dodger pitching great Carl Erskine said the Braves' third baseman had the fastest bat of anyone he had ever seen.[18]

Like Aaron, Mathews was pretty much a low-key guy, one who did almost all of his talking with his performance on the field. He did not mind jumping into fights, but he did not start them. He did finish his share, though, and was the Braves' unofficial enforcer.

"Eddie was direct, honest, and stubborn," Logan said. "He was the kind of teammate you wanted on your side. He was a tough guy, but he didn't know how to start a fight. I started them, and he finished them."[19]

"With Eddie," Lew Burdette said, "you never worried about anything. If somebody charged the mound when you were pitching, you knew Eddie was going to be there. He used to tell me, 'Let the son of a gun charge you, and then get out of the way.'"[20]

"Eddie was a tough competitor and a tough guy," said Warren Spahn, Mathews' teammate for thirteen years. "He didn't back down from anybody. I remember the day he got into a fight with Frank Robinson (then of the Cincinnati Reds) at third base. Eddie hit him with three punches that not even Muhammad Ali could have stopped."[21]

"He was a very strong hitter," Aaron said, "and had a very quick bat. He hit so many big home runs for us, and he was such a hard worker. He hated to lose."[22]

"I think Eddie was one of the greatest third basemen of all time," Logan said. "He had one of the sweetest swings I ever saw. There was only one Eddie Mathews."[23]

Seemingly a moody man who was thought to be aloof, he was voted one year by Milwaukee baseball writers the Braves' most temperamental player, and Mathews admitted he could be difficult to get to know.

"I'm not the type to make a big production out of everything I do," he said. "I think it's a joke when a guy strikes out and throws his bat. If I have to do that to show the fans I'm mad, to heck with it. I shouldn't have to fling bats or kick water coolers. Hustling to me means taking the extra base, beating out the slow roller, breaking up a double play, knocking the ball out of the catcher's glove, backing up throws, and keeping my mind on the game at all times."[24]

Mathews was the only member of the Braves to play for the team in Boston, Milwaukee, and Atlanta. In 1966, the club's first year in Atlanta, he batted .250 with sixteen home runs and fifty-three RBI. Following the season, he was dealt to Houston with a player to be named later and pitcher Arnold Umbach for strikeout-prone outfielder Dave Nicholson and Bob Bruce, a pitcher who won forty-nine games in nine big league seasons. It had not been that long ago that Mathews was one of those "untouchables," players who would never be considered for a trade.

"When the Braves traded me to Houston," he said, "I cried like a baby. I am not ashamed of crying. I had totally wanted to play with the Braves, period. Those years in Milwaukee were just tremendous. There was nothing like Milwaukee when we played there. We had great support from the city and from the whole state of Wisconsin as well as surrounding states. It was a joy to go to the ballpark in those days."[25]

Late in the 1967 season, Houston sent Mathews to the Detroit Tigers, who were looking for a veteran hitter to bolster the bench down the stretch of the American League pennant race. Mathews hit six home runs in thirty-six games for the Tigers, but they finished one game behind the Boston Red Sox. The next year, he managed just three homers in thirty-one games as Detroit won the AL flag and then the World Series, defeating the St. Louis Cardinals. In the fourth game of the 1968 Fall Classic, the last time he would play third base, Mathews had one hit in three tries against Bob Gibson, the Cards' right-hander who was perhaps the nastiest pitcher batters faced in that era. Mathews narrowly missed hitting a home run off Gibson when he pulled a ball over the right field roof in Tiger Stadium, but the smash was foul by five or six feet.

Mathews worked as a scout, then as a hitting coach for the Atlanta Braves and Oakland A's, returning to the Braves' bench as a coach in 1971. During the '72 season, at the age of forty, he replaced Lum Harris as manager and stayed on until he was fired after ninety-nine games of the 1974 season. He was in the dugout when his old power partner, Aaron, belted home run number 715 in April of 1974. Mathews' jersey number 41 was retired by the Braves in 1969. He was elected to the Hall of Fame in 1978.

7

Spahn Keys Torrid August

As the Milwaukee Braves began the month of August, Warren Spahn was not a very happy man. He was happy enough with his Milwaukee Braves and the way they were playing; their four-game winning streak had them even with the St. Louis Cardinals atop the National League standings. The problem was with himself. The left-hander was not at all pleased with the way he had been pitching. He was in a slump. What troubled him was the duration of the slump. Spahn had endured bad times before and realized that was part of baseball. In a long season that covers 154 games, there will be good and bad stretches. But his bad one had grown to puzzling proportions. His record in July was 2–3 to go with two no-decisions. He had more hits allowed than innings pitched, his earned run average was over four, and he had only pitched one complete game. That came on July 16, and Spahn did not get another win the rest of the month. While he was struggling, Bob Buhl had pitched brilliantly and, at least for a six-week period, had become the ace of the Braves' staff. Spahnie, though he gave Buhl ample credit, had his pride. His teammates, and the rest of baseball, for that matter, looked to him to be the mound mainstay in Milwaukee. He looked forward to a new month as a new beginning, determined to turn his season around. Spahn would do just that, and how!

The Gene Conley show gave the Braves their fifth straight win. The tall right-hander pitched his first shutout of the season and singled in the game's only run. Conley allowed the Dodgers just four hits in winning his third decision in a row. Two of his three strikeouts came with a runner on third base. He out-pitched Brooklyn lefty Johnny Podres, who had posted six successive complete-game road wins entering the contest. Conley's RBI hit off Podres came with two strikes and two outs in the fifth inning. County Stadium was overflowing with a record crowd of 45,840, including 2,500 who were glad to watch even though they did not have seats.

The Dodgers evened the series by erupting for six runs in the last two innings to break up what had been a pitching duel between their young southpaw, Danny McDevitt, and Lew Burdette, whose personal four-game win streak came to an end. Ed Roebuck threw three hitless innings of relief as the Bums sneaked within three games of league-leading St. Louis. Milwaukee trailed by a game and a half.

After having their winning streak ended by the Dodgers the previous day, the Braves started a new one as they blasted four home runs to take a 9–7 victory and the series from Brooklyn. The attendance was 43,109, sending the three-day County Stadium total over 128,000. Eddie Mathews, Hank Aaron, Del Rice, and Johnny Logan left the park, and Wes Covington added three singles. Aaron's thirty-first homer of the season was a three-run shot. Mathews and Logan both hit two-run jobs. Dodger nemesis Bob Buhl picked up his fourteenth win, thanks to some nice relief from Spahn. He came into the game with one out in the ninth inning and the bases full of Dodgers, who already had one run in the frame and had the tying runs in scoring position. Spahn got pinch-hitter Don Zimmer on a foul popup to first baseman Frank Torre and then whiffed switch-hitter Jim Gilliam to end the game. But it did not end quietly. The last pitch was a called strike, and neither Gilliam nor his teammates thought the call a good one. They felt Rice, who always was behind the plate in games started by Buhl, had swayed home plate umpire Ed Sudol. The Dodgers streamed out of their dugout and followed Sudol to the tunnel which led to the umps' dressing quarters. Buhl beat Brooklyn for the fourth time in 1957, with Spahn notching the save.

The Braves did not play the next day, and that allowed their thirty-six-year-old left-hander to catch his breath and make his scheduled start. Not only did Spahn start, but he finished, scattering nine hits for his eleventh win. He stranded the potential tying and winning runs in the ninth by striking out Smoky Burgess. The Braves sandwiched the one-run win and a two-run triumph around a 12–2 whipping of the Redlegs. Wes Covington led the slaughter by smashing a pair of home runs and driving in four runs after getting two hits and two RBI the previous day. Red Schoendienst lined a bases-loaded triple and Andy Pafko had a double that plated two runs. Conley pitched his third straight complete game to earn his seventh win in his last eight starting assignments. It was a big night all around for Conley, whose wife gave birth to the couple's third child two hours before the game. Schoendienst came through with a two-run single in the eighth inning and knocked in a third run with a sacrifice fly in the series finale, while Del Crandall hit his fourteenth homer. Burdette improved his record to 10–1 against Cincinnati over the past two years and helped himself with an RBI single. When the series opened, Milwaukee was one game behind first-place St. Louis. When it ended, Milwaukee held a two-game lead over the Cardinals, who were swept at home by the Cubs.

Fred Hutchinson and his Cards were glad to see the Braves coming to Busch Stadium. There is nothing like going head-to-head with the team you are trying to catch. A sweep of the three-game series would put St. Louis back in first place. The problem for the Cardinals was that the Braves were playing at a level far above everyone, having won nine of their last ten games. St. Louis ran into Milwaukee's hottest pitcher, Bob Buhl, in the series opener, and they found the Braves' hitters even hotter. Buhl made it six wins in a row and the Braves made it five straight, with the hurler's record improving to 15–6. Schoendienst rapped out four hits in four at-bats and Aaron had two hits to lift his league-leading batting average to .334. One of his hits was his thirty-second home run that allowed him to pull even with Stan Musial in the NL RBI chase with eighty-seven. Bob Hazle also had four hits, including a towering home run. Eddie Mathews and Wes Covington both clouted long homers in the eighth inning as Milwaukee made the game a laugher, 13–2. Buhl once again preferred to talk about his hitting to sportswriters. He joked about his "key" two-run single, which came with his club leading by six runs.

It was more of the same in game two. Spahn tossed a five-hit shutout and proved he was back on track by turning in his second straight complete game. Milwaukee's offense scored nine runs, the sizzling Hazle knocking in three with a pair of singles and a double. Aaron went 2-for-2 and scored four times. Logan added a two-run triple. For Spahn, the shutout was the fortieth of his career as he beat the Cardinals for the forty-fifth time.

Conley stayed on beam, winning his fourth in a row and not giving up a run until St. Louis managed one in the ninth inning. The Braves made five hits count for five runs. Mathews ripped a solo homer and an RBI single, Frank Torre smacked a run-scoring double, and Logan lined a two-run double. Since replacing Bob Trowbridge in the Milwaukee rotation in late July, Conley had won five of six starts, and all five victories were complete games.

Gene Conley was quite an athlete, good enough to play prominent roles on world championship teams in two sports. Standing 6-foot-8, he was an imposing sight for batters when he kicked up his left leg and delivered a fastball. He was a factor under the backboards on the hardwood, a tough competitor who could mix it up with the best. Legendary Boston Celtics coach Red Auerbach once called Conley, "The toughest guy I ever had in a fight."

Conley was selected first-team All-Pacific Coast Conference in basketball while playing for Washington State for the 1949–50 season and then pitched the Cougars into the College World Series, where they finished as the runner-up to Texas. He was inducted into the Pac-10 Hall of Honor in 2005. Conley played six seasons in the NBA and came off the bench from 1959–61 for the Boston Celtics as they won the league championship all three years. Sometimes he backed up Celtics center Bill Russell, who is one of the NBA's all-time greatest players, but more often than not, he played alongside Russell. Conley averaged 5.9 points and 6.3 rebounds, while playing about seventeen minutes a game during his NBA career. Conley is the only athlete to play on world championship teams in the major leagues and the National Basketball Association. He played with the Celtics in 1953 before the Braves' front office pressured him into quitting basketball. He returned in 1959 because, with three children and baseball nowhere near the lucrative profession it is now, he needed the money.[1]

The Boston Braves signed Conley in 1951, and he pitched so well on their farm teams that *The Sporting News* twice named him the Minor League Player of the Year, selecting the big right-hander for the honor in 1951 and 1953. He pitched for the Hartford Chiefs his first season. The Braves brought him up for the end of the 1952 season and gave him three starts. National League hitters knocked him around as he gave up twenty-three hits and eleven earned runs in less than thirteen innings. In 1953, he was with the Milwaukee Brewers. It was obvious he had the potential and the stuff for a bright future, and the next year, he was back in Milwaukee with the Braves. When they headed north following their 1954 spring training, Conley was with them. His rookie season was fantastic. He started twenty-seven games, had a record of 14–9, threw two shutouts, and posted a fine 2.96 earned run average over 194.1 innings.

Conley had ten wins in June of 1955 when he felt a twinge in his right arm. He managed one more victory before shutting down for the last six weeks of the season. He struggled the next year, but won four straight at one point and finished 8–9 with a 3.13 ERA in 158.1 innings. Conley pitched ten fewer innings in 1957; however, for a while, he joined Bob Buhl as the most effective pitchers on the Milwaukee staff. Conley pitched his best baseball at a very important time, when Warren Spahn and Lew Burdette were both scuffling a bit. Conley was an extremely important cog in the Braves' drive to the pennant as he finished with nine wins and a 3.16 earned run average.

Following an 0–6 season in which he threw just seventy-two innings, Milwaukee traded Conley to the Philadelphia Phillies in March of 1959. He was dealt with infielders Joe Koppe and Harry Hanebrink for infielders Ted Kazanski and Johnny O'Brien and catcher Stan Lopata. After winning twenty games in two years for the Phils, they traded him to the Boston Red Sox for another tall right-handed hurler, Frank Sullivan. Conley won twenty-five games in two seasons with the Red Sox, including a career-high fifteen in 1962 when he also had a career high with 241.2 innings pitched.

Highlighting Conley's career was his performance in the 1955 All-Star Game, which was played in front of more than 45,000 fans in County Stadium. The American League led, 5–0, after six innings before Braves shortstop Johnny Logan singled in the first run for the National League, which scored two runs in the seventh inning and three in the eighth as the game eventually went into extra innings. Conley came in to pitch the twelfth inning, and he struck out Detroit right-fielder Al Kaline, Washington first baseman Mickey Vernon, and Cleveland third baseman Al Rosen. On the way to the dugout, Conley received a long and loud ovation from the huge crowd, most of which was comprised of Braves fans. In the bottom of the inning, Stan Musial hit a home run to make Conley the winning pitcher and to give the NL a 6–5 victory in perhaps the greatest comeback in All-Star Game history.[2]

The showdown series was mainly a showcase for the Braves, who extended their winning streak to seven games and their National League lead over St. Louis to five games. The Cardinals, meanwhile, had lost six in a row, their longest skid of the season.

Milwaukee traveled to Cincinnati for three games in Crosley Field, where the Braves played as if it was their second home. In truth, it did not matter where the Braves played the Redlegs because they owned them. The hex continued and so did Milwaukee's scorching pace. The Braves swept the three games convincingly, winning by scores of 12–4, 13–3, and 8–1, while amassing forty-one hits that included eight home runs. Burdette won the opener in a route-going performance and was the hitting star as well. He belted two home runs, including his first as a major leaguer. The second was a three-run blow that broke a 4–4 tie. Schoendienst had three hits and three RBI and Andy Pafko had a 3-for-3 day with a double.

For nearly a month, Bob Buhl had been unbeatable. During the first half of July, he could not win. Since then, he could not lose. After losing four straight decisions, the right-hander had won his last six. He and the Braves had a two-run lead before the Redlegs scored in the eighth, and Fred Haney brought in Don McMahon. The mainstay of the Milwaukee bullpen since

Gene Conley played on world championship teams in pro baseball and basketball. His best outings of 1957 came as a starter during an important stretch when other Braves hurlers were not faring so well.

his arrival in the majors on the last day of June, McMahon slammed the door. And then the Braves' offense slammed as they exploded for eight ninth-inning runs. Wes Covington bashed a grand slam and McMahon, who seldom got a chance to bat (he had two hits in eight at-bats for the season), lashed a three-run double. Hazle had three more hits and an RBI, and Logan smacked a two-run homer, his tenth. Buhl's victory was his seventh in a row and his sixteenth against six losses.

In the series finale, Spahn allowed eight hits and an unearned run in pitching his third successive complete game. Milwaukee hit the power switch with four home runs, two by Hank Aaron. He cracked a three-run shot in the first inning and later added a two-run clout, giving him thirty-four roundtrippers. Mathews and Hazle joined the homer parade, with Hazle also getting a pair of singles. Spahn improved his lifetime record against the Redlegs to 44–14, his best against any team. The Braves had won ten in a row, fifteen of their last sixteen games, and had a 71–42 record. They were threatening to make a shambles of the National League race with an eight-game lead over both St. Louis and Brooklyn. Cincinnati, which looked like a contender early in the season, trailed by ten and one-half games. Philadelphia was twelve games out of first place.

The Cardinals were reeling. They carried a nine-game losing streak into Milwaukee. They also carried memories of having been swept at home by the Braves a week earlier, while being outscored in the three setbacks, 27–3. County Stadium was not a place any National League team wanted to be visiting at that time; no one relished meeting up with a club that was hitting on all cylinders, one that was scoring runs in bunches and allowing very few. Old Hutch, the St. Louis skipper, knew another sweep by the Braves could, for all intents and purposes, knock his Cards right out of the pennant chase. On the other hand, it was a chance for them to climb back into the race and make it interesting.

That is exactly what the Cardinals did. With a crowd of over 45,000 looking on and anticipating the kill, St. Louis jumped on Gene Conley right away. The tall right-hander had, in recent weeks, stayed in step with Buhl, Spahn, and Burdette in giving Milwaukee — at least, for that period of time — the best four starting pitchers in the big leagues. His good pitching and good fortune came to a sudden end. Conley got leadoff batter Ken Boyer to open the game, gave up a single to Wally Moon, and retired Stan Musial for the second out. But he walked Joe Cunningham, bringing Walker Cooper to the plate. Cooper, the forty-two-year-old catcher, was able to catch in only thirteen games in 1957. He drove in ten runs, and two of them came on a double off Conley. Alvin Dark singled home Cooper for a 3–0 Cardinal lead before the Braves batted. Conley walked two in the second inning and was replaced by Juan Pizarro, who pitched shutout relief until Del Ennis hit a three-run homer in the seventh. Milwaukee staged a mini-rally in the bottom of the seventh inning, getting run-scoring singles from Schoendienst and Torre. After giving up the two runs, St. Louis starter Lindy McDaniel departed and got shutout help from three relievers to close a crucial 6–2 win. Musial had two hits in five at-bats to raise his average to .3333. That gave him the NL batting lead over Aaron, whose hitless night dropped him to .3326.

The injury bug bit the Braves once again as shortstop Johnny Logan had to leave the game because of a painful shin bone in his left leg. A doctor said Logan's shin was badly inflamed and that he would need to be hospitalized and treated with antibiotics. Logan's leg was hurt when Cincinnati's Frank Robinson slid into him at second base two days earlier.

Milwaukee regained the game it had lost to the Cardinals by nipping them in eleven innings the next day, 5–4. The Cards jumped on Lew Burdette to score three runs in the first inning just as they had the night before. Larry Jackson was perfect through five innings, setting down all fifteen Braves he faced. But the St. Louis right-hander ran into trouble in the sixth. Del Crandall singled and, two batters later, Red Schoendienst got hold of a Jackson curve ball and deposited it into the right-field seats for his thirteenth home run of the season. The Braves bunched singles by pinch-hitter Carl Sawatski, Schoendienst, and Torre in the eighth to tie the score. When the Cardinals put men on second and third with only one out off of Milwaukee relief ace Don McMahon in the top of the ninth inning, Haney walked to the mound, pointed to the bullpen, and tapped his left arm. In walked Warren Spahn, who had pitched nine innings less than forty-eight hours earlier. Ennis, batting for Moon, was walked intentionally, and Musial then bounced into a double play. The Cards scored a run in the eleventh, and the Braves answered. With one out, Torre singled and was replaced by pinch-runner Hawk Taylor. Mathews also singled. Aaron then belted a long double off the right-centerfield wall, scoring Taylor and Mathews, to give Milwaukee the victory. Aaron's game-winner made a loser out of Billy Muffet (remember that name) and a winner out of Spahn, who worked the final two and two-thirds innings.

Newspapers reported that Aaron had accused St. Louis pitchers of throwing at him. He singled out Larry Jackson and Sam Jones, noting a ninth-inning pitch from Jackson that was thrown near Aaron's head. "They have been doing that all season," he said. "Jackson has done it before, and Jones has done it in St. Louis. I know neither of them is that wild. It's on purpose. I can tell when they are throwing at me. I've got a family just like they've got. If that's the only way they can win a ball game, then they ought to get other jobs. I don't mind being brushed back—you expect that—but I don't like pitches aimed at my head. I'm just like a rabbit. Every time I go up there, I've got to jump around and look for a hole. Jackson gets the first pitch over for a strike. Now I have to protect the plate. I can't let him get ahead of me. So what does he do? Throws the next one at my head. You're not looking for it after the first strike, but that's when they throw it. We don't knock Stan Musial down, so why do they do it to me?" Asked what he planned to do about the situation, Aaron said, "It just makes me more determined to go up there and get a hit."[3]

Cardinal manager Fred Hutchinson responded by calling Aaron's charges "A lot of nonsense," adding, "He doesn't know what it is to be knocked down." St. Louis coach Terry Moore labeled Aaron's remarks "Bush League," and said, "A big leaguer doesn't say those things."[4]

Sunday was a very long day for everybody at County Stadium. A double-header was scheduled, and it got under way at 1:30 in the afternoon. The second game was over at 9:48 p.m. In between, there was a rain delay of more than two hours, a ten-inning game that lasted nearly three and a half hours, and, finally, a game that moved quickly. The Cardinals did what they had to do, sweeping Milwaukee, 8–6 and 6–0. Bob Hazle singled and poled a three-run homer. Eddie Mathews also had a roundtripper and a single. The Braves saw a five-run lead evaporate as St. Louis torched the Milwaukee bullpen for thirteen hits. Musial smacked a game-winning two-run homer in the tenth off Juan Pizarro, the fourth of five Braves pitchers. Wilmer "Vinegar Bend" Mizell dominated the nightcap. The southpaw blanked the Braves on four hits and allowed only two runners to get as far as second base. Musial had four hits in the doubleheader to grab the NL batting lead from Aaron, who got just one hit in nine at-bats.

St. Louis, by winning three of four in Milwaukee, trimmed two games off its deficit and moved within six games of the Braves in the National League standings. And, while that did not make for a lively home team locker room, there was far worse news to ponder. Bob Buhl, the Braves' most consistent starting pitcher for much of the season, faced only two batters in the opener of the twinbill. He walked both, then left the game holding his right shoulder.

Milwaukee had a day off to recover from the grueling twin defeats to the Cardinals, and that gave Spahn an extra day of rest. One of his four days between starts, however, was spent pitching more than two innings of relief. All that did was make the lefty even sharper for his August 20 start in Pittsburgh. He shut out the Pirates for seven innings and scattered seven hits to win, 3–1. The victory was his fifteenth against eight losses. The Braves only managed one run off of Vernon Law, but they scored twice on reliever Luis Arroyo in the ninth. A single by Schoendienst, a triple by Mathews, and a single by Aaron produced the runs. Still, the Cardinals gained ground as they took two one-run victories from the Giants in the Polo Grounds. Musial homered in each game. St. Louis slipped a half-game closer and trailed by five and one-half.

The Braves got that half-game back along with a day of rest while the Cards were getting thumped by the Giants, 13–6. Milwaukee and St. Louis both won the next day, leaving the Cardinals six games behind the Braves. Brooklyn was in third place, seven and a half games out of the lead. Cincinnati and Philadelphia were barely above .500 and all but forgotten as both were thirteen and one-half games behind Milwaukee. The Braves' 6–1 win was in Ebbets Field, where Lew Burdette pitched a neat seven-hitter for his twelfth victory. Hank Aaron gave him all the offense he would need with a three-run home run in the first inning. The blast, which was Aaron's thirty-fifth, came off Sal Maglie after the Dodgers' right-hander walked Frank Torre and gave up a single to Eddie Mathews. Red Schoendienst poked his fourteenth roundtripper over the screen in right field and just inside the foul pole. Burdette singled and scored on a double by Mathews. Hazle doubled and later crossed the plate on Crandall's sacrifice fly.

Fred Haney checked the daily injury report, and he did not like what he saw. The prognosis on Buhl was that he had an inflamed tendon in his right shoulder, and he was flown back to Milwaukee to receive further medical attention. Wes Covington, who had been swinging such a hot bat for almost a month, had hobbled off the field after grounding out to Brooklyn second baseman Junior Gilliam in the fourth inning. It was scary because Covington's injury was to his left Achilles tendon, and a tear would end the outfielder's season for sure. It turned out that the tendon was pulled, and Covington would miss only two games. Logan was scheduled to leave the hospital that day after being treated for a shin infection. There was a chance he could take ground balls and batting practice four days later.

Gene Conley was in total command of the Dodgers for eight innings as he out-dueled Sandy Koufax. Aaron was the whole show offensively, crushing a long home run in the fourth and a run-scoring triple in the seventh. The RBI were the 100th and 101st for Aaron. His triple followed a walk to Mathews. Aaron was on third base with nobody out, but Koufax retired Crandall, Andy Pafko, and Felix Mantilla to prevent further damage. Crandall was playing right field because of the injury situation, with the left-handed hitting Hazle on the bench since Haney platooned him and used him only against right-handed pitchers. Milwaukee threatened to break the game open in the eighth when it loaded the bases with no outs. Catcher Del Rice coaxed a walk from Ed Roebuck, who relieved Koufax after seven innings. Conley singled, and so did Schoendienst, with the slow-footed Rice holding at third. Roebuck got Torre on a fly ball to right that was too short for Rice to tag and score. He struck out Mathews and struck out Aaron. Don Drysdale, who would eventually combine with Koufax to form one of baseball's all-time best righty-lefty pitching duos, made a rare relief appearance and retired the Braves in order in the ninth. Sandy Amoros, one of the Dodgers' 1955 World Series heroes, led off the bottom of the inning with a double off the right-field screen. Charlie Neal singled home Amoros, and Conley was finished, having allowed eight hits. Hard-throwing Don McMahon entered the game and promptly whiffed Pee Wee Reese. But Carl Furillo, pinch-hitting for John Roseboro, drew a walk and with it, thunderous applause from nearly 22,000 Ebbets Field faithful who smelled a winning rally. Their hopes came down to the last out when another pinch-hitter, Randy Jackson, flied to Pafko in left. Gilliam then beat the ball into the dirt, and it bounded high into the air. There was really no time for McMahon to get the speedy Gilliam at first, but he tried anyway. The throw was bad, and Neal scored the tying run from second base, with Furillo going to third and Gilliam to second. Gino Cimoli then lined a base hit to center to plate Furillo with the deciding run in a 3–2 Brooklyn victory. The Dodgers' comeback spoiled a fine outing by Conley and made a losing pitcher out of McMahon.

The Braves won the August 24 rubber match, which was also their last game ever in Ebbets Field. They said good bye, 13–7, with a power barrage that included four home runs and two doubles. Milwaukee's Bob Trowbridge and Brooklyn's Johnny Podres matched zeroes for three innings before both teams' bats heated up. Nippy Jones led off the fourth for the Braves with his second home run of the season. Podres retired Mathews, then Aaron walloped a tape-measure blast, his thirty-seventh of the season, into the left-center field bleachers. Crandall made the second out before Pafko unloaded the Braves' third roundtripper of the inning. Drysdale, the second of eight pitchers used by Walter Alston, had to come in to get the final out. Not to be outdone, the Dodgers entered the home run-hitting contest in their half. Gil Hodges led off with a drive into the left-field seats, and singles by Amoros, Neal, and Roseboro cut Brooklyn's deficit to a run. Milwaukee broke the game open by scoring five times in the sixth on five hits and an error. Hazle and Mantilla contributed RBI singles, with Ernie Johnson, who relieved Trowbridge in the fourth, getting a run-scoring double. The Dodgers scored once in the bottom of the inning and four times in the seventh, slicing the Braves' lead to 8–7. Milwaukee sealed the verdict with one run in the eighth and four in the ninth, capped by Mantilla's homer, a towering three-run shot. Burdette threw two and two-thirds innings of shutout relief to earn his thirteenth win. Two guys playing because of injuries to teammates combined to drive in seven runs, with Mantilla getting four RBI and Pafko three.

The Dodgers, who began the series with hopes of getting within three and a half games of the Braves, trailed them by seven and one half and were nine games behind Milwaukee in the loss column. The Bums only had three games remaining with the National League leader, and those would be played in County Stadium two weeks before the end of the season.

As it turned out, the report on Johnny Logan was overly optimistic. He was not able to play again until September. The shortstop was replaced by Mantilla in a game with St. Louis August 16 because of a shin injury that proved much more serious than anyone originally thought. Mantilla's performance during Logan's absence and the previous month, as a fill-in for Schoendienst, was one of the most overlooked contributions to the Braves' pennant drive. When names like Aaron, Mathews, Schoendienst, Spahn, Burdette, and Buhl show up big in the box score every day, and then a Hurricane Hazle comes blowing in with a booming bat, steady everyday play by a backup infielder gets lost in the shuffle. Mantilla, although shaky at times in the field, made most of the plays, and he came through with several key hits. In the seven games he played at second base in the end of June, when Schoendiest was out, Mantilla batted .333 with two doubles, two home runs, and six runs driven in. He hit safely in all seven of those games. Playing shortstop every day over the last two weeks in August, Mantilla batted over .300 with two home runs and two doubles.

Spahn continued being Spahn as he pitched the Braves past the Phillies, 7–3, to put his club thirty games over .500. Again, he hurled nine innings, giving him complete games in five straight starts. Spahn produced the first run of the game when he socked his second homer of the season in the third inning. Hazle took care of the rest of Milwaukee's scoring with a pair of three-run bombs. In the fourth, following singles by Torre and Aaron, Hazle sent a Robin Roberts offering over the right-center field fence. Facing Warren Hacker in the sixth, Hazle blasted one deep over the wall in right after a walk to Mathews and a single by Wes Covington.

The Phillies nipped Milwaukee, 4–3, and split the two-game set when pinch-hitter Ron Northey singled in the winning run in the bottom of the ninth off of Ernie Johnson. Eddie Mathews had a two-run single and a triple, with Wes Covington and Hazle both adding a single and a double.

The Braves made their final visit to the Polo Grounds, but it certainly was not like the old days. The Giants, their record six games under .500, were not in the pennant race, and they were signed and sealed as a 1958 West Coast team, the delivery set for the coming winter. Crowds for Milwaukee's two late-August games in New York totaled just over 26,000, with most of them on hand just to see Willie Mays. The Say Hey Kid was enjoying a season that

would see him finish with thirty-five home runs, thirty-eight stolen bases, and a .333 batting average.

Home runs accounted for all of the Braves' scoring in a 4–3 win, and Don McMahon pitched two perfect innings to save it for Lew Burdette. Red Schoendienst led off the game with a home run off Al Worthington, Eddie Mathews connected with Frank Torre on base in the sixth inning, and Torre hit an opposite-field blast into the upper deck in left field in the eighth.

The Giants earned a split in the two-game series by winning the second contest, 12–6, exploding for eight runs in the third inning. Gene Conley was rocked for eight hits and nine runs in two and two-thirds innings. Five of the runs were unearned as Felix Mantilla booted a grounder at short and Bob Hazle let a base hit scoot past him in right field.

Spahn capped a sensational August with a win in Cincinnati as the Braves prevailed, 9–5. This time, he was not as sharp. He left after six innings, having given up eight hits, five walks, and three runs, all earned. Four home runs made it easy for Milwaukee. Mathews, Torre, Carl Sawatski, and Wes Covington went deep, with Mathews and Torre driving in two runs apiece. Spahn had a record of 7–0 with a save in August, pitching five complete games, and posting a dazzling 1.80 earned run average. He allowed only forty-seven hits in 54.2 innings during the month, finishing with a 17–8 record.

The Braves continued their home run barrage in a 14–4 trouncing of the Redlegs. Five Braves belted roundtrippers to highlight a fifteen-hit attack, with Schoendienst rapping out four singles. Mathews hit a home run in his fourth game in a row, giving him twenty-eight for the season, and had three RBI. Aaron clouted his thirty-eighth homer and Covington homered for the second straight game, with Mantilla and Rice joining the long ball parade. Rice's blow was a three-run job, while Mantilla hit a two-run shot. The Braves scored five runs in the first inning, and when the Redlegs jumped Burdette for three hits, two walks, and two runs in one-third of an inning, Fred Haney came out of the dugout with a quick hook. Juan Pizarro got the call, and the rookie left-hander worked out of a bases-loaded jam without further damage. Pizarro struck out nine Reds in eight and one-third innings to notch his fifth victory. Seeking a little pay-back in recalling Frank Robinson's hard slide into Johnny Logan that resulted in the Braves' shortstop missing half of August, Covington went hard into Cincinnati second baseman Johnny Temple.

Opposite: **Felix Mantilla was a valuable utility infielder for the Braves, filling in at second base, shortstop, and third. He blossomed as a hitter after leaving Milwaukee and getting a chance to play every day. (©Brace Photo. Used by permission.)**

The Redlegs' scrappy infielder did not take kindly to being dumped, and he jumped up and into Covington's face. Both dugouts and bullpens emptied, but the confrontation was more pushing and shoving than it was a full-fledged brawl.

Covington filled what had been a huge void for the Braves. For the first two months of the 1957 season, left field was a revolving door. Covington was one of four Braves who took a turn at the position, and after a slow start, he was sent to Milwaukee's Triple-A team in Wichita on May 15. A native of Laurinburg, North Carolina, the left-handed hitter was batting under .100 at the time. Covington was recalled on June 17, and he belted a home run in his second game back in the majors. He had one more roundtripper, but hit just .244 for the rest of the month.

Then he got hot. Covington homered in two of the first three games in July and went on to hit seven home runs and bat .310 with 22 runs batted in over his first full month with Milwaukee. He added five triples, getting at least one extra-base hit in eleven of thirty games. Playing every day, Covington batted fifth in the Braves' lineup against right-handers and was dropped to seventh or eighth against lefties. He missed six games in August because of injuries, but that did not cool him off as he had a .304 average, with six home runs and eighteen RBI. Covington batted .284 for the season, with eight triples, twenty-one home runs, and sixty-five runs batted in. He homered once in every 15.6 at-bats, behind Aaron, who had a home run for every 13.9 at-bats, and ahead of Mathews, who hit one homer in every 17.9 at-bats. One important thing about Covington's offensive production, one that did not show on the stat sheet, was that he helped Aaron get better pitches to hit. Knowing a powerful hitter was coming up next, hurlers could not pitch around Aaron. Mathews, Aaron, and Covington were a formidable trio in the middle of the Milwaukee lineup as they combined to hit ninety-seven home runs for the season.

Before Covington nailed down the left field spot, Bobby Thomson, Andy Pafko, and Chuck Tanner were given a whirl at the position. Thomson, a right-handed hitter, batted .236 with four home runs before being traded to the Giants on June 15. Tanner, who batted from the left side, hit .246 with two homers before he was swapped to the Cubs on June 8.

Pafko, who was thirty-six years old, was a valuable and productive player for the Braves in 1957. He was one of the club's best pinch-hitters, and after center fielder Billy Bruton was lost to the team in mid-season, Pafko saw frequent duty in right field following Aaron's switch to center. Pafko, a right-handed hitter, platooned with Bob Hazle in right field over the final two months of the season.

Although his best years were behind him, Andy Pafko was still a dependable outfielder in 1957, and he came through with some big defensive plays and clutch hits for the Braves.

Once a consistent power hitter, Pafko smacked eight home runs and drove in twenty-seven runs, while batting .277. Over his career, he had double-figure homer totals in ten consecutive seasons, with a high of thirty-six in 1950, when he hit .304. He played for the Chicago Cubs from 1943 through part of the 1951 season. Pafko drove in 110 runs in 1945, and he had 101 RBI while batting a career-high .312 with twenty-six home runs in 1948. Pafko was traded to the Dodgers one-third of the way through the 1951 season, when he totaled thirty home runs for the two teams that year. The Braves obtained him from Brooklyn in the winter of 1953 for Roy Hartsfield and $50,000.

Injuries forced Fred Haney to plug holes in the outfield with players who seldom saw action out there. Del Crandall, the Braves' regular catcher, played nine games in right field. Second baseman Red Schoendienst, who started his career as an outfielder with the St. Louis Cardinals, fellow infielder Felix Mantilla, and first baseman Nippy Jones also played some outfield for the Braves. Thirteen different Milwaukee players were used in the outfield in 1957.

Milwaukee's ten-game winning streak keyed a 19–7 August, which was the team's best month of the season. When it started, the Braves shared first place in the National League with St. Louis. When it ended, the Braves owned a seven-game lead over second-place Brooklyn, with the Cardinals trailing by seven and a half games.

8

The Clincher

Cousin is a baseball term that refers to a team which constantly loses to another team. A prime example would be the old Kansas City Athletics, who were the New York Yankees' "Cousins." The Athletics not only were doormats for the Yankees, but they were practically a farm team for New York as well. In 1957, Cincinnati was Milwaukee's "cousin" as the Braves defeated the Redlegs eighteen times in twenty-two meetings. It was the best record Milwaukee had against any team that year.

So it was unusual that the Reds not only defeated the Braves, but shut them out to close the series and begin September, a month that would prove to be Milwaukee's worst since May and one that would see the National League pennant race take some surprising turns in a bit of a rollercoaster ride to the finish. Brooks Lawrence, who was a nineteen-game winner in 1956, shut out the Braves on five hits, while his teammates got to Gene Conley for five hits and four runs in three innings.

The Braves went into Wrigley Field and swept three games from the Cubs, first winning a slugfest and then throwing back-to-back shutouts. Milwaukee amassed twenty-six hits in taking the first game of a doubleheader, 23–10, with Frank Torre and Bob Hazle getting four safeties apiece. Three of Hazle's hits were doubles. Torre scored six runs to tie a major league record previously shared by Johnny Pesky of the Boston Red Sox and Mel Ott of the New York Giants. Wes Covington singled twice, hit a home run, and drove in six runs. Hank Aaron also knocked in six runs with a pair of singles and a double. Eddie Mathews drove in three with two singles and a long home run. For the second straight game, Lew Burdette could not stand prosperity and blew a chance to get an easy win. The Braves scored six runs in the first inning, two in the second, and five in the third, but the Cubs put seven runs on the scoreboard in three innings. Burdette was yanked without being able to get out of the third, having given up seven hits and all seven of the Chicago runs. Ernie Johnson relieved and calmed the seas considerably. He finished up, surrendering three runs over six and a third innings, while striking out seven, to get his seventh win in nine decisions. The Braves scored in every inning except the fifth, with Mathews and Aaron both crossing the plate four times. Johnson even chipped in two hits and an RBI. The second contest was much different as Bob Trowbridge blanked the Cubbies on three hits. He fanned a season-high nine batters and walked only one in improving his record to 5–4. Covington had three more hits and two more RBI, giving him eight runs batted in for the day. Meanwhile, St. Louis lost twice to Cincinnati and Brooklyn dropped two to Philadelphia. The Braves were on the verge of running away with the National League pennant as they led the Cardinals by eight and a half games and the Dodgers by nine.

Warren Spahn, who pitched an eight-hitter for his shutout of the Cubs, won his eighth decision in a row to lift his record to 18–8. Left-hander Dick Littlefield threw six shutout innings before Milwaukee erupted for five runs in the seventh. Mathews, Aaron, Covington, Felix Mantilla, and Del Crandall all contributed run-scoring singles in the inning. Aaron blasted his thirty-ninth home run with two teammates aboard in the eighth. The shutout was the forty-first of Spahn's career, giving him the all-time lead for NL lefties in that category. He had shared the record with Eppa Rixey and Larry French.

Milwaukee turned right around and lost three in a row, two in St. Louis. The Cardinals won, 5–4, in twelve innings and then trounced the Braves, 10–1, the following night. In the first game, the Cards knocked Juan Pizarro out of the box before he could retire a batter. They scored four runs off of the rookie and did not get another run until the twelfth when Del Ennis plated the game-winner with a sacrifice fly off of losing hurler Don McMahon. Del Rice ripped a three-run homer and Mathews added a solo shot, his thirtieth. Sam "Toothpick" Jones threw a four-hitter at the Braves as the Cardinals broke open a scoreless game with three runs off Burdette in the fifth inning on the way to their easy win. St. Louis, which was playing without an injured Stan Musial, was within six and a half games of Milwaukee.

It stayed that way next day as both the Cardinals and Braves lost, but the Dodgers won their third straight to trail St. Louis by a half game and Milwaukee by seven. The Braves started a twelve-game home stand, but were handed their third loss in a row by the Cubs, who scored all of their runs in the seventh inning on the way to a 5–4 win. Bob Hazle hit a home run. It was the 177th roundtripper of the season for the Braves, equaling their total for 1956.

Every club needs a stopper, a pitcher who can put an end to a losing streak, and Spahn took great pride in filling that important role for the Braves. He did that in the second game of the series with Chicago, pitching a five-hitter in a 7–2 victory. Spahn's ninth consecutive win was his nineteenth on the season, and his complete game was his seventh in his last eight starts. Red Schoendienst ignited Milwaukee's five-run third inning with a single. After two were out, Aaron walked, and Covington followed with a three-run blast into the right-field seats. Mantilla and Crandall both singled home a run. Pinch-hitter Andy Pafko gave the Braves extra insurance by cracking a two-run homer in the seventh. Spahn fanned a half-dozen Cubs, walked one, and had one of Milwaukee's fourteen hits.

The last-place Cubs won the next day, 5–3, to take the series in Milwaukee. Chicago scored twice in the tenth inning when Ernie Johnson walked four batters. Covington drilled a home run, and the Braves scored the tying run in the ninth after trailing, 3–0. Bob Buhl returned to action. Making his first appearance in three weeks, he pitched three scoreless innings of relief. The Cardinals nipped the Redlegs and trailed Milwaukee by five and a half games.

Lew Burdette finally got his fifteenth win and went the distance despite giving up twelve hits. Hank Aaron and Eddie Mathews slugged back-to-back home runs in the fourth inning, and the Braves edged Pittsburgh, 4–3. After seeing his club lose four of five games, Fred Haney juggled his lineup. He moved Aaron into the second slot, batted Covington in the cleanup spot, and dropped Torre to fifth in the batting order. Aaron, who normally hit fourth, smacked his fortieth homer. Mathews, who also had an RBI single, hit his thirty-first. Wes Covington singled in a run, giving the left fielder fourteen runs batted in over nine games. Milwaukee turned three double plays, all started by shortstop Johnny Logan. St. Louis also won, downing the Phillies.

The Cardinals clobbered the Phils the next day, while the Braves lost. The Cards' fourth straight win pulled them within four and a half games of Milwaukee. Warren Spahn pitched another beauty, a seven-hit complete game, but was denied his twentieth win. Pirates catcher Hank Foiles homered in the third inning and singled home a run in the ninth for a 2–1 victory. The Braves managed only six hits off of Ronnie Kline, their run coming on a Pafko roundtripper.

Milwaukee opened a three-game home series with Brooklyn on September 12 and nipped the Dodgers, 2–1. Crandall drove in the winning run with a pinch single in the bottom of the ninth inning. Pafko singled in the other run for the Braves and made three outstanding plays in right field. Bob Trowbridge earned the victory by pitching five and two-thirds innings of shutout relief. Buhl started, but was taken out after allowing three hits and four bases on balls. He left in the fourth with one out and the bases loaded. Junior Gilliam, the first hitter to face Trowbridge, hit a line drive that Pafko appeared to catch. Charlie Neal tagged and ran home. But Pafko, who was unable to hold onto Gilliam's shot, quickly threw the ball into Schoendienst at second base. Roy Campanella, who had been on second, returned to the bag when he thought Pafko had caught the ball in the air. Schoendienst, thinking fast, tagged the Brooklyn catcher and then stepped on second to force Dodger pitcher Danny McDevitt, who was on first. Because the double play was executed without the force being removed, Neal's run was not counted. The Brooklyn dugout went berserk as did the team's general manager, Buzzie Bavasi, who was sitting nearby. Dodger players threw towels onto the field to show their displeasure.

Pafko also made a leaping catch near the fence in right and played Duke Snider's double off the wall perfectly in the ninth. Pafko rifled a throw to the cutoff man that prevented Pee Wee Reese from scoring. In the Braves' half of the inning, Logan drew a walk from McDevitt, and Covington tried to sacrifice him to second. After not getting the bunt down, Covington grounded into a double play. At least, it looked like a double play. But Dusty Boggess, the plate umpire, ruled that he had called time before the pitch. Again, towels sailed from the Dodgers' dugout. Covington singled to right, and after Nippy Jones hit into a force play, Crandall plated Logan with the deciding run. Milwaukee cashed in on the Cardinals being idle to add a half-game to its lead and increase the margin to five full games.

The Dodgers filed an official protest of the game, saying that the confusion by the umpires caused Brooklyn to lose, and asking that it be replayed. The next day, National League president Warren Giles denied the protest and said he was notifying Bavasi, "I can't take seriously a request that the game be replayed." Giles said he was adding that it was hard to seriously consider a request that came "simply because the base runners became confused over an umpire's decision." Bavasi had asked Giles to order a replay "in the interest of justice and integrity of baseball," adding, "Your action on this should be taken in fairness to all clubs in contention for the pennant." What amounted to a dare on the part of the Brooklyn GM was basically ignored.

Joe Adcock was back in the Milwaukee lineup at first base for the first time since June 23, when he fractured a bone in his ankle. He was hitless in four at-bats in the win over the Dodgers, but the Braves welcomed his return. At the same time, they appreciated the great effort Frank Torre had given.

During the time Adcock, was out, spanning seventy-six games, Torre performed admirably. Playing just about every day at first base, he batted .244 in Adcock's absence, with eight doubles, three triples, and two home runs. Torre scored thirty-three runs and drove in twenty-three in that stretch. His bat was the hottest in July, when he had an eight-game hitting streak. Included was a game in which he smashed three doubles and another when he went 4-for-4. Over a span of two weeks, Torre hit safely in twelve games, getting twenty-one hits in fifty-nine at-bats for a .356 average with eleven RBI. A left-hander all the way, he played first base gracefully, making the first-to-short-to first double play as smoothly and as well as anyone.

Heroes come in many forms, and the biggest ones are not athletes, but people who selflessly give to make a difference in the lives of others. It may be the act of saving a life, and that, too, happens in many ways. Frank Torre is such a hero because of what he meant to his family.

His famous brother, Joe, once an MVP while playing for the St. Louis Cardinals and more notably the very successful manager of the New York Yankees, has explained why his older brother is so special. Joe Torre went public in 2003 about domestic violence in his family. There were four children — Frank, Joe, and two sisters — and their father, a detective, terrorized their mother. The children watched as their dad beat their mother, threw her down stairs, and threatened her life with a knife because of the way she had cooked eggs.

The children lived in constant fear, more for their mom than themselves. She was the object of their father's violent attacks, but everyone was the target of his verbal abuse. He made the children feel as if they were nothing, telling them they were no good.

Eventually, big brother Frank left the Brooklyn home to play baseball in the minor leagues. Without him, life was even more frightening for the rest of the family. They would phone Frank, who was traveling to play baseball, late at night and share terrible experiences. He was all they had. Joe, in telling about the terrible situation, recalled how brave Frank was and how he saved the family. What he did was to have a lawyer draw up a document in which the father would sign the house over to the mother, pack his belongings, and leave. In return, he would not be required to provide any financial support. Frank saw to it that his father got out and never came back. Joe has always looked at Frank as a father figure.[1]

Frank Torre's big league baseball career was short, ending when he was only thirty-one years old. It was highlighted by two straight trips to the World Series, and he appeared in all seven games for the Braves in 1957 and 1958. He hit .300 with two home runs in the '57 Fall Classic. His lifetime batting

Frank Torre, a silky smooth first sacker, came up with some big hits in his stint as an everyday player. He slugged two home runs in the Braves' World Series triumph over the New York Yankees.

average was .273, with a high of .310 in 1962 when he had just 168 at-bats for the Philadelphia Phillies. Torre's best year was 1958 as he posted career bests of 138 games, 372 trips to the plate, six home runs, and fifty-five runs batted in, while hitting .309. Milwaukee sent him to Philadelphia in an "unknown transaction" prior to the 1962 season.

Adcock was a slugger. A strapping six-foot-four, 220-pounder from Louisiana, he attended Louisiana State University, where he studied agriculture and was a standout in basketball and baseball. He broke in with the Cincinnati Redlegs in 1950, and starting the next year, he had at least ten homers in each of his sixteen remaining seasons. He came up as an outfielder and played there most of his first three years in the majors because the Redlegs had Ted Kluszewski at first base. From 1954 on, Adcock was strictly a first baseman, except for 1958–59, when he played a total of forty-three games in the outfield for the Braves.

Cincinnati traded Adcock to Milwaukee in February of 1953 as part of a four-team deal that saw the Braves send cash to the Redlegs and first baseman Earl Torgeson to Philadelphia. Brooklyn sent outfielder Jim Pendleton to the Braves and infielder Rocky Bridges to the Redlegs. The Phillies sent cash to Milwaukee and pitcher Russ Meyer to the Dodgers. Adcock stayed with the Braves until November of 1962, when they swapped him to Cleveland. He played with the Indians for two seasons and with the California Angels his last two years.

Adcock enjoyed two gigantic seasons. He clouted thirty-eight home runs, drove in 103 runs, and batted .291 in 1956. In 1961, he smashed thirty-five homers, had 108 RBI, and hit .285. His lone All-Star Game selection was in 1960, a season that would see him finish with twenty-five roundtrippers, ninety-one RBI, and a .298 batting average. He hit 336 home runs, 199 of them on the road, and drove in 1,122 runs in his big league career. Adcock belted some tremendous shots, and in 1953, he became the first player to hit a ball into the center-field bleachers at the Polo Grounds, a blast that traveled more than 450 feet. In 1956, he launched a drive at Ebbets Field that went over the eighty-three-foot wall at the 350-foot mark in left field and landed on the roof. He put together a terrific four-year stretch from 1959–62, when he hit 114 home runs and had 353 RBI.

He always hit well against the Dodgers, especially in Brooklyn, and in 1954, he smacked nine home runs at Ebbets Field, tying a record for homers by a visiting player in one season. Four of those home runs came on July 31, when he also had a double, giving him what was then a major-league-record eighteen total bases in a contest. (Shawn Green of the Dodgers broke the record in 2002 when he had a single, a double, and four home runs for nineteen total bases against the Milwaukee Brewers.) The previous day, Adcock singled, doubled, and homered to knock in three runs, so he had twenty-five total bases in two successive games, equaling Ty Cobb's major league record.

Adcock drove in seven runs in his four-homer game, giving him ten RBI in two games. The day after he smashed four home runs against Brooklyn,

The Braves missed Joe Adcock's big bat for much of the '57 season as a broken leg limited the big first baseman to sixty-five games and a dozen home runs.

Adcock lined a double as the Braves were on their way to a third straight pounding of the Dodgers. When he stepped to the plate in the fourth inning, Clem Labine had seen enough of the big first baseman. The Brooklyn reliever beaned him, hitting Adcock in the head with a fastball that left him unconscious for fifteen minutes. Adcock was carried from the field on a stretcher, but he was back in the lineup the next day. A batting helmet saved him from serious injury. The Braves had started wearing the protective caps just two months earlier.

Getting hit was not uncommon for Adcock, who crowded the plate and invited inside pitches, and neither were injuries. Jim Hearn of the Giants plunked him in July of 1955, breaking Adcock's arm and ending his season. Adcock got off to a slow start in 1956, and when his batting average dipped under .200 in the middle of May, Milwaukee manager Charlie Grimm sat the first sacker on the bench and left him there much of the time. When Fred Haney replaced Grimm in mid-June, one of the first things he did was to insert Adcock into the lineup on an everyday basis. The move paid off as Adcock hit home runs in five successive games. He homered in eight of nine games and finished with thirty-eight roundtrippers.

One of the funniest things any of the Braves saw on a baseball field involved Adcock and his getting hit by a pitch. It was in July of 1956 when Ruben Gomez of the Giants threw a fastball that hit Adcock on the arm. Remember, Hearn, also of New York, had hit the first baseman one year earlier, and it had ended his season. Adcock, normally an extremely mild-mannered man, was understandably upset. After taking a few steps toward first base, he yelled something out to Gomez, and then he headed for the mound. By that time, Gomez had the baseball back, and he threw it at Adcock and hit him again. Then Gomez, who could run, took off, with the plodding Adcock chasing him. Gomez dashed all the way to the fence in center field and back, finally retreating to the dugout and then to the locker room. Adcock continued his chase, which ended in the Giants' dugout. Both players were fined, and Gomez was hit with a suspension. In future years, when Gomez pitched against the Braves, the incident would be brought up, and Adcock would be teased about running all over the field.

Adcock became part of the answer to a trivia question when he hit a home run that was not a home run in 1959. It was May 29 in Milwaukee, the night Pittsburgh left-hander Harvey Haddix pitched twelve perfect innings. Meanwhile, Lew Burdette had shut out the Pirates for thirteen innings. In the bottom of the thirteenth, following a walk, a sacrifice bunt, and an intentional walk to Hank Aaron, Adcock hit the ball out of the park for a three-run home run. Only, it was not a home run. Seeing that the Braves had scored, Aaron rounded second base and headed for the dugout. When Adcock passed him on the basepaths, he was called out and credited with a double as Milwaukee won, 1–0, instead of 3–0.[2]

Before he was hurt in 1957, Adcock was batting .280 with nine home runs and thirty-two RBI in fifty-one games. In fourteen games after his return, he hit .317 with three homers and six runs batted in.

The series continued on September 13, and the Dodgers beat the Braves two straight times to make the National League race interesting. A crowd of almost 41,000 fans attended each game in County Stadium, but they went home shaking their heads. What they witnessed was outstanding Brooklyn pitching as Don Drysdale and Carl Erskine tossed back-to-back complete games. Drysdale threw a five-hitter for his fifteenth win, while losing pitcher Gene Conley fell to 8–9. Wes Covington stayed hot with two hits, and Red Schoendienst also had two. Erskine allowed just four hits and one run in pitching his first complete game in more than a year. He would go the distance just two more times in his career. Burdette suffered his fourth bad outing in his last five starts. He was rocked for seven hits and six runs before leaving in the fifth inning. Strangely, Burdette was 0–4 against the Dodgers in Milwaukee after beating them twice at Ebbets Field. St. Louis split a pair at home with the Giants to gain another game on the Braves, who led the Cardinals by four and the Dodgers by six.

Milwaukee lost its third in a row and another chunk of its National League lead. The Phillies nipped the Braves in ten innings, 3–2, as Curt Simmons and Dick "Turk" Farrell combined on a six-hitter. Milwaukee hitters remained in a deep slump. The Braves had managed a meager twenty-five hits and seven runs in a five-game stretch that saw them lose four times. Spahn pitched into the tenth inning and absorbed the loss as he came up empty for the second straight time while bidding for his twentieth victory. His chances looked good this time as he carried a one-run lead into the ninth. But the Phillies rallied to tie it before light-hitting Ted Kazanski singled in the winning run off Bob Trowbridge, who relieved Spahn with two men on and nobody out in the tenth inning. In two failed attempts at number twenty, Spahn had pitched eighteen innings and allowed only five runs.

It was a time for worry in Milwaukee. The Cards won both ends of a doubleheader from Pittsburgh to pick up a game and a half and trailed the Braves by only two and one-half games. With thirty-seven-year-old Stan Musial leading the way, the Cardinals emerged from desperation mode to play their best baseball in two months. Musial batted .500 during a two-week stretch that saw St. Louis get itself back in the National League pennant race after it had appeared that the Braves might run away with the flag.

Milwaukee manager Fred Haney was looking back, not just at the Cardinals who were coming on fast, but at the previous season. He remembered all too well that his Braves led the National League standings for most of the 1956 season — 122 days overall, to be exact — only to finish in second place, one game behind the Brooklyn Dodgers. Bob Buhl felt things would have been different if he had not hurt his finger in August and missed some starts. Hank Aaron, however, said the Braves choked, that they had the pennant won and let it get away. All of these thoughts were going through Haney's mind, and even though he put up a good front, he was worried. Milwaukee had twelve games left to play. St. Louis had eleven remaining.

If the Braves were feeling any pressure, they did not show it. Instead of crumbling, they started winning again and just kept on winning. The Cards did not play on September 16, and Milwaukee took advantage of the opportunity to pad its lead a little. The Braves led by three games after downing the Phillies, 5–1, to stop a three-game skid. Bob Buhl won for the first time in over a month as he pitched a complete game and scattered eight hits. His batterymate, Del Rice, gave the Braves' offense a much needed jump start. Buhl's personal catcher, who hit a home run every sixteen at-bats in 1957, led off the bottom of the third inning with a drive over the left-field fence. Rice also doubled in a run in the fourth. Logan had three of the Braves' fourteen hits. Buhl's control was shaky at times as he walked five, but he struck out six in pitching out of frequent trouble to earn his seventeenth victory.

Adcock picked a great time to get back on the home run track. Big Joe hit his first roundtripper in almost 100 days, and it helped Milwaukee maintain a three-game lead over the Cardinals. Hank Aaron doubled to lead off the second inning, and Adcock followed with his tenth homer of the season and his first since June 11. Aaron also connected, belting his forty-first in the eighth to give the Braves a little breathing room in what was to be a 3–1 win over New York. The home run tied the Cubs' Ernie Banks for the major league lead. Aaron added a second double as he ended a week-long drought of extra-base hits. Adcock had a pair of singles to go with his homer. Bob Trowbridge pitched a complete-game five-hitter and got some nice defensive support from Eddie Mathews. The third baseman made a diving back-hand catch just inside the foul line to rob Daryl Spencer of a double. Mathews ran down a foul pop by losing pitcher Curt Barclay and made the catch over his shoulder with his back to the plate. Both gems came in the fifth inning and prevented some damage as they were sandwiched around a couple of Giants hits. The triumph was not without worry for the Milwaukee bunch. It seemed someone was getting hurt every week, and this time, it was Rice. The catcher came up limping while running out a ground ball in the fourth inning. Rice pulled a muscle and had to be replaced by Del Crandall, the Braves' starting backstop who was trying to take an extra night off. The Cards kept pace by bombing Brooklyn for their fourth straight win and their eighth victory in nine games.

Burdette came up with a timely work of pitching art. He painted the corners all day, threw a four-hitter at the Giants, and bagged his sixteenth win, 8–2. Burdette got a dozen outs on groundballs and walked one in pitching a complete game. He also drove in a run and scored one in continuing his hex over the Giants, who had not beaten the Braves' right-hander in three years. A crowd of more than 31,000 was in County Stadium for the game, putting the club over the two million mark in attendance for the fourth year in a row. The victory gave the Braves a 6–6 record for what was a disappointing home stand, but most importantly, it lengthened their lead over the hard-charging Cardinals. The Dodgers downed the Cards, who fell four games behind Milwaukee. Haney reminded reporters that while the memory of one that got away may still have been dancing in his players' heads, the pressure was really on St. Louis and not Milwaukee. He pointed out that the Braves had been playing good baseball; they just were not hitting for a while. The skipper also noted that the Braves would be sending their big three to the mound for Milwaukee's upcoming series in Chicago, and Haney liked his club's chances of taking all three games. And that is precisely what happened.

Warren Spahn won his twentieth game, but it was not easy, even though the final score of 9–3 would indicate otherwise. It was a chilly, cloudy day in Chicago's Wrigley Field, with rain delaying the start of the contest. Spahn and Cubs right-hander Bob Rush locked into a pitcher's battle through six innings. The Braves scored first, a bases-loaded walk to Eddie Mathews sending the run home in the third inning. Wes Covington clouted his twentieth home run in the fourth, making it 2–0. Frank Ernaga played in only forty-three major league games over parts of two seasons, but he seemed to always come up with big hits against Milwaukee. He did it twice in this game, rapping an RBI single in the fourth and a run-scoring double in the sixth that tied the score. The Braves broke the game wide open in the seventh when they scored five times in an inning spiced by a questionable umpire's call and temper tantrums.

Bob Hazle smacked a double to open the inning. He went to third on a single to short right field. Spahn struck out. Red Schoendienst hit a bouncer to Cub shortstop Ernie Banks, who tossed the ball to second baseman Bobby Morgan. The ball was hit too slowly for a double play, so Hazle scored the go-ahead run for the Braves. Morgan had the ball in plenty of time for the force-out, however, umpire Ken Burkhart had his arms spread as he was giving the safe sign. Chicago players poured out of the dugout and onto the field, converging at second base where Burkhart explained that Morgan had been off of the base. Rush charged off the mound and shoved the umpire. Morgan heaved the ball into the air. The second baseman was ejected from the game, while Rush, surprisingly, was allowed to continue playing. But the Cubs' pitcher appeared to come unglued. Johnny Logan singled Crandall home with the second run of the inning, and lefty Dick Littlefield was summoned from the bullpen. He was greeted by an RBI single from Mathews. Turk Lown, a righty, came in to pitch, and Aaron welcomed him with another RBI single. Covington was intentionally walked, and Lown was replaced by southpaw Ed Mayer, the Cubs' fourth pitcher of the inning. Mayer promptly hit Frank Torre to bring in the fifth and last run of the inning.

When the Cubs put two runners on base with one out in the seventh, Haney called on McMahon. The burly right-hander struck out John Goryl and former Brave Chuck Tanner to douse the threat. McMahon did give up a run in the ninth, but he was spectacular as he fanned six batters in two and two-thirds innings. Milwaukee added insurance in the ninth on a run-scoring single by Torre and a sacrifice fly by Pafko. Logan, Mathews, Aaron, Hazle, and Crandall had two hits apiece as the club totaled fourteen. Spahn was a twenty-game winner for the eighth time in his career after allowing three hits and one earned run. The Braves inched closer to a pennant even though St. Louis also won. They were the only teams remaining in the National League race as the Dodgers had plunged nine games out of first place and were eliminated.

The Braves won their fifth straight game and drove another nail into the proverbial coffin of the Cards, who lost in Cincinnati. Bob Buhl and Joe Adcock were the big guns in Milwaukee's 6–2 win in Wrigley. Buhl pitched a complete-game eight-hitter for his eighteenth win, matching his total of the previous season and his career best. He survived a bout with wildness as he walked four and threw a wild pitch, but Buhl was bailed out by three double plays which came in the second, seventh, and eighth innings. Adcock belted a pair of long home runs, giving him nine hits in twenty at-bats since returning to action. Del Rice also homered. Schoendienst opened the game with a sliding triple and scored when Mathews grounded out. Adcock's solo home run made it 2–0, Braves, in the second, but Ernie Banks tied the score with a two-run shot in the third. Covington walked in the fourth and trotted around the bases ahead of Adcock's second homer of the afternoon. Milwaukee added a run in the eighth on Aaron's RBI single and one in the ninth when Rice connected.

Haney and his players were breathing easier. With seven games remaining on the Braves' schedule, their magic number for at least sharing the NL championship was two. That meant any combination of Milwaukee wins and St. Louis losses totaling two would assure the Braves of at least a tie for first place in the final standings. Three was their magic number for claiming the title outright. So, no matter what the Cardinals did, if the Braves could win three of the seven games left on the schedule, they would be going to the World Series.

The Braves' winning streak continued as they completed a sweep by out-slugging the Cubs, 9–7. It took ten innings, and Milwaukee had to overcome a four-run first-inning deficit, but a sixteen-hit attack highlighted by four home runs did the trick. Starter Bob Trowbridge did not make it through one inning. He retired just one batter before being lifted, having walked one and given up three hits. Taylor Phillips pitched shutout ball for one and one-third innings, and fellow left-hander Juan Pizarro gave up three runs in three innings. Ernie Johnson pitched two scoreless innings and McMahon whiffed four batters in putting up two more zeroes. Meanwhile, the Braves' bats were playing catch-up. Aaron hit his forty-second homer, tying Banks for the league lead, to key a four-run fourth for Milwaukee and also tying the score, 4–4. The Cubs jumped back in front by getting three runs in the fifth. The Braves answered with two in the sixth on Covington's twenty-first roundtrip-per and an RBI groundout by pinch-hitter Carl Sawatski. Mathews' ninth-inning home run sent the game into extra innings. Bob Hazle culminated a four-hit day with his seventh homer in the tenth, Mathews' RBI single providing some padding. The last run was scored by McMahon, who had walked, and running the bases seemed to take something out of the normally reliable relief ace. He walked two Cubs, and with one out, Haney signaled for Joey Jay.

Jay was a hefty guy, a right-hander who stood six-foot-four and weighed 230 pounds. A $2,000 bonus baby, he was the first former Little Leaguer to reach the majors.[3] In the early sixties, he would become the workhorse ace of the Cincinnati Reds. Jay pitched 247 innings in 1961 and 273 in 1962, winning twenty-one games both years. The Braves' front office was frequently criticized for allowing him to get away. Prior to his September call-up by Milwaukee, Jay had pitched a total of forty-seven innings for the Braves in three different seasons. As a seventeen-year-old, he had thrown a shutout in his very first big league start, in 1953, and then toiled in the minors for three years while reading about veterans Spahn, Buhl, and Burdette, and promising youngsters named Conley, Crone, and Trowbridge. Most of Jay's work with the Braves was in relief and most of it was in September, when rosters were expanded. Now, at the still tender age of twenty-two, Jay was coming into a game that counted. Indeed, he was in the heat of a pennant race. He was up to the challenge, inducing Goryl and Bob Will to ground into force-outs that ended the game after nearly three and a half hours. Jay earned the save in what was his only major league appearance of 1957. The victory went to McMahon, his first in the major leagues.

While the Braves were pulling one out in Chicago, the Cardinals were winning in Cincinnati's Crosley Field. But time was running out on St. Louis, which needed to win all of its remaining six games and have Milwaukee lose five of its last six. And that would be just for a share of first place.

It was with great trepidation that the Cardinals traveled to Milwaukee for a three-game must series. The Cards knew they must win all three to keep their dim hopes alive. The drama, along with the St. Louis hopes, ended fast. The Braves clinched the National League pennant with a 4–2 win, their seventh straight. The winning streak came at a time some sportswriters were predicting that Milwaukee would go into the tank and blow a big lead and the title. It is one thing to write about athletes not producing in the crunch. It is quite another to make big pitches and get big hits when so much is on the line. The Braves played some of their best baseball of the season in perhaps the toughest week of the season.

The night of September 23 was what might be expected in Milwaukee at that time of the year. It was cold, temperatures dipping into the low forties, and many of the nearly 41,000 County Stadium fans took blankets with them to the game. The Cardinals even had a fire going in their bullpen.[4] The Braves' faithful were counting on a celebration, thinking that it would be the night their beloved Braves would become champions of the National League. The huge crowd was kept in suspense as Milwaukee wasted one scoring opportunity after another. Milwaukee scored a run in the second inning, with the Cardinals getting two in the sixth, and the Braves knotting the score in the seventh. In what was an omen, Lew Burdette was on the mound for the Braves. Southpaw Wilmer "Vinegar Bend" Mizell started for St. Louis, but he only lasted into the second inning. Relieving him was Larry Jackson, the right-hander Hank Aaron had accused of throwing at him earlier in the season.

The Braves were on the verge of blowing the game wide open when they loaded the bases with no outs in the second. Aaron and Adcock singled, and Andy Pafko, attempting to sacrifice, laid down a perfect bunt that he beat out for another hit. Wes Covington lifted a fly ball to center that was deep enough to score Aaron. Moon dropped it as Covington was credited with a sacrifice fly, and the bases remained loaded. Jackson was in a stew, but he escaped with no further damage. Burdette threw five shutout innings before the Cardinals got to him. Moon singled, Stan Musial doubled, Irv Noren was

All-time home run king Hank Aaron was a fine defensive outfielder who moved to center field in the middle of the season. In addition to his power, he hit for average, batting .322 with 198 base hits in 1957.

intentionally walked, and Alvin Dark delivered a two-run single. St. Louis had a 2–1 lead until the seventh when Red Schoendienst singled, went to second on Johnny Logan's sacrifice bunt, and scored on Eddie Mathews' ringing double to right. St. Louis had its own chance to break the game open in the eighth when Moon walked and Musial singled him to third. Noren, who had been swinging a hot bat in recent games, hit the ball in the dirt to Logan, who went home with his throw, nailing Moon at the plate. Del Ennis and Dark both grounded out, and Milwaukee had dodged a bullet.

Billy Muffett came on to pitch for the Cards, with Jackson leaving after working seven strong innings. Muffett set the Braves down in order in the ninth, but he got into deep trouble in the tenth when Milwaukee loaded the bases with only one out. A fly ball would probably end the game and the season as would a ground ball that caused an infielder to range far to his right or left. But Torre, pinch-hitting for Burdette, grounded into a double play, and St. Louis had lived to play another inning. It was the fourth twin killing Milwaukee hit into in ten innings. The Braves, who left thirteen runners on base that night, wasted one scoring opportunity after another, leaving Haney to wonder if it would come back to haunt them. Gene Conley pitched an uneventful eleventh. Logan singled to start the bottom of the inning and stayed put as Mathews flied to Moon in center. Aaron stepped to the plate, and on the first pitch from Muffett, he clouted a drive to deep center field. Moon went back to the wall and leaped, but the ball was gone. The game was over, and so was the National League pennant chase. The Braves' 4–2 win clinched the league championship. The home run was Aaron's forty-third, and the one he often called his favorite of the 755 that he hit in his career. It was the only home run Muffett allowed in his 1957 Cardinal season that spanned twenty-three appearances and forty-four innings. After the game, Aaron recounted to reporters how he had stayed home from school in 1951 when Bobby Thomson hit his famous "shot heard 'round the world." Aaron told about how he had always dreamed of hitting a home run like the one Thomson had smacked, one that won a pennant. Now, Aaron had done just that.[5]

Winning a pennant is always special, and the manner in which the Braves clinched the 1957 National League flag was especially gratifying. They had knocked second-place St. Louis out of the picture themselves, not getting any help from another team. Making the whole deal even sweeter was the fact that the Cardinals had spoiled the Braves' pennant dreams the year before, taking two out of three games in St. Louis on the final weekend of the 1956 season.

Although they had clinched the pennant, the Braves' regulars were back in the lineup the next night. Aaron smashed another momentous home run, this one off Sam Jones with the bases loaded in the first inning. Schoendienst and Logan singled, and Mathews walked before Aaron hit his forty-fourth and final homer of the season. It was the first grand slam of his career. Third-string catcher Carl Sawatski and Spahn drove in runs in the seventh, and the six runs were more than enough for the southpaw marvel. He allowed five hits and one run, pitched a complete game, and notched his twenty-first win. The Braves' 6–1 win was their eighth in a row. They had played down the stretch like the champions they were.

The winning streak came to an end the following afternoon even though Buhl went the distance. His teammates scored just once, while St. Louis bunched all four of its runs in the eighth inning and wrapped up second place, ahead of the Dodgers. Aaron extended his hitting streak to eleven games with a single and a double. During that time, with the Braves attempting to wrap up the league title, he had twenty hits in forty-eight at-bats for a .417 average. Aaron had four doubles and clouted four home runs in that stretch, including homers in three straight games.

There was bad news about Billy Bruton, but it was not unexpected. Doctors were recommending that the center fielder see a specialist who would make further recommendations regarding possible surgery on his injured right knee. It appeared almost certain that Bruton would not be able to play in the World Series. He had not played since colliding with Felix Mantilla on July 11. Bruton had been on his way to an outstanding season. In seventy-nine games, he had eighty-five hits, including sixteen doubles, nine triples, and five home runs. He was batting .278 with forty-one runs scored, thirty RBI, and eleven stolen bases. Bruton did indeed undergo knee surgery, and it prevented him from being ready at the start of the 1958 season, when he played in 100 games. He did have several more solid seasons. And, although he swiped between thirteen and twenty-two bases in each of his final six years in the majors, he never regained all of his speed. Bruton had stolen a total of eighty-five bases in his first three years in the big leagues. He appeared destined for even more success in that department, but the injury seemed almost to put reigns on his thievery. Still, he remained a fine player. Bruton enjoyed his best all-around season in 1960, when he had 180 hits, including thirteen triples and twelve home runs, scored 112 runs, and batted .286 with twenty-two stolen bases. It was his final season with the Braves, who traded him during the winter to the Detroit Tigers.

Fred Haney obviously missed Bruton and his speed, but the Braves had been playing without him for more than half of the season. And their outfield was set with Aaron in center, flanked by Covington in left, and a platoon of Hazle and Pafko in right. Pafko was the oldest player on the Milwaukee roster, having been born two months before Spahn. At thirty-six, he had two years on Schoendienst as the oldest position player on the team. Pafko had a fine September, hitting half of his season total of eight home runs. His fourth of the month came in a 2–1 home win over Cincinnati in a game that saw the Braves set a National League attendance record of 2,145,926. Milwaukee held the old record as well, setting it in 1954. Del Crandall's homer came in the fifth inning as did Pafko's. Those were all the runs Burdette needed to get his seventeenth win. He pitched a four-hitter and the third straight complete game by a Braves hurler.

Johnny Klippstein shut out Milwaukee on one hit the next-to-last day of the season, with the Braves closing the 1957 schedule with a 4–3 win over the Redlegs. Haney cleared his bench, sending twenty-four players into the game as 45,000 County Stadium fans further boosted the Braves' attendance mark. Schoendienst drove in the tying run with a ninth-inning single that was his 200th hit of the season. Mantilla lined a base hit to plate the game-winner and cap a two-run rally. Buhl tuned up for the World Series by pitching five shutout innings and allowing five hits. McMahon, the sixth Milwaukee pitcher, got the victory. The win did not mean much other than adding a little icing to the cake and sending the team into the Series on a winning note. The Braves went 16–11 in September to finish with a record of 95–59.

9

Bring On the Yankees

Milwaukee withstood the St. Louis Cardinals' best shot coming down the home stretch of the 1957 season and held on; in fact, the Braves took total control of the pennant race during that period to win the National League championship by a comfortable margin. The Braves either held first place or shared it for nearly all of the last two months of the season and rode a pair of long winning streaks to stagger the Cardinals and then knock them out.

After bolting out of the starting gate, Milwaukee was only a so-so ball club until June. Then the Braves played .636 baseball over the next three months, and after stumbling to a 6–9 record in the first half of September, they used a 10–2 finish to turn back the St. Louis Cardinals. The Braves' pitching was fantastic over the final twelve games, allowing two or less runs seven times and throwing seven complete games. The Milwaukee bats, which had been so cold while the Cardinals closed to within two and one-half games, averaged twelve hits and six runs during the eight-game win string that wrapped up the pennant.

Milwaukee, which played .500 baseball in games with second-place St. Louis (11–11), fared better against every other National League team: 18–4 vs. Cincinnati; 16–6 vs. Pittsburgh; 13–9 vs. both New York and Chicago; and 12–10 vs. both Brooklyn and Philadelphia.

The Braves had started to think about the New York Yankees weeks before the regular season ended. The Bronx Bombers were always on the minds of teams making World Series plans in the 1950s. In fact, the Yankees had become practically synonymous with the Fall Classic, having played in twenty-two up until that time while winning seventeen world titles. The Yanks have kept a constant October presence over several decades as they played in six World Series in the 1920s, five in both the thirties and forties, five more in the sixties, and six in the late nineties and into the early years of the twenty-first century. Never, however, were the Pinstripes more dominant than in the fifties, when they appeared in eight of ten World Series, while winning six world championships.

New York began its fantastic run at the end of the forties. The Yanks won the World Series from 1949–53, finished second behind the Cleveland Indians in the 1954 American League standings, were beaten by the Dodgers in the 1955 Fall Classic, and then defeated Brooklyn in 1956. They would beat Milwaukee in seven games in the 1958 Series.

When Casey Stengel was named the Yankees' manager prior to the 1949 season, he was looked upon by the baseball world as more of a clown than anything else. In nine previous years as a big league skipper, only one of his teams posted a record of .500 or better, and that was the 1938 Boston Braves, who went 77–75. After five years of wearing the pinstripes with the number thirty-seven on his back, Stengel was hailed as a genius. He was lauded for taking good ball players and getting great seasons from them by utilizing them in a platoon system that allowed them to make the most of their hitting skills. His pitching staffs were seldom over-worked, a credit to their tremendous depth as well as old Casey's shrewd maneuvering. And, no matter how he shuffled his cards, Stengel had terrific talent in Mickey Mantle, Yogi Berra, Bill Skowron, Elston Howard, Hank Bauer, Tony Kubek, Gil McDougald, and Bobby Richardson. There were other big names earlier, but those were New York's prime-time position players in the fifties. Stengel may have pushed the right buttons most of the time, but he had some pretty nice buttons to push.

The Yankees won the 1957 pennant with a record of 98–56, finishing eight games ahead of the second-place Chicago White Sox. The Braves finished eight games in front of St. Louis, posting a record of 95–59. New York had won by nine games the year before and by five or more games two other times in the decade, so breezing to the American League flag was customary for the Yanks. It was a luxury that allowed time for injured players to heal and tired ones to rest.

To say the New York Yankees were feared in the postseason would be accurate, although a big league club would never admit feeling scared. The company line would be that the Yankees had everyone's respect because of their many World Series titles and their tremendous tradition. It might be closer to the truth to say that the Braves, and other National League teams, were a bit afraid of getting swept away by the undertow created by the combination of New York's winning habit, its talent-laden roster, and even the sense that — in big games, in close games, and particularly in October games — the baseball gods seemed to smile upon the Pinstripes.

Milwaukee manager Fred Haney ascribed to most of the old baseball superstitions and he knew enough to pay proper allegiance to The Yankee Dynasty. And, while there was something to be said for the almost-hypnotic stupor the rest of baseball found itself in regarding the Yankees, there was more to be said for winning seventeen championships in twenty-two trips to the World Series. This was a team that knew how to win. The Yanks were beyond confident; they looked at October as an annual bonus for their paychecks.

In 1957, the Chicago White Sox, behind Minnie Minoso, Nellie Fox, and Billy Pierce, gave the Yankees a pretty good run for their money during the American League regular season. Chicago led the Yanks by four games at the end of May before Stengel's boys put together back-to-back months of superb baseball. The Yankees were absolutely sizzling in June and July, going 21–9 each month, for a .700 winning percentage over a span of nearly nine weeks. New York led the ChiSox by three and a half games entering August, lengthened that to five and a half by the end of the month, and stayed safely in front the rest of the way. The Yankees won ten in a row in the middle of June. They had another string of victories that reached seven, starting late in June, carrying into early July, and igniting a stretch in which they won thirteen of fourteen games.

Mickey Mantle had the kind of season fans felt he should have had every year. The switch-hitting center fielder played 144 games, scored a league-leading 121 runs, slammed thirty-four home runs, drove in ninety-four runs, drew 146 bases on balls, had a .512 on-base percentage, and batted .365. Normally, that figure would have led the American League in batting, but in 1957, an elder statesman in Boston was defying nature as he turned back the clock. Ted Williams, at the age of thirty-eight, hit a truly amazing .388, missing his second trip to the magical .400 circle by just five hits. Mantle nipped the Splendid Splinter in first-place votes, six to five, and finished ahead of him, 233 points to 209, to win his second straight AL Most Valuable Player award. The Mick earned the 1956 MVP by winning the triple crown.

Catcher Yogi Berra hit twenty-four home runs and drove in eighty-two runs, but batted just .251. First baseman Bill "Moose" Skowron hit .304 with seventeen roundtrippers and eighty-eight RBI. Shortstop Gil McDougald hit a solid .289 with thirteen homers, eighty-seven runs scored, and sixty-two runs batted in. Leadoff batter Hank Bauer, the right fielder, batted .259 with eighteen home runs and sixty-five RBI. Tony Kubek, the American League Rookie of the Year, batted .297.

The Yankees' home run production was not as impressive as usual as their 145 roundtrippers were third-most in the American League behind Kansas City and Baltimore. But the Yanks' 723 runs were the most scored by any AL club, and their .268 team batting average was also the best in the league. Their .409 slugging percentage was tops in the AL as well. New York depended on its bats and not its legs; the club did not run much and stole just forty-nine bases. The real key for the Yanks, however, was their pitching.

Five New York starting pitchers won at least ten games, and four them posted an earned run average under the team figure of 3.00, which led the league. Tom Sturdivant had a 16–6 record with a 2.54 ERA; Bob Turley was 13–6, 2.71; Bobby Shantz was 11–5, 2.45; Whitey Ford was 11–5, 2.57; Don Larsen was 10–4, 3.74; and Johnny Kucks was 8–10, 3.56. Shantz, at thirty-one, was the oldest of the six starters; the other five were in their twenties. Four of the six were right-handers, with Ford and Shantz the lefties. All started at least twenty games, with the exception of Ford, who made seventeen starts. Right-hander Bob Grim was the number one reliever. He had nineteen saves, a 12–8 record, and a 2.62 ERA in forty-six appearances, all out of the bullpen. Art Ditmar, another righty, also pitched in forty-six games, including eleven starts. He went 8–3 with a 3.25 earned run average. Grim and Ditmar were both in their late twenties. It was a very young, very deep, and very impressive pitching staff.

Second baseman Bobby Richardson and third sacker Andy Carey were excellent glove men, and McDougald and Kubek were both fine shortstops who made the routine plays consistently. They were the reasons the Yankees turned a league-high 183 double plays. During the 1957 World Series, veteran Jerry Coleman played second for New York, with left-handed hitting Jerry Lumpe platooning at third with Carey. Mantle and Bauer were joined in the outfield by Elston Howard, Berra's backup behind the plate, and old salt Enos Slaughter as they got most of the innings in left field. Slaughter, forty-one, could still hit, and he was a tough out in the clutch.

The Yankee bench included Harry "Suitcase" Simpson, who played first base and the outfield; Joe Collins, who also played at first and the outfield; and infielder Billy Martin, who was always one of Casey's favorites. Thirty-seven-year-old southpaw pitcher Tommy Byrne, who did not have a particularly good year on the mound, hit three home runs during the season and was sometimes used as a pinch-hitter.

New York's players had a habit of rising to the occasion, and none was more special than the World Series. Mantle, who played in a dozen of them in his career, belted eighteen home runs, scored forty-two runs, and had forty RBI, with 123 total bases — all World Series records. Berra, in fourteen Fall

Classics, hit twelve homers and drove in thirty-nine runs. Ford won ten, lost eight, and posted a 2.71 ERA in eleven World Series.

Milwaukee stacked up nicely with New York, and on paper, the Braves appeared to have more power than the Yankees and just as good if not better pitching than the defending world champs. The Yanks' defense may have been better, but just by a shade, with the main advantage being that New York's outfielders were more experienced than Milwaukee's.

The Braves led the majors in runs scored with 772, in home runs with 199, in triples with sixty-two, and with a .442 slugging percentage. Their team batting average of .269 was second in the National League behind the Cardinals' .274. The Braves ran even less than the Yankees, finishing next-to-last in the National League with thirty-five stolen bases, but speed was not their forte. Milwaukee's pitching was outstanding, with three stopper-type starters and a handful of solid hurlers who could either start or relieve. The Braves pitched a major league-leading sixty complete games and recorded a 3.47 earned run average, second in the NL to Brooklyn's 3.35.

Spahn was voted the Cy Young Award winner (there was only one back then instead of one in each league) after leading the majors with twenty-one wins and the National League with a 2.69 earned run average. He worked 271 innings, had eighteen complete games, pitched four shutouts, and had four saves. Bob Buhl might have been the Cy Young recipient had he not missed three weeks with a sore arm. He had an 18–7 record, a 2.74 ERA, fourteen complete games, and four big "stops." (A stop is a starting pitcher's win that ends his team's losing streak.) Lew Burdette went 17–9 with a 3.72, fourteen complete games, and three saves. Buhl was third in the NL in victories behind the nineteen by Philadelphia's Jack Sanford, and Burdette was fourth. Buhl ranked fourth in the NL in earned run average and shared fourth place with Burdette in complete games.

Gene Conley was 9–9 with a 3.16 ERA and six complete games. Bob Trowbridge was 7–5 with a 3.64 and three complete games, while starting sixteen games and coming out of the bullpen to finish eight. Lefties Taylor Phillips and twenty-year-old Juan Pizarro were also versatile hurlers. Phillips started six games and finished nine. Pizarro started ten games and finished seven. All thirty of Ernie Johnson's appearances were in relief as he went 7–3 with a 3.88, four saves, and sixteen games finished. Don McMahon led the Braves with nine saves, while posting a 1.54 and finishing nineteen games.

Defensively, Milwaukee had the second-best fielding percentage in the National League, its .981 figure just a point behind Cincinnati. The Braves turned 173 double plays. First baseman Frank Torre and second baseman Red

Twenty-win machine Warren Spahn led the 1957 Braves with twenty-one victories, a 2.69 earned run average, and 271 innings pitched. He notched another win in the World Series. (©Brace Photo. Use by permission.)

Schoendienst were both tops at their position in fielding percentage. Torre made four errors for a .996 percentage. Schoendienst committed twelve miscues and had a .986 percentage. Shortstop Johnny Logan led the league's shortstops with 440 assists. Spahn did not make an error. The catching was not only reliable, with the two Dels handling Milwaukee pitchers beautifully; the receiving and the defense had been sparkling. Between them, Crandall and Rice committed just eight errors and were charged with only five passed balls. Both catchers had strong arms, quick releases, and they could throw out would-be base stealers.

The Braves' outfield defense raised questions. Hank Aaron was a fine outfielder, but he was not as experienced in center as in right, his normal position. Andy Pafko, once a standout fielder, had slowed a step or two at age thirty-six, although he was still dependable. Wes Covington and Bob Hazle were both considered defensive liabilities. Neither got good jumps on fly balls, and Hazle had made six errors in only forty games.

Aaron deservedly won the National League Most Valuable Player award. His votes totaled 239 points to 230 for Stan Musial, Schoendienst placed third with 221, and Spahn finished fifth. Aaron edged Schoendienst in first-place votes, nine to eight, while Musial received five. Only twenty-three years old, the Milwaukee outfielder belted forty-four home runs and drove in 132 runs to lead the league in both categories. His .322 batting average was fourth as Musial won the title with a .351 mark. Aaron also led the NL with 369 total bases and 118 runs scored, while getting 198 hits, two less than league leader Schoendienst. Seventy-seven of Aaron's hits were for extra bases.

In looking back now at the '57 Milwaukee club, it was arguably one of the best all-around and best balanced squads of all time. An everyday lineup with three future Hall of Famers, including two of the greatest sluggers in baseball history, grabs anyone's attention. Throw in a pitching staff headed by another sure-fire Cooperstown candidate, a prize left-hander who combines with two righties to win fifty-six games, and one sees this edition of the Braves was not just a one-year wonder. They hit more home runs than any team in the majors, scored more runs than anyone, and allowed the second fewest runs in the National League.

It is interesting that despite losing two of their key offensive weapons for more than half the season — their speediest runner who was the team's only legitimate base-stealing threat and a power hitter who averaged close to twenty-eight home runs a season when he was healthy — the Braves continued to roll. The main reason was that Spahn, Buhl, and Burdette formed an anchor that kept Milwaukee from drifting into an extended slide. Very seldom did all three have a bad outing one after the other, and even less frequently did that happen twice in succession. In the course of a week, one of the big three would provide an outstanding performance, and that helped the Braves avoid long losing streaks. A three-game skid was the worst they experienced all season because pitchers did what was necessary to halt the slides.

Milwaukee lost three straight games eight times in 1957, and Buhl was the man on the mound four times following the Braves' third loss in a row. He won all four games, pitching three complete games and going eight innings in the fourth outing. One of his "stops" was a four-hit shutout. What may have proven more important was the fact that two of Buhl's stops came in succession, thus preventing what could have been a very long and disastrous losing streak. After he blanked the New York Giants on June 19, the Braves lost three more games in a row before Buhl beat Philadelphia on June 23. Had he not come through both times, Milwaukee could have dropped eight consecutive games. Spahn twice halted three-game slides by throwing shutouts, one of them a five-hitter. Both of the other three-game losing streaks were ended in wins in which the Braves scored ten runs, with Juan Pizarro going the distance with a nine-hitter in one.

Injuries are an accepted part of any sport, and the Braves sure had their share. A broken bone in his ankle limited Joe Adcock to 209 at-bats and a dozen home runs. Johnny Logan's shin became infected in the middle of August, causing him to eventually be hospitalized and miss twenty-two games. Right-hander Bob Buhl hurt his pitching shoulder with two weeks left in August and missed three weeks and at least four turns, probably costing him a twenty-win season. Red Schoendienst fell down the dugout steps in late June and was out a week. Lew Burdette and Ernie Johnson experienced arm trouble that kept them off the mound for a while. Frank Torre, Wes Covington, and Eddie Mathews all sat out a handful of games with minor ailments. The biggest loss, of course, was center fielder Billy Bruton for over half of the season and the World Series.

Hank Aaron sprained an ankle in the middle of July, and it looked like he would be out for at least a week. But with Bruton already sidelined, Aaron knew the Braves needed him, and he returned to the lineup earlier than he probably should have. In fact, Milwaukee manager Fred Haney said after the season that playing on a bad ankle for several days likely cost Aaron points on his batting average and possibly the triple crown. It should also be noted that Aaron played out of position for more than half of the season as he switched from right to center field following Bruton's injury. Aaron never complained or looked back with regret on changing positions or playing hurt. He did it for the team, knowing the Braves needed him in the lineup. His main goal was for Milwaukee to win the pennant. Personal achievements took a back seat. That obviously speaks volumes of Aaron's character and of the time he played. The game and its players really were different then.

Aaron played in 151 of the Braves' 155 games. (Rain stopped a May game with Philadelphia after five and one-half innings, with the score 1–1. It was an official game, and statistics counted, but the contest was replayed rather than resumed.) Mathews played in 148 games, with Logan and Torre both appearing in 129. Del Crandall played in 118 games. Covington, who spent more than a month with Milwaukee's triple-A team in Wichita, played in ninety-six games for the Braves. When Schoendienst joined Milwaukee in a June 15 trade deadline deal with the New York Giants, the Braves had 100 games remaining. He played in ninety-three of them.

After being banged up and bruised throughout the season, the Braves were in pretty good shape for the World Series. With the exception of Bruton, no Milwaukee player was questionable for the October 2 opening game. Everyone else on the Braves was healthy. Adcock was back to full strength. Mathews had missed a game with a bad cold near the end of the season, but he was feeling strong. Milwaukee was physically fit and ready to play.

The same could not be said of the New York Yankees. On the day before the World Series opened, Yanks manager Casey Stengel did not know whether Mantle and steady Skowron would be able to play. Mantle, who was plagued by knee problems most of his career, was slowed by shin splints the final week of the season, and he was still hurting. The switch-hitting slugger took batting practice at Yankee Stadium two days before Game One of the Series, and he hit the ball hard. Mantle said he intended to play, but that the decision rested with his manager. Skowron was experiencing back pain that had kept him out of the lineup the last three weeks of the season. The Moose said that, surprisingly, bending to field ground balls did not really bother him, but that running was quite painful.

If Skowron was unable to play, there was talk that Stengel might go with Howard at first base. He had played two games at first during the final weekend of the season and had handled himself well. Howard, like Skowron a right-handed hitter, had been behind the plate in thirty-two games and in the outfield for seventy-one. Collins, a left-hander all the way, was New York's other first baseman by trade, but with southpaw Warren Spahn scheduled to pitch the opener for Milwaukee, Stengel would likely try to get as many right-handed hitters in his lineup as possible.

Platooning was one of Casey's favorite managing tools. Others had tried alternating left- and right-handed batters based on the opponent's starting pitcher, but Stengel became famous for it — some sportswriters even seemed to think he invented it. The truth is, the Old Perfessor was more successful with the platoon system because he had better players.

One big advantage the Yankees had was in versatility, which increased the number of moves Stengel could make. McDougald played 121 games at shortstop, twenty-one at second base, and seven at third. Kubek played fifty games in the outfield, forty-one at shortstop, and thirty-eight at third base. Simpson played sixty-three games in the outfield and forty-eight at first base. He was acquired from the Kansas City Athletics on June 15 and would be traded back to Kansas City on June 15, 1958. Berra, like Howard, saw action in the outfield as well as behind the plate.

There was quite a bit of gamesmanship going on between the Braves and Yankees. Near the end of the season, when it was learned Bruton would almost surely not be able to play in the World Series, the Braves talked about making a special request to Commissioner Ford Frick to be allowed to add outfielder Ray Shearer to their World Series roster. Shearer was not eligible, according to major league rules, because he was not on the Milwaukee roster on August 31. Upon hearing about that, Stengel said that would be fine with him as long as he could put pitcher Sal Maglie in uniform for the Series. The Braves' front office quickly retracted its request, saying the club would use rookie John DeMerit as a backup outfielder.

Maglie pitched most of the season for the Brooklyn Dodgers, compiling a 6–6 record with a 2.93 earned run average. The Yankees got him on waivers on September 1, one day too late to include him on their World Series roster. Maglie pitched well for New York, making three stars and three relief appearances. He went 2–0, with a shutout, three saves, and a 1.73 ERA.

Since he was not eligible to play in the World Series, Maglie pitched batting practice for the Yankees and also served as a scout of sorts. He shared his knowledge of the Braves' hitters, having faced them all a number of times while pitching five and a half seasons for the New York Giants before joining the Dodgers.

The automatic assumption by many fans and writers was that the Yankees had the advantage in the managerial department. After all, Stengel had a living room full of World Series championship trophies, while Haney had just one pennant to his credit. His background was mostly with terrible ball clubs. Prior to taking over the Braves during the 1956 season, Haney had managed six years in the majors, with his teams finishing last four times and sixth twice in eight-team races.

Haney's first big league managing job was with the St. Louis Browns, who had a 43–111 record in 1939, followed by 67–87. They were 15–29 in 1941 when he was fired. He did not get another major league job for twelve years. He was the skipper of the pitiful Pirates from 1953–55, Pittsburgh going 50–104, 53–101, and 60–94. In his first six years as a manager, Haney's record was 288–526, a .354 winning percentage.

Like Stengel, Haney became a much better manager when he got a team with talent. Taking over the Braves in the middle of June in 1956, his record was 68–40. Milwaukee was 95–59 in his first full season, then 92–62 and 86–70 in Haney's last two years. His record with the Braves was 341–231, a .596 winning percentage. In four years, his Milwaukee teams won two pennants, tied for first place, and finished second, one game behind the Dodgers.

Haney played seven years in the major leagues, mostly with the Detroit Tigers and Boston Red Sox. Primarily a third baseman, he played just fourteen of his 622 games in the National League with the Cubs and Cardinals. His best season was 1923, when he went to bat 503 times for the Tigers, hit four home runs, drove in sixty-seven runs, scored eighty-five, and had a .282 batting average. His career average was .275. His first managing assignment was with the 1936 Toledo Mud Hens of the double-A American Association. Toledo was a farm team of the St. Louis Browns, who promoted Haney in 1939. Two years later, they let him go and hired Luke Sewell.

He returned to Toledo as manager before leaving the field for the broadcast booth in 1943. Haney worked six years announcing games for the Hollywood Stars, a Pittsburgh farm team. He went back to the dugout to manage the Stars in 1949, remaining with the Hollywood team four years and winning two Pacific Coast League titles. The Pirates elevated Haney to be their manager in 1953. He became a member of the Braves' coaching staff for the 1956 season, and by the midway point, he was their skipper.

Haney was much more of a low-profile guy than Stengel, who loved to talk, hear himself talk, and read what he talked about in the newspapers. And, whereas Stengel made some unusual moves like pinch-hitting for an infielder early in a game, Haney kind of sat back and let his players play. In fact, that was his strength, according to many of the Braves. He left them alone, not making too many rules or speeches, and let them play the game. Bob Buhl called Haney "a real gentleman and a good manager who knew baseball, a smart manager who found ways to win."[1]

In his book, *I Had a Hammer*, Aaron wrote that Haney was intent on making sure the Braves did not let the pennant get away in 1957 as they had in 1956. "Haney seemed to think that all we needed was some toughening up, so when we reported to Bradenton, it was boot camp. We ran sprints and did push-ups and sit-ups — things that athletes do when they're in training. It was sort of a new concept for baseball, and to us it made Haney seem more like a drill sergeant than a field manager. We called him Little Napoleon.

"I never quite figured Haney out. On one hand, he was a military man, very concerned with fitness and motivation. One of his friends was Pat O'Brien, the actor who played Knute Rockne, and in the heat of the pennant race he would bring in O'Brien and have him give us his 'Win one for the Gipper' speech. On the other hand, I sometimes thought that after he got us in shape, Haney didn't do much managing at all — that he more or less let the team run itself. Maybe that was his philosophy. But I didn't go along with most of his methods and never really warmed up to him."

Aaron added that "Nonetheless, I have to admit that I had some of my best years when Haney was the manager, starting with 1957. I was the type of player who responded well to praise, and now and then Haney would provide it, whether he intended to or not. During the spring of 1957, he commented to some newspapermen that he thought I'd soon be taking my place with the great right-handed hitters of the game. Comments like that excited me."[2]

On the eve of the first game of the World Series, Haney predicted his Braves would win it. In naming Spahn as his Game One starting pitcher, the Milwaukee manager said he planned to give the ball to Burdette in Game Two. But Haney added that, if necessary, he would use Burdette in relief in the opener. If that was the case, Haney said Buhl would then be the Game Two starter. Haney also said he would stick with his right-field platoon, with Andy Pafko playing against left-handers and Bob Hazle against right-handed pitchers. The Braves' skipper said he was considering the same system with right-handed batting Joe Adcock and lefty-hitting Frank Torre at first base, but that he might go with Adcock against all hurlers if he was hitting well.[3]

Stengel announced Whitey Ford as his opening-game pitcher, and said his Game Two starter would be either Bobby Shantz or "Bullet" Bob Turley. Most observers figured Shantz would get the call since Stengel liked to use left-handers as often as possible when playing at Yankee Stadium.

Pafko was one of only two Braves to have played in Yankee Stadium, having patrolled the outfield for the Brooklyn Dodgers in the 1952 World Series.

Here is the way the Braves and the Yankees lined up at each position:

	BA	2B	3B	HR	RBI	OBP
CATCHER						
Crandall	.253	11	2	15	46	.308
Rice	.229	1	1	9	20	.309
Sawatski	.238	4	0	6	17	.316
Berra	.251	14	2	24	82	.329
Howard	.253	13	4	8	44	.283

	BA	2B	3B	HR	RBI	OBP
FIRST BASE						
Adcock	.287	13	2	12	38	.351
Torre	.272	19	5	5	40	.339
Jones	.266	2	1	2	8	.293
Skowron	.304	15	5	17	88	.347
Simpson	.270	16	9	13	63	.321
Collins	.201	1	0	2	10	.310
SECOND BASE						
Schoendienst	.309	31	8	15	65	.344
Richardson	.256	11	1	0	19	.274
Coleman	.268	7	2	2	12	.354
Martin	.241	5	2	1	12	.257
SHORTSTOP						
Logan	.273	19	7	10	49	.319
McDougald	.289	25	9	13	62	.362
THIRD BASE						
Mathews	.292	28	9	32	94	.387
Carey	.255	6	5	6	33	.309
Lumpe	.340	6	2	0	11	.389
UTILITY						
Mantilla	.236	9	1	4	21	.296
Kubek	.297	21	3	3	39	.335
OUTFIELD						
Aaron	.322	27	6	44	132	.378
Covington	.284	4	8	21	65	.339
Pafko	.277	6	1	8	27	.308
Hazle	.403	12	0	7	27	.477
Mantle	.365	28	6	34	94	.512
Bauer	.259	22	9	18	65	.321
Slaughter	.254	7	1	5	34	.369

10

October Sunshine

The crowd of 69,476 that jammed into Yankee Stadium for Game One of the 1957 World Series was treated to a baseball art show. On exhibit were Warren Spahn and Whitey Ford, a pair of crafty left-handers who were not just two of the all-time best southpaws, but two of the all-time best pitchers. It was a duel for the ages, and neither hurler disappointed. Both were on their game as zero after zero went up on the scoreboard.

It was a beautiful October afternoon, a bit crisp as was normal for that time of year in New York. The sky was bright blue, with big fluffy clouds drifting slowly overhead, hovering as if watching the action below. All World Series games were played in the afternoon back then, and, of course, in games played at The Stadium, shadows figured to become a factor as they crept toward home plate in the late innings. That would not happen on this day, though, because the game moved too fast.

Mickey Mantle and Bill Skowron were both in the Yankees' starting lineup. Both had been questionable, but neither was going to miss a World Series game if he could help it. Playing in October might have been old hat for the men in pinstripes, but the boy in each of them still became excited about what would be the thrill of a lifetime for any kid.

Ford retired the Braves in order in the first inning without a ball being hit out of the infield. Hank Bauer skied to Andy Pafko in right field and Gil McDougald singled to right. Mantle then smacked a sharp ground ball to shortstop Johnny Logan. It looked like Milwaukee would easily force McDougald at second base, but Logan could not get the ball out of his glove. It stuck in the webbing, and Mantle was credited with an infield hit. New York, getting the kind of break other teams came to feel were somehow

161

dropped into the Yanks' laps by the baseball gods, had immediately mounted a threat. It was the type of freak thing that might have rattled a lot of pitchers. But not old Spahnie, who got Skowron to ground into a forceout and disposed of Yogi Berra on a pop out. Milwaukee went one, two, three in the second. In the bottom of the inning, after one out, Jerry Coleman lined a double to left field, but the second baseman was stranded on harmless flies to Wes Covington in left by Tony Kubek and Ford.

As the Yankees took the field for the third, there was a buzz in the stands as fans realized number fourteen was no longer playing first base. Skowron was in agony with back pain and was not able to continue. In his place was Elston Howard, the twenty-eight-year-old third-year Yankee. He was a catcher who had spent most of the '57 season in the outfield, and now, in the major leagues' center ring, he was shoved into action at a position he had played for only sixteen innings all summer.

Ford struck out Covington before allowing his first base runner when Del Crandall singled sharply to center. Spahn rolled to short, forcing Crandall, and Schoendienst lifted an easy fly to Mantle. Spahn then retired Bauer on a ground ball to short, McDougald on a fly ball to medium left, and Mantle on another fly to left field, this one carrying to the warning track. In the fourth, the Braves got something brewing after Johnny Logan bounced to McDougald at short. Eddie Mathews walked and went to third on Hank Aaron's single to right. A fly ball of any distance from slugger Joe Adcock, and Milwaukee would grab the lead. Adcock, however, hit a hard ground ball to McDougald. It was a tailor-made double play ball, and the Yankees turned it, McDougald to Coleman to Howard. When Howard, Berra, and Andy Carey went down quietly, the game was scoreless heading into the fifth.

The Braves made some more noise with some help from the Yankees. Andy Pafko hit a shot up the middle, but McDougald — an immensely underrated player who always seemed to make defensive plays and get hits at the most crucial of times — gloved the ball behind second base and nailed his man at first base. Covington then singled. He was forced on Crandall's roller to McDougald on what should have been New York's second twin killing in as many innings. Coleman's relay throw to first was perfect, but Howard dropped the ball. He was charged with an error, offering no excuses later when explaining he was simply nervous. Spahn then worked Ford for a walk, bringing clutch-hitting Red Schoendienst to the plate. The Redhead chopped a bouncer to third baseman Carey, who easily beat Crandall to the bag for the third out.

Coleman led off the bottom of the fifth with a single between third and short. Tony Kubek and Ford both grounded out, sending Coleman to third with two outs. Bauer then smashed a drive to deep right-center field, the ball bouncing off the wall for a double for the first run of the game. Often, when a ball is hit so far, it is because of a mistake by the pitcher, whether a fast-ball up in the strike zone or a hanging breaking pitch. Spahn told reporters after the game that he put the pitch right where he wanted it, low and away from the right-handed hitter, but that Bauer just mashed it. McDougald made the last out of the inning, but the run New York had scored looked awfully big the way Ford was pitching.

Then, all of a sudden, the little lefty seemed to lose his concentration in the top of the sixth inning. Certainly his control deserted him temporarily as he walked Logan and Mathews, putting Braves at first and second with nobody out and Aaron coming to the plate. The question going through many minds in Yankee Stadium was, "Will he be bunting?" Cleanup hitters are not called on to sacrifice very often, but it appeared as if runs would be difficult to come by off of Ford, and perhaps playing for one run would be good strategy. Aaron was not bunting, and he struck out on three pitches. Adcock then grounded out to Howard at first, with both runners moving up, but they were left standing when Pafko struck out. The Braves had wasted a golden opportunity to at least get even, and in the last of the sixth, their hole grew deeper.

After Mantle flied to center, Berra worked Spahn for a base on balls, and Howard lined a shot into center field for a single. Carey also singled to center, driving in Howard, and sending Berra to third. Right-hander Ernie Johnson had been warming up in the Milwaukee bullpen, and Fred Haney waved him in. It was a bit of a surprise that he took Spahn out so early, especially when he had given up just two runs and did not appear to be tiring (something the left-hander would attest to following the game). Coleman figured on swinging away, but with one out and the Braves' infield playing back, he started thinking otherwise. So he walked down and talked with Yankee third base coach Frank Crosetti, telling him to let Berra know that he might drop down a bunt. It would be a safety squeeze, meaning Berra would not start home until he saw Coleman's bat make contact with the ball.

However, by the time Coleman returned to the plate, he saw the Braves' infield had drawn in, so he swung away and fouled off Johnson's first pitch. Coleman then glanced at Crosetti, who was going through his signals, and saw the sign for the squeeze. It was the suicide, meaning the runner on third would dash for home when the pitcher released the ball, and the batter was required to get his bat on the ball no matter what. Berra took off when Johnson threw the ball, and Coleman laid down the bunt, with Berra scoring

Wes Covington provided left-handed power while plugging a hole in left field. Not known for his defense, he contributed two fielding gems that helped Milwaukee win the World Series.

easily. The Yankees led, 3–0, and with Ford pitching as he often pitched in October, those three runs looked huge to both the Yankees and Braves.

Milwaukee finally broke through in the seventh, scoring once on Wes Covington's opposite-field double to left and an RBI single by Schoendienst. Ford fanned Logan for the third out and then set down the last six Braves he faced, retiring seven straight batters to end the game. Don McMahon pitched the last two innings for the Braves, with the only excitement involving Mantle and his speed. His beautiful drag bunt in the eighth became his second infield hit of the day, but Mantle was erased trying to steal second when Crandall gunned a strike to Logan.

Ford, in earning his fifth of what would be ten World Series victories, threw 128 pitches. And, while he was certainly the top story of Game One, Jerry Coleman was not far below the main headline. During the regular season, the 33-year-old veteran played in fifty-seven games, forty-five of them at second base. Bobby Richardson, who was twenty-two, played in ninety-three games at second base. It raised a few eyebrows when Coleman got the starting nod over Richardson in the Series opener, but those who followed the Yankees closely knew Stengel liked to go with experience in the biggest games. Coleman showed why as he got two hits in three at-bats and drove in a run, while handling seven chances in the field flawlessly.

Covington was the lone bright spot for the Braves, getting two of his team's five hits off Ford. After the game, Haney took on the horde of second-guessing sportswriters, explaining that he never bunts, especially on the road, with his best hitter at the plate.

Game Two pitchers were right-hander Lew Burdette, the old fidget master, for Milwaukee and lefty Bobby Shantz, with small stature and a big curve ball, for the Yankees. Skowron was unable to play for New York, doctors saying that after a couple of days' rest, the best he could do would be to pinch-hit. Stengel loaded his lineup with left-handed batters, inserting forty-one-year-old Enos Slaughter in left field, where Kubek had played in the first game, moving Kubek to third, and using "Suitcase" Simpson at first base. There were no changes for the Braves.

Shantz started like gangbusters, striking out the side, as Milwaukee continued to find New York southpaws puzzling. Burdette also retired the side in order. But things quickly changed as both teams scored a run in each of the next two innings.

Leading off the second, Aaron clobbered the ball over Mantle's head in center for a triple on a ball the Mick said he misjudged badly. Aaron scored on Adcock's single, Adcock taking second when Mantle booted the ball. After two were out, Crandall was walked, but Burdette tapped back to Shantz to end the inning. In the Yankees' half, a ground out and strikeout were sand-wiched around a walk to Slaughter before Kubek and Coleman put together back-to-back two-out hits that tied the score. Coleman, whose hit was of the infield variety, had his second RBI in two days and was quickly becoming one of those little guys to have a big Series. Shantz made the last out on a sensa-tional catch by Covington. The Yanks' pitcher, a right-handed batter, caught hold of a Burdette fastball and lined it toward the corner, but Covington raced to his right and made a back-handed catch to rob Shantz of a hit and the Yankees of two runs. Logan belted a change-up into the left-field seats in the third, with Bauer answering for New York with a blast of his own as he smoked a Burdette sinker that did not sink. The score was tied, 2–2, but Haney was a bit concerned because the last four outs recorded by Burdette were on fly balls, and he was known as a groundball pitcher.

The Braves hammered Shantz for three straight singles to open the fourth inning. Adcock picked up his second straight hit, followed by a Pafko sin-gle, and a run-scoring base hit to left by Covington. Pafko also scored on the play, an unearned run resulting from Kubek's error. Shantz' day was finished as Stengel brought in right-hander Art Ditmar, who got Crandall and Bur-dette on pop-ups to Simpson and Schoendienst on a bouncer to McDougald at short. Milwaukee led, 4–2, and that would be the final score.

Burdette retired the Yankees in order in the fourth and pitched around a walk to Coleman in the fifth. Ditmar hit Logan with a pitch to start the fifth, then threw a double-play ball to Mathews, and encountered no prob-lems through the sixth inning. Burdette found himself in plenty of hot water in the bottom of the sixth. He walked Mantle, who was forced by Berra on a ground ball to Logan at short. Slaughter sliced a double to left, putting run-ners at second and third with one out.

Simpson then hit a slow roller, a swinging bunt, down the third-base line. Burdette, a good athlete, got off the mound and pounced on the ball. But with his momentum carrying him away from first base, getting Simpson appeared unlikely. The Braves' pitcher somehow whirled and got enough on his throw to nip the runner, with both runners holding their bases. First base-man Joe Adcock also made a nice play on his end. Burdette's throw pulled him off the base, but Adcock was able to swipe-tag Simpson before his foot hit the bag. Instead of having the bases loaded with one out, New York still had two runners in scoring position, but needed a two-out hit to score. It did not happen as Kubek grounded to Schoendienst at second to end the threat.

Looking for insurance, Crandall beat out a bunt to start the seventh and was sacrificed to second by Burdette. Schoendienst bounced out and Logan flied to left as Ditmar completed four innings of one-hit relief. Coleman grounded out to Mathews in the Yankees' half of the inning before pinch-hitter Jerry Lumpe singled to right. The threat was a mild one as Bauer popped to Logan and McDougald sent a soft fly to Pafko in right field.

Relief ace Bob Grim pitched the last two innings for New York and allowed only a harmless single to Covington. The Yankees' bullpen did a terrific job, giving up two hits while walking no one in six shutout innings.

Burdette got three easy outs in the eighth inning and another to start the ninth before Kubek banged a single to right. Joe Collins pinch-hit for Coleman, who had three hits in five at-bats so far in the Series, and popped out to Logan. Howard kept the Yankees' hopes alive when he singled to put the potential tying runs on base. Richardson ran for Howard. Burdette induced Bauer to hit a ground ball to Logan, who tossed to Schoendienst for the game-ending force-out. The Braves had evened the World Series at a win apiece.

Burdette pitched a complete-game seven-hitter, getting a dozen outs on ground balls and striking out five. The Braves got eight hits, two each by Adcock and Covington. Milwaukee played errorless baseball for the second time. The Yankees committed two errors, giving them three in two games.

In the Milwaukee locker room, Haney said he considered taking Burdette out in the ninth inning and bringing in the fire-balling McMahon. The Braves' skipper said he would have made the change had Burdette not handled Bauer. Not worrying about possibly providing the Yankees with extra incentive in the form of blackboard material, Burdette told reporters, "There are several clubs in our league as good as the Yankees."

Crandall, referring to his batterymate's escape from hot water in the sixth and ninth innings, said, "When Lew gets into trouble, that's when he gets kind of ornery. He just won't let those guys score on him."[1]

A champion seldom makes excuses, and that was the case with the Yankees. After the game, with reporters offering the "Burdette throws a spitball" charge on a platter, New York players refused to bite. They did not accuse him of doctoring the ball, just praised him for being a fine pitcher. The men in pinstripes credited the Milwaukee right-hander for a superbly pitched game, complimenting him on his control and command of his sinker and screwball.

After drawing nearly 135,000 fans for two games in Yankee Stadium, the Series moved to County Stadium for the third game, following a Friday travel day. The Braves were going home, and so was Tony Kubek, the Yankees' versatile rookie who was born in Milwaukee and grew up there.

And a grand homecoming it was, for Kubek and not the Braves. A crowd of 45,804 roared as twenty-nine-year-old Bob Buhl took the mound for Milwaukee, and the noise grew louder when he zipped a strike past Hank Bauer, then fielded his easy tap back to the box and threw to first. Batting second in a lineup shaken up by Stengel, Kubek took a ball and a strike before shooting a line drive to right field. Bob Hazle went back to the wall 355 feet from home plate, and jumped in vain. The ball cleared the fence, giving the Yankees a sudden lead and the County Stadium fans a sudden disappointment.

Buhl never recovered. He walked Mantle and Berra, then had Mantle picked off second, but threw wildly into center field as both runners moved up a base. Gil McDougald sent a fly to deep center, and Aaron ran back, tripped, and fell. Miraculously, he still made the catch, with Mantle tagging and scoring easily. "Suitcase" Simpson singled into center to score Berra and finish the day for Buhl. Juan Pizarro, the twenty-year-old rookie lefthander, came in and retired Jerry Lumpe on a fly to Hazle. It was 3–0, Yankees.

"Bullet" Bob Turley, a fast-balling right-hander started for New York, and he ran into immediate trouble. Schoendienst singled to right and Logan walked, but Mathews and Aaron both popped out to the infield. Covington walked to load the bases for Adcock, but he took a called third strike to end the threat and the first inning.

Pizarro pitched around a walk to Bauer in the second before the Braves again jumped on Turley. He walked Hazle, and Del Rice followed with a solid single to center. Pizarro, a good hitting pitcher, flied to left for the first out. Schoendienst then got his second hit in as many innings, an RBI single to right, as Hazle scored. Logan struck out looking, and when Mathews walked to load the bases, Stengel had seen enough. He removed Turley and called in Don Larsen from the bullpen. The man who has pitched the only perfect game in World Series history inherited a full-blown jam with Aaron coming to the plate. But Larsen retired Aaron on a fly ball to Bauer in right, and the Yankees led, 3–1.

They tacked on two runs in the third off Pizarro when Lumpe lined a two-run single. Mantle smashed a homer following a Kubek single in the fourth off Gene Conley, New York pulling away to a six-run lead. Meanwhile, Larsen was mowing down the Braves as he set them down in order both innings, while striking out two. Larsen had pitched eleven and one-third innings of perfect World Series baseball over two years.

Ernie Johnson entered the game in the fifth and pitched two scoreless innings for Milwaukee. He did not allow a hit, walked one, and struck out two. Johnson gave the Braves a chance to get back into the game, and they did make a little noise. Johnny Logan singled to lead off the fifth, ending Larsen's streak of retiring thirty-four consecutive Series batters. Mathews flied to left before Aaron showed his tremendous power to the opposite field by blasting a home run to right-center. The two-run shot cut New York's lead to 7–3, but that would be as close as the Braves would get.

Following Aaron's homer, Larsen walked Wes Covington, bringing Stengel out of the dugout to remind his right-hander that with a big lead, he needed to throw strikes. Larsen fanned Adcock and induced Hazle to hit a soft fly ball to Kubek in left for the third out. The Braves loaded the bases in the sixth on base hits by Schoendienst and Logan and a walk to Mathews, but Aaron grounded out to Lumpe at third. Mathews drew his third base on balls, and Aaron singled to start the ninth. When pinch-hitter Andy Pafko was hit by a pitch, Milwaukee had loaded the bases once again. Larsen, however, left them that way for the third time as he got Hazle to pop up to McDougald and then struck out Del Crandall to end the game. Milwaukee left fourteen runners on base for the game.

The Yankees had sealed the deal with a five-run seventh inning keyed by back-to-back homers, all of the damage coming off pitches from Bob Trowbridge. Kubek's second roundtripper of the contest, a three-run shot, highlighted the eruption. Mantle followed with a clout of more than 400 feet into the Milwaukee bullpen. For the day, Kubek had three hits, scored three times, and drove in four. Schoendienst had three of Milwaukee's eight hits. Larsen was superb in relief, throwing seven and one-third innings, scattering five hits, and giving up two runs. The Yanks' 12–3 laugher gave them a 2–1 Series edge.

The next game looked for a long time like it would be decided by Milwaukee's top pitching and hitting stars. Ultimately, though, a bit player proved a key to the outcome by doing a little creative umpiring. Game One starter Warren Spahn was back on the mound for the Braves to start Game Four, while the Yankees went with right-hander Tom Sturdivant, whose sixteen wins were tops on the New York staff. Haney made a lineup change, inserting the left-handed hitting Frank Torre at first base in place of Joe Adcock. In the first three games, Adcock had two singles in eleven at-bats, with one RBI. Stengel switched the first two batters in his lineup, using Kubek in the leadoff spot with Bauer hitting second.

Kubek beat out a bunt to open the game and advanced to second on Bauer's slow roller to short. Mantle bounced to Spahn, who gloved the ball and trapped Kubek between second and third, where the Braves tagged him in a rundown. Berra walked, with Mantle moving to second and then scoring on McDougald's single to left. That was the only run in the first three innings as Sturdivant gave up just one hit and worked out of one mild jam.

That was in the second inning when Aaron led off with a sharp ground ball in the hole between third and short. McDougald, the Yankees' shortstop, ranged far to his right and knocked the ball down, but could not make a play. Covington bounced to Carey at third, with Aaron forced at second. Covington then stole second base and reached third on Torre's groundout to second baseman Jerry Coleman. Hazle stranded Covington as his bouncer was gobbled up by McDougald, who threw to Elston Howard at first.

Spahn got the Yankees one-two-three for three straight innings, bringing Milwaukee to the plate in the bottom of the fourth, trailing, 1–0. Sturdivant began his own demise by issuing his only free pass of the day. Logan drew the walk to lead off the inning and went to third on Mathews' double, a bullet down the right-field line that was his first hit of the Series. That brought Aaron to the plate, and the general feeling in the press box was that Stengel would have the National League home run champ walked intentionally, setting up a play at any base.

But Stengel, who frequently ignored "the book" and managed by instinct, decided to let Sturdivant pitch to Aaron. The count went to one and one before Aaron flicked those lethal wrists and belted a drive that cleared the left-field wall with plenty to spare. After Covington grounded out, Torre launched a blast to right. It was his first home run all season in County Stadium as all five of his regular-season homers were hit on the road. Sturdivant recovered to fan Hazle and get Crandall on a comebacker to the mound, but the Braves had taken a 4–1 lead.

When Spahn got Andy Carey on a grounder to Logan to start the fifth inning, the stylish southpaw had retired eleven Yankees in a row, nine on ground balls. Jerry Coleman broke the spell with a single to right field; however, Spahn got right back in the groove by getting Simpson, pinch-hitting for Sturdivant, to ground into a double play, Schoendienst to Logan to Torre. Bobby Shantz came on in relief for New York and re-captured his first-inning magic of Game Two. The little lefty pitched three hitless innings, issuing one walk, while striking out four Braves as he kept the Yankees in the ball game.

Spahn continued his mastery of the New York hitters, pitching three more scoreless innings for a total of seven straight. He got two ground balls and struck out Mantle in the sixth. Berra singled to start the seventh, and after a fly out by McDougald, the Yankee catcher was erased when the Braves turned a double play, Logan to Schoendienst to Torre, on a bouncer by Howard.

Carey led off the Yankees' eighth by lining a two-base hit. He stayed at second as Coleman grounded to Logan at short, then advanced to third when Lumpe roped a pinch single to center. Spahn then did what he had been doing all afternoon. He threw a low breaking pitch to Kubek, and the result was a ground ball to Logan, who started the Braves' third double play of the game and kept them in front, 4–1.

Johnny Kucks, who was making his first appearance of the Series, was greeted by a Schoendienst double. The right-hander, realizing another run might have proven too much for his Yankees to overcome, bore down to strike out Logan and get Mathews on a routine fly to Kubek in left field. After Kucks walked Aaron, left-hander Tommy Byrne was brought in to face the left-handed hitting Covington. The thirty-seven-year-old veteran of three previous World Series with the Yankees, who was playing in his final major league season, did his job, striking out Covington.

Bauer flied out to Aaron in center and Mantle bounced to Logan at short in the ninth, and it looked as though Spahn would breeze to victory. He had a three-run lead and needed one out. The Yankees, of course, were known to possess an almost mystical ability to rally, and once again, they used their last breath to stay alive. Berra singled to right, and so did McDougald. Up came Howard, who had hit three harmless ground balls against Spahn that day, with the Braves turning one of the grounders into a double play. On a three-and-two pitch, Howard jumped all over a screwball and crushed a three-run homer into the left-field bleachers to knot the score, 4–4. It was as if Howard had stuck a dagger into nearly 41,000 hearts at County Stadium. As the saying goes, the silence was deafening. Spahn gathered himself to retire Carey, but he walked to the dugout a stunned warrior.

Byrne set the Braves down in order in the bottom of the ninth, sending the game into extra innings. Yankee fans were hopefully thinking their team had Spahn on the ropes. Braves fans were fearfully thinking the same thing. Sure enough, more trouble was on the horizon for the lefty. Coleman bounced out to Logan and Byrne struck out, but again New York came up with what old-timers liked to call two-out lightning. Kubek topped a slow roller to second, and by the time Schoendienst charged the ball and threw to first, the rookie had beaten it out for an infield hit. Bauer followed with a booming triple over Aaron's head in center field, extending his World Series hitting streak to eleven games. Bauer drove in Kubek, and New York led, 5–4.

Now it was Milwaukee that had to come from behind or face a 3–1 Series deficit. Nippy Jones, in what was to be his final major league appearance, pinch-hit for Spahn and took a low, inside curveball from Byrne, then headed for first base. Jones claimed the ball had hit him on the left foot. Plate umpire Augie Donatelli disagreed and called him back, ruling the pitch was simply a ball. The baseball had rolled to the backstop, and both Jones and Yankee catcher Yogi Berra went to retrieve it. Jones won the race and brought the

ball back to show Donatelli. Jones pointed to a spot of black on the ball, noting that it was polish from his shoe. Convinced, the ump rewarded Jones' detective work by pointing him toward first base. The clubhouse boys always polished all of the players' shoes before every game, and the Braves were mighty glad they did.

New York relief ace Bob Grim came in to pitch for the Yankees, who had also made a defensive change because Mantle's right shoulder was hurting. Kubek moved from left field to center, and forty-one-year-old Enos Slaughter took over in left.

Mantle recalled how badly his shoulder hurt. "It happened in the bottom of the tenth. We had scored the tie-breaker and were up by a run. Now the Braves had a man on second. My shoulder was throbbing so badly I flagged the dugout. Casey called time, took me out, and moved Kubek to center. Moments later, I watched Eddie Mathews club one a mile high and into the right field bleachers to win the game."[2]

Felix Mantilla went into the game to run for Jones and was sacrificed to second base on a dandy bunt from Schoendienst. Johnny Logan smacked a shot past Slaughter and into the left-field corner for a double, driving in Mantilla with the tying run. Mathews, using a borrowed bat, ended the game and evened the Series by pulling a Grim fastball into the right-field seats. Spahn induced nineteen batters to hit the ball into the dirt, resulting in twenty-two outs as the Braves turned three double plays in their 7–5 victory. Logan equaled a World Series record for shortstops with nine assists in nine innings, getting a tenth in the extra frame. The record had been set by the Yankees' Roger Peckinpaugh in 1921.

Mathews explained afterward that he used one of Joe Adcock's bats the entire game because it did not have a knob at the end. Mathews displayed a callous on his right palm and said the knob of his own bat rubbed against the sore spot and bothered him.[3]

Mantle did not start Game Five as the pain in his right shoulder persisted and was unbearable when he tried to throw a ball or swing a bat. The injury had occurred in Game Three when Mantle was on second base and Bob Buhl tried to pick him off. Mantle dove back to the base and Braves second baseman Red Schoendienst came down on top of him. No one knew the Yankee center fielder was hurt until after Game Four. Without Mantle, Kubek

Opposite: **Nippy Jones provided depth at first base while Joe Adcock was injured. His final major league at bat produced the famous shoe polish incident that keyed the Braves' win in Game Four of the '57 World Series. (©Brace Photo. Used by permission.)**

moved to center field and Slaughter played left. Gil McDougald moved into the third slot in the lineup normally occupied by Mantle. Game One winning pitcher Whitey Ford started for New York. Game Two winner Lew Burdette was on the mound for Milwaukee.

As good as the sinkerballing right-hander was when he pitched in Yankee Stadium, he was even better this time. Ford matched his earlier outstanding Series performance, resulting in a splendid pitching duel that saw only fifteen batters reach base and took just two hours to play.

Hank Bauer gave his teammates cause to think things would be different with Burdette the second time around when he led off the contest with a sharp single to left. Kubek laid down a sacrifice bunt that sent Bauer to second, and McDougald hit the ball right on the nose, but Andy Pafko caught the line drive in right field. Yogi Berra grounded to Logan at short. Schoendienst bounced out and Logan popped out before Mathews drew his seventh walk of the Series. Aaron lined to Slaughter in left, and the first inning was quickly over.

The Braves were dealt a terrible blow in the top of the second, although Burdette put another zero on the scoreboard. Slaughter smacked a lead-off single to center and was running when "Suitcase" Simpson struck out. Del Crandall's throw to Logan was in plenty of time to nail Slaughter and complete the double play. Then, all of a sudden, Schoendienst motioned toward the Milwaukee dugout and started limping off the field. It turned out he had pulled a groin muscle in his right leg while diving for Slaughter's hit. The Redhead later said that he had originally hurt himself the day before and that he woke up feeling stiff and sore. He said the quick move he made attempting to catch Slaughter's hit had worsened the previous injury. Felix Mantilla came in to play second base.

Burdette and Ford kept things uneventful except for a Pafko single in the second and a Bauer infield hit in the third. In the fourth inning, Burdette escaped some serious trouble that might have proven disastrous if not for a pair of splendid defensive gems. Gil McDougald led off by sending a blow to deep left that looked like it might be gone. Wes Covington, not known for his fielding, went back to the wall, leaped, and made the catch near the top of the railing. He slammed into the fence, fell to the turf, and came up holding the ball. At the very least, McDougald would have had a double. So, Covington's play looked mighty big when Joe Adcock booted Berra's grounder to first and Slaughter followed with his second base hit of the day. New York was threatening with one out. Simpson, a left-handed batter, hit a high chopper toward third that looked as though it may bound over Mathews' head. The Braves' third baseman jumped high, stabbed the ball, and whipped it to Mantilla, who relayed to Adcock to complete a pretty twin killing. The Yankees pulled off a double play of their own in the bottom of the inning, Adcock's grounder to McDougald at short rubbing out Aaron, who had singled.

Burdette retired the Yankees in order over the next two innings, while Ford allowed a harmless Pafko single in the fifth. But in the bottom of the sixth, the Braves strung together three hits — half of their total for the day — to break the scoring ice. It all started with two outs on what looked like an inning-ending ground ball. Mathews hit a bouncer to Jerry Coleman, and the veteran second baseman made an error in judgment. Rather than charge the ball, he waited on it, and the extra bounce gave Mathews time to beat the throw to first. Coleman had not realized how fast Mathews was. Aaron hit a little pop fly that fell between right fielder Bauer and Coleman, with Mathews racing to third. Adcock ripped a solid single to right that plated Mathews for what would be the only run of the game.

Berra singled to center to start the Yankee seventh, Slaughter then banging into a double play, Logan to Mantilla to Adcock. There were no other baserunners until the eighth when Coleman's one-out single to right put the tying run on base. Mantle pinch-ran, and after Elston Howard took a called third strike, was cut down stealing. It was the second time in the Series Crandall had gunned Mantle down attempting to swipe second.

Burdette had plenty left for the ninth inning. He struck out Bauer and struck out Kubek before McDougald rifled a single to center field. Berra popped weakly to Mathews for the final out, giving Burdette his second complete-game victory and the Braves a 3–2 World Series lead. His 1–0 win was fashioned with eighty-seven pitches, with seventeen outs coming on fifteen ground balls as no Yankee made it as far as third base. Milwaukee executed three double plays for the second straight game.

The teams traveled back to New York nursing injuries and illnesses. Mantle, diagnosed with a strained tendon in his right shoulder, could barely lift his arm and was not expected to play in Game Six. Neither was Schoendienst, who had a groin pull in his right leg. In addition, Warren Spahn was in bed with some sort of a virus as was Yankee right-hander Johnny Kucks, who had a fever and a headache.

Bob Buhl would be the starting pitcher for Milwaukee, and he was anxious to make amends for his third-game showing in which he lasted less than one inning. Stengel named Bob Turley as his starter. Bullet Bob had his own share of problems in that same game, when he could not survive the second inning after being staked to a three-run lead. However, Turley was overpowering in an inning of relief in Game Five. He retired the Braves in order in the eighth and struck out two, getting Logan and Mathews looking at third strikes.

Turley, the pressure of his team's possible elimination on his shoulders, breezed through five innings. After being wild in his first start of the Series, walking four batters in less than two innings, he was putting the ball where he wanted it. Turley allowed a single to Frank Torre in the second and a double to Eddie Mathews in the fourth, while issuing no free passes and striking out four over four innings.

Buhl fanned the first two batters he faced before walking Slaughter. Berra singled, and both runners advanced on a wild pitch before Buhl whiffed McDougald, thereby striking out the side. Jerry Lumpe singled to start the second for the Yankees, and he attempted to steal second. New York was no more successful against Del Rice than against Del Crandall as Rice fired to Logan to cut down Lumpe. Coleman walked, but was left on base as Buhl had four strikeouts through two shutout innings.

Turley appeared to get stronger in the third when he struck out two more batters, and Buhl began the bottom of the inning as if he would match his mound opponent pitch for pitch. He retired Bauer on a pop-up and Kubek on a ground ball, and then the roof caved in. Buhl walked Slaughter for the second time, and Berra followed with a home run into the right-field seats. Playing in what was then a record fifty-third World Series game (Berra holds the record with seventy-five), the Yankee catcher whacked the tenth Series homer of his career. McDougald got a base hit, and when Buhl walked Lumpe, he was finished after lasting two and two-thirds innings. Ernie Johnson came in to strike out Simpson. The Yankees led, 2–0, and it stayed that way until the fifth inning. Torre led off with his second home run of the Series, slicing the Milwaukee deficit in half.

Johnson, meanwhile, held the Yankees right where they were by throwing three shutout innings. After Coleman's lead-off double in the fourth, a blooper down the left-field line, Johnson retired ten batters in a row, four on strikeouts and five on ground balls. He became the pitcher of record in the top of the seventh when Aaron hit a blast that landed in the Milwaukee bullpen more than 400 feet from home plate. Aaron's home run was his third of the Series and tied the score. Hank Bauer broke the tie and Johnson's hold on the Yankees in the bottom of the seventh when he smashed a hanging curve ball down the left-field line just inside the foul pole for his second Series homer. The roundtripper extended Bauer's World Series hitting streak to thirteen games. Johnson got the last two outs, completing a fine day of relief work. Turley seemed stronger than ever in the eighth, striking out the first two Braves he faced, walking Mantilla, and getting the last out on an easy pop-up.

Don McMahon came in to pitch for Milwaukee and found himself in quick trouble when Berra lined an opposite-field double to left. McDougald bunted him to third base, and New York was in business for a possible insurance run. Lumpe lifted a fly ball near the left-field foul line, and Wes Covington made his third sparkling defensive play of the Series. He caught the ball on the run and fired a perfect throw to Rice at home plate, doubling up Berra and keeping the Braves within a run of the Yanks. Mathews started the ninth by coaxing a base on balls, but Aaron was called out on strikes, and Covington bounced back to Turley. The pitcher threw to McDougald, who tossed to Joe Collins, a defensive replacement for Simpson, at first base to end the game. The Series was tied, three games apiece, following New York's 3–2 win.

Turley, using a no-windup style made famous by Don Larsen during his perfect game in the previous year's World Series, was in command almost the entire contest. After walking four in his brief Game Three appearance, Turley issued only two bases on balls, while striking out eight. He pitched a four-hitter, though two of the hits left the park. Johnson was tagged with the loss, despite surrendering just two hits and one run in four and one-third innings, while striking out five and walking no one. Berra enjoyed a big day at the plate, with a single, double, and two-run home run in four trips.

The 1957 World Series had come down to the seventh game, and Warren Spahn, Milwaukee's ace pitcher, was the obvious choice to start for the Braves. He had three days' rest, which was his norm during most of the regular season. But Spahn, though improved, was still not full strength. So Fred Haney decided to start Lew Burdette with only two days of rest. It did not seem that big of a gamble since Burdette had pitched with less than three days rest in the past, and he not thrown all that many pitches in Game Five. The Yankees' ace, Whitey Ford, had opposed Burdette in that contest, but would not get the ball to start the deciding game. Stengel was going with Don Larsen, who was brilliant in Game Three. There were four days between that shining relief job and Game Seven.

The Yankees appeared to have every advantage. In addition to playing at home, their pitching was deeper and better rested. The Braves were hitting under .200 as a team entering the seventh game, and they were playing without their sparkplug, Red Schoendienst.

Mantle, although not 100 percent, was back in the Yankees' lineup, hitting in his familiar third spot and playing center field. Stengel kept the old pro, Slaughter, in left field, moving him up to the second slot in the batting order. Kubek, not Lumpe, played third, and Collins, not Simpson, was at first base. Haney shook up his lineup as well. With Schoendienst still unable to play, Mantilla was again at second base. But after going hitless so far in the Series, he was dropped from leadoff to number seven in the batting order. Leading off was Bob Hazle, who had always hit in the fifth, sixth, and seventh holes, and who did not yet have a base hit in the Series. Torre, who had come through with two surprising home runs, remained at first base.

There were 61,207 fans at Yankee Stadium on October 11, and most of them thought the Yankees would beat Milwaukee. So did most of the sportswriters covering the game. Many of them were from New York, and many of them were smug in their analyses, feeling deep down that that the Yankees were kings and that no team was their equal, especially in big games. And, after all, the World Series title belonged in New York as teams from the city had won the last eight championships. The Yankees themselves had six of the world titles, winning the Series from 1949–53 and again in 1956. The Giants had won in 1954 and the Dodgers had done it in 1955. Besides, in addition to the tradition, the odds were on the Yanks' side because Burdette was not well rested and the Bronx Bombers were due to have their way with the right-hander who had held a spell over them for eighteen innings.

Burdette's spell over the Yankees would continue, although they threatened very early to change their luck against the Braves' right-hander. Larsen was tough at the outset as he struck out two batters and retired the side in order. Bauer led off for New York and lined Burdette's first pitch for a double to left, stretching his World Series hitting streak to fourteen games. The noisy Yankee Stadium crowd scarcely had a chance to get excited, however, before the picture changed drastically. Slaughter hit a bouncer back to the mound, and Burdette fielded it, then turned to hold Bauer at second. But the veteran right fielder had bolted toward third, and he was trapped. Burdette ran Bauer toward third, flipped the ball to Eddie Mathews, who ran the runner back toward second, then tossed to Johnny Logan. Logan threw back to Burdette, who had gone over to cover third, while Bauer scrambled back to second. By that time, Slaughter was also arriving at second base. Burdette threw to Logan for the tag on Slaughter, with Bauer ending up on second where he had started. The Braves did not handle the rundown very well, so the Yanks still had a runner in scoring position. It did not matter, though. Mantle also tapped back to the pitcher for out number two, Berra was intentionally walked, and McDougald popped out to Mathews.

Aaron singled to open the second inning and was bunted to second by Covington. Torre walked, but Mantilla flied out and Crandall grounded into a force out. Burdette got the Yankees one, two, three with two ground balls and a strike out.

Larsen retired Burdette on a foul pop to begin the third inning. Then came a Milwaukee uprising that decided the Series, but it would not have occurred without help from the Yankees. Bob Hazle lined an opposite-field single to left, and Logan followed with a smash to Kubek at third that looked like a double play. Kubek's throw to second pulled Jerry Coleman off the base. So instead of having to go back out on the field, the Braves had two men on and the heart of their order coming up. Mathews made the Pinstripes pay by scorching a double into the right-field corner, driving in Hazle and Logan. Stengel called left-hander Bobby Shantz in from the bullpen, and Larsen was headed to the showers, trailing 2–0. He should have been sitting in the dugout still nursing a shutout

The Braves were not finished. Aaron singled Mathews home. Covington continued to go with the pitch as he had most of the Series and singled to left-center, Aaron taking third. Torre picked up an RBI on a groundout to second that forced Covington, with Aaron crossing the plate. Mantilla flied softly to Bauer in right to end the inning. Milwaukee had sent eight men to bat, and four of them scored. Burdette then made quick work of the Yankees.

Art Ditmar took over on the mound for New York and pitched around another single by Hazle and an error by McDougald. Burdette pitched a perfect fourth. Ditmar put up another zero in the fifth, and when Burdette took care of Kubek on a fly to left, he had set down eleven batters in a row. Coleman broke the string with a single, but he was forced at second on Collins' bouncer to Logan at short. Bill Skowron pinch-hit for Ditmar and grounded to Logan for another force out. It was the first action since Game One for Skowron, who stayed in the game to play first base in place of Collins.

Game Four starter Tom Sturdivant became the Yankees' fourth pitcher, and he threw two shutout innings of two-hit relief. Burdette worked out of a mild jam in the sixth. With two outs, Mantle lined a base hit to right field and Berra reached when Mathews bobbled his grounder to third. Mathews immediately got the chance to redeem himself when McDougald slapped a bouncer his way, and the Braves' third sacker made the play to end the threat. Kubek singled to lead off the seventh, but Burdette disposed of the Yanks on two ground balls and a strike out.

Lefty Tommy Byrne came on to pitch for New York in the eighth, making what would be his final big league appearance. Del Crandall belted a two-out home run to provide Milwaukee with more breathing room. It was a long drive to left that barely eluded Slaughter's glove as he leaped at the fence. The Yankees went out meekly in the eighth as did the Braves in the ninth.

And, so, it came down to the bottom of the ninth inning, with the Yankees staring at a 5–0 deficit and at a hurler who had owned them for nearly three whole games. Burdette had thrown sliders, hard sinkers, and screwballs.

He had mixed his pitches well, and he had put the ball where he wanted it. On top of all that, he had made great pitches when he needed them most, very seldom giving New York hitters anything in the middle of the plate or up in their eyes where they could tee off.

The Yankees did not win all of those pennants and World Series championships by throwing in the towel when they fell into a hole, and they were not about to do that now. They were notorious for spoiling opponents' parties with last-ditch rallies, and their comebacks were expected as well as feared.

Berra opened the ninth with a pop fly to Torre at first. McDougald singled right up the middle. Kubek skied to Aaron in center field. Two were out. Burdette needed one more. Coleman kept New York's hopes alive with a single to right. Byrne then batted for himself. To those who did not know much about him, there may have been shock that a pitcher would be sent to the plate by a team down to its last out of a World Series. But Byrne, who batted as he threw — left-handed, had a career batting average of .238, which was pretty good for a pitcher. He had fourteen career home runs, including three during the 1957 season. Byrne did not let Casey and his teammates down. He ripped a shot toward center field, a sure hit that looked like it might spoil Burdette's shutout. But second baseman Mantilla dove for the ball and knocked it down. He could not make a play, but he kept the ball in the infield and kept McDougald from scoring.

Skowron approached the plate, with Yankee fans thinking grand slam. "I wasn't really that worried," Burdette would say after the game. "Even if he hit the ball in the seats, we would still have been leading by a run."[4] Skowron did not hit the ball in the seats, but he did hit it hard. He smashed a sizzling grounder to Mathews' right, between him and the third-base bag. It looked like a possible double which would score at least two runs and bring the tying run to the plate in the person of Hank Bauer, who had two home runs in the Series. Mathews saw to it that none of those things happened. He glided to his right, back-handed the hard shot, and raced to third base ahead of Coleman. Mathews always called that force-out his proudest moment in baseball.[5] The Braves had won, 5–0, and had won the championship in their very first World Series. Burdette pitched his second straight shutout and did not allow a run in his last twenty-four innings. His seven-hitter included three strikeouts and one walk.

Burdette was nothing short of sensational throughout the Series. He pitched and won three complete games, all in an eight-day span. In twenty-seven innings, he gave up twenty-one hits, walked four, surrendered two runs, both earned, and struck out thirteen. His earned run average was 0.67. He was a landslide selection as the Most Valuable Player of the World Series.

Any other time, Hank Aaron would have won the award. He led both teams in hitting with a .393 batting average, getting eleven hits in twenty-eight at-bats and at least one in all seven games. He clouted three home runs and drove in seven runs, both highs for the Series. His five runs scored equaled the totals of Johnny Logan and Yogi Berra. Frank Torre batted .300, with two of his three hits home runs, and knocked in three runs. Red Schoendienst, who left early in Game Five and did not play again, hit .278. Eddie Mathews hit just .227, but he drew eight walks, had four RBI, scored four runs, and his five hits included a home run and three doubles.

Jerry Coleman led the Yankees with a .364 average and Berra batted .320. They both had eight hits as did Hank Bauer and Tony Kubek. Bauer drove in six runs and hit two homers, matching Kubek's total, which came in one game. Mantle ended up with nineteen at-bats, five hits, one homer, three runs scored, two RBI, a .263 batting average, and he was caught stealing twice.

New York out-hit Milwaukee, .248 to .209, and scored more runs, 25–23. The Braves hit eight homers, the Yankees hit seven. New York committed six errors, resulting in three unearned runs. Milwaukee made three errors, resulting in one unearned run. The Yankees' earned run average was 2.89. The Braves had a 3.48 ERA.

All four of the Braves' wins were complete games, with Warren Spahn turning in a ten-inning job in Game Four. The southpaw had a 1–1 record and a 4.78 earned run average in two games covering 15.1 innings. Don McMahon threw five strong innings in three relief stints, allowing three hits and no runs, while striking out five. Ernie Johnson was also outstanding out of the bullpen. He, too, appeared in three games. He gave up two hits and one run, with an ERA of 1.29 and eight strikeouts in seven innings.

Burdette was interviewed by hordes of newspaper, radio, and television reporters following his brilliant World Series performance. He was asked more than once if his tremendous success against the Yankees was the result of his having a special incentive or a grudge since they once had him and let him go. Burdette's answer to all that was about as good as his pitching: "I should say not. The Yankees gave me the best break in my life when they shipped me to the Braves." Asked once more if he threw a spitball, Burdette feigned extreme seriousness and responded, "I am not a cheating pitcher." But he added, "Let them keep thinking I throw a spitter. Things have reached a point where it's the best pitch I have, even though I don't throw it."[6]

New York columnist Red Smith included the following in his report after the Braves' seventh-game win: "It was the third victory for Chief Rubber Arm — to enemy batters he is known as Chief Slobber on Stitches — and

Lew Burdette kept hitters guessing with his fidgety mannerisms, his strategic mix of pitches, and his way of making them think he might be throwing a spitball. The right-hander was the 1957 World Series hero with three complete-game victories.

his second successive shutout. After the third inning of the second game, which Burdette won, 4 to 2, the Yankees never made a run against him. Alternately embraced and abused by his ever-loving playmates, he departed with an unfinished string of twenty-four consecutive scoreless innings.

"It is necessary to go back more than a half century, to the World Series of 1905 and the princely Christy Mathewson, to find a record of better pitching under pressure. That year Matty pitched three shutouts, twenty-seven scoreless innings in a row. Last man to start and win three games in a World Series was Cleveland's Stan Coveleski against the Brooklyn Robins of 1920, though the Cardinals' Harry Brecheen beat the 1946 Red Sox three times, once in relief."[7]

Here is what Casey Stengel said about the man who had done so much to take away the Yankees' world title: "He did a big job. He was the big man in the Series. He took care of us all the way. He stopped all of our hitters. He held us to two runs in three games, and he was just as good in the third game as he was in the second and as he was in the first. He was better than any pitcher I've seen in a long time. He gave us a few scoring chances. He made us hit the ball on the ground in nearly every tight spot. He was great.

"I have to say the other team outplayed us in the Series," Stengel continued, "even though our pitching, especially by Whitey Ford, was very good. In the main, though, I must credit their pitcher (Burdette). He beat us three times."[8]

After his clubhouse speeches, the Old Perfessor paid a visit to the joyous Braves' locker room, where he shook hands with Braves owner Lou Perini and manager Fred Haney, congratulating them and saying, "You fellers did splendid."[9]

The 1957 World Series set a seven-game attendance record of 394,712, surpassing the 389,763 total of the 1947 Yankees-Dodgers Fall Classic. The total receipts (not counting radio and television revenue) were $2,475,978, another record. Thirty members of the Braves were voted a full share of $8,924.36. The Yankees' individual share cut was $5,606.06. Red Schoendienst and Billy Bruton were voted full shares. Bob Hazle and Nippy Jones were voted three-quarter shares of $6,693.27 apiece. John DeMerit, who played in thirty-three games, received a one-third share of $2,974.78. Hawk Taylor, like DeMerit, a bonus baby, received $1,000 after playing in just seven games.

On the day the World Series concluded, the Braves reported that surgery on Bruton's right knee was successful. The operation included removal of cartilage and the repair of two torn ligaments. Bruton had injured his knee exactly three months earlier.

11

Almost a Dynasty

The nucleus of the 1957 Milwaukee Braves returned the next season, and although the offense was not quite as imposing, the pitching was even better. The end result was the same — or, almost the same — as the Braves again won the National League pennant and again reached the seventh game of the World Series against the mighty Yankees. There, Milwaukee came up short, as New York took the decisive game and the World Championship.

Over the last four years of the decade, the Braves were almost a dynasty. They finished a game out of first place in the 1956 pennant race, won everything in '57, narrowly missed a second straight World Series title in 1958, and tied for first place in the National League standings in '59. They were four outs from winning back-to-back World Championships and one win from playing in three World Series in a row.

A club with young sluggers like Aaron and Mathews, and with pitchers like Spahn and Burdette, can make that kind of mark on a league when those players stay healthy. And the Braves' stars stayed healthy.

Twenty-two members of Milwaukee's 1957 champions were back with the Braves in '58. Gone were pitchers Taylor Phillips and Dave Jolly, but their replacements, Joey Jay and Carlton Willey, proved to be more talented and more productive. Also missing was Nippy Jones, a third-string first baseman.

The 1958 Braves did not hit as many home runs or score as many runs as the previous year. They only got five wins from Bob Buhl. Red Schoendienst showed signs of slowing down. Bob Hazle was no longer a hurricane. Billy Bruton did not return to center field as early as the club had hoped.

Still, Milwaukee won the National League pennant by the same eight-game margin as the year before, winning ninety-two games — just three fewer than 1957.

During the winter, the Braves made two deals, one of which proved instrumental in the club repeating as NL champion. They sold pitcher Dave Jolly, who was used mostly in mop-up situations, to the San Francisco Giants in October. Then, in December, they traded left-handed pitcher Taylor Phillips and minor league catcher Sammy Taylor to the Chicago Cubs for pitcher Bob Rush and outfielder Eddie Haas.

Rush, a thirty-two-year-old right-hander, had won 110 games in ten seasons with the Cubs. He was in the Milwaukee starting rotation much of the 1958 season, winning ten games, losing six, and posting a 3.42 earned run average.

The Braves' pitching was absolutely brilliant, just as it was in 1957, as it led the league with a 3.21 earned run average, with sixteen shutouts, in fewest runs allowed with 541, and in complete games for the fourth year in a row. The Milwaukee staff recorded an amazing seventy-two route jobs, Warren Spahn leading the majors with twenty-three and Lew Burdette placing third in the NL with nineteen, two less than the Phillies' Robin Roberts.

Buhl, an eighteen-game winner the two previous seasons, suffered arm problems in 1958 and pitched in only eleven games, going 5–2 over seventy-three innings. Gene Conley, like Buhl, had arm troubles that limited him to seventy-two innings pitched, and he failed to register a win in six decisions. Veteran reliever Ernie Johnson also was hurting, and after being a key man out of the bullpen the year before, he appeared in just fifteen games.

As a result, a shot of youth was infused into the Braves' staff, and a pair of right-handers picked up a lot of the slack. Carlton Willey, twenty-seven, won nine games, threw nine complete games, had a 2.70 ERA, and led the National League with four shutouts. Joey Jay, twenty-two, had seven wins, six complete games, a 2.14 ERA, and three shutouts. Juan Pizarro, a second-year lefty, won six games, had a 2.70 ERA, and threw seven complete games. Seven Milwaukee pitchers started at least ten games.

Spahn led the league with twenty-two wins, setting a major league record for left-handers with his ninth twenty-victory season. He also led NL pitchers by working 290 innings and shared the best winning percentage of .667 with teammate Lew Burdette. The fidgety right-hander became a twenty-game winner for the first time, had the fewest walks per nine innings with 1.63, and pitched three shutouts. His 2.91 earned run average was third lowest in the league, while Spahn's 3.07 was fourth (among pitchers who worked enough innings to qualify).

After leading the league in runs scored and home runs in 1957, the Braves

fell to fourth in both categories. Eddie Mathews led the team in home runs with thirty-one. Hank Aaron belted thirty homers, while driving in ninety-five runs and batting .326. Wes Covington enjoyed a big season, hitting .330 with twenty-four roundtrippers and seventy-four RBI. Joe Adcock added nineteen home runs and Del Crandall had eighteen.

Bruton rejoined the Braves, but missed a big chunk early, and played in 100 games. Schoendienst went through some nagging injuries and played in 106 games. Hazle started slowly and never got going. He had a .179 batting average with no extra-base hits when Milwaukee sold him to the Detroit Tigers on May 24. Carl Sawatski had one hit in ten at-bats before the Braves traded him to Philadelphia on June 13.

Felix Mantilla again was a valuable and versatile utility man. An infielder by trade, he played forty-three games in the outfield and saw action in twenty-eight others at second base, shortstop, or third base. He smacked seven home runs and had fifty hits in 226 at-bats. Mel Roach, filling in for Schoendienst, made just one error in twenty-seven games at second base, while batting .306 with three homers in 136 trips to the plate. Harry Hanebrink added some pop from the left-handed side of the plate with four home runs in 133 at-bats, while playing the outfield and a little third base.

Spahn, who was used as a pinch-hitter three times, helped the offense by batting a career-high .333 at the age of thirty-seven. He cracked two homers and drove in seven runs. Burdette had fifteen RBI and belted three home runs, while hitting .242. Spahn had thirty-six base hits and Burdette had twenty-four.

Fred Haney was second-guessed a bit for platooning Adcock with Frank Torre at first base. Only thirty years old, the right-handed hitting Adcock had averaged twenty-five home runs over three seasons before missing much of 1957 with a broken ankle. He had clouted thirty-eight homers and driven in 103 runs in 1956. Torre had few equals defensively, but he was never going to be a big threat to hit the long ball. Adcock ended up playing twenty-two games in the outfield and seventy-one at first base, batting .275 with nineteen home runs and fifty-four RBI in 320 at-bats. Torre made his manager look good by hitting .309 and knocking in fifty-five runs, but produced just six homers in 372 trips to the plate. Although his overall numbers were solid, Torre's power shortage provided fuel for Haney's critics.

In addition to the injuries, Milwaukee overcame sub-par seasons from

Opposite: **Juan Pizarro showed loads of promise as a rookie in 1957. The left-hander started ten games in both of Milwaukee's pennant-winning seasons, but his best years came after he left the Braves. (©Brace Photo. Used by permission.)**

Mathews, who batted .251 and drove in seventy-seven runs, and Logan, who hit .226. Andy Pafko, thirty-seven, batted .238 with three home runs in 164 at-bats.

The Braves played fine defense, committing 119 errors and compiling a .980 fielding percentage, both figures second in the league. Aaron, Mathews, Spahn, Burdette, Crandall, and Logan all made the National League All-Star team.

The Giants, who were settling into their new home on the West Coast as were the Dodgers, surprised everyone with a 9–5 April that left them a half-game in front of Milwaukee and Chicago. At the end of May, the Braves led San Francisco by percentage points, but the teams were in a virtual tie for first place in the National League, four games ahead of a bigger surprise, the Pittsburgh Pirates.

The Braves won a wild one in early June at San Francisco's Seals Stadium. Leading the Giants by percentage points entering the game, Milwaukee trailed, 7–1, after three innings. The Braves scored a run in the seventh inning, another in the eighth, then rallied to tie the score when Wes Covington blasted a three-run homer in the ninth off left-hander Pete Burnside. Milwaukee appeared on the way to victory by getting two runs in the tenth inning, but San Francisco answered with two runs in the bottom half. In the tenth, Spahn pinch hit and delivered an RBI single that proved to be the game-winner. The win put the Braves a full game ahead of the Giants.

The Braves played .500 baseball (13–13) in June, but finished the month with a two-game lead over St. Louis. San Francisco, after a 10–17 month, fell three and a half games back. The Giants went 17–11 in July and moved within a half-game of Milwaukee, but the Braves pulled away in August and remained comfortably in front of the National League pack the rest of the way.

Milwaukee strung together six straight wins starting July 30 and had a seven-game winning streak later in August. The Braves won twenty-three of thirty-four games in the month and began September leading the second-place Pirates by seven and one-half games and the third-place Giants by nine. Burdette and Spahn pitched pennant-deciding wins for the Braves, both triumphs coming at Cincinnati's Crosley Field. For the second straight year, Milwaukee owned the Redlegs, beating them seventeen of twenty-two meetings.

Burdette's six-hitter in a rain-shortened game clinched a tie for first place as the Braves downed the Redlegs, 5–1. Billy Bruton's two-run double capped a three-run sixth inning for Milwaukee. The game was stopped in the seventh following constant rain that had fallen since a half an hour before the first pitch. The win was Burdette's nineteenth, matching his career high from 1956. The next day, on September 21, the Braves made it back-to-back NL pennants by nipping Cincinnati, 6–5.

Spahn notched his twenty-first win with outstanding relief help from Don McMahon, who pitched two and two-thirds shutout innings. For the second time in as many years, Hank Aaron swung the big bat in the clincher. He doubled in a pair of runs and slugged a two-run homer. Red Schoendienst had three hits and an RBI, while Spahn helped his own cause with a single, a double, and a run scored.

The Braves became the first team other than the Brooklyn Dodgers to win two straight National League pennants since the St. Louis Cardinals took three in a row in 1942, '43, and '44.

Milwaukee again met the New York Yankees in the World Series after both teams finished with a record of 92–62. The Braves and Lew Burdette picked up where they left off in 1957.

Warren Spahn outlasted Whitey Ford in the opening game, which was played in County Stadium. Moose Skowron's fourth-inning home run put the Yankees in front, but the Braves came right back to score two runs. Hank Aaron walked, and with two outs, Del Crandall, Andy Pafko, and Spahn singled, Pafko and Spahn each getting an RBI.

Spahn issued a one-out walk to Ford in the fifth, and Hank Bauer bashed a two-run homer to left field. It was just a preview of the fireworks show the New York right fielder would stage throughout the Series. Bauer's home run gave the Yanks a 3–2 lead, and Ford kept it that way by pitching three shutout innings after the blast. In the eighth, Eddie Mathews walked, went to third on a double by Aaron, and scored the tying run on a long sacrifice fly to center by Wes Covington.

Meanwhile, Spahn seemed to get better as the game grew longer. He pitched five straight shutout innings, bringing Milwaukee to bat in the bottom of the tenth. Joe Adcock singled off fireballer Ryne Duren with one out, and Covington skied to Elston Howard in left for out number two. Crandall singled Adcock to second. Billy Bruton, who had pinch hit for Pafko and stayed in the game to play center field, ripped a single to right-center. Bruton drove in Adcock with the winning run, giving Spahn and the Braves a 4–3 victory.

The Yankees began Game Two by scoring their first run off Burdette in twenty-five innings. It was an unearned run, but things could have been much worse as New York had the Braves' right-hander on the ropes in the opening inning. Bauer singled, Gil McDougald reached on Mathews' throwing error, and Mickey Mantle walked to load the bases with nobody out. Howard forced

Mantle at second and got an RBI before Berra bounced into the first of two Milwaukee double plays, Schoendienst to Logan to Frank Torre.

Bullet Bob Turley was on the mound for the Yankees, and he retired just one batter, while getting raked for four runs on three hits and a walk. The Braves exploded for seven runs in the biggest first inning in World Series history. Bruton slammed a leadoff home run. Schoendienst doubled and scored on Covington's single, with a walk to Aaron sandwiched in between. Duke Maas relieved Turley and got Torre to fly out to right. Crandall drew a walk to load the bases, and Logan came through with a two-out, two-run single. Burdette smashed a three-run homer to left, giving Milwaukee a 7–1 lead. Covington knocked in another run and Mathews also plated a pair, with Pafko, Torre, and Crandall all driving in a run apiece. Bruton and Covington finished with three hits each, Schoendienst, Mathews, and Aaron all adding two as the Braves pounded out fifteen hits. Mantle clouted two home runs and Bauer socked his second in as many games. The final was 13–5, Braves, as Burdette improved his Series record to 4–0. More importantly, Milwaukee had won the first two games.

Back home in Yankee Stadium, New York rode the right arm of Don Larsen and Bauer's booming bat to a 4–0 win. Larsen scattered six hits and struck out eight over seven innings, with Duren throwing two hitless innings. Bauer had three hits in four at-bats and drove in all four Yankee runs. Milwaukee starter Bob Rush, locked in a scoreless duel with Larsen, walked Norm Siebern and McDougald in the fifth inning. Bauer singled them both home, then walloped a two-run homer following a walk to pinch-hitter Enos Slaughter in the seventh. Bauer had three home runs in three Series games, while extending his Fall Classic hitting streak to seventeen games.

Game One pitchers Spahn and Ford were on the mound again in Game Four. Spahn pitched a masterpiece as the Braves won, 3–0. The thirty-seven-year-old southpaw threw a two-hitter, striking out seven and walking two. Spahn also singled in a run. Crandall and Aaron had two hits each. Five of Milwaukee's nine hits were for extra bases, with Aaron, Pafko, Mathews, and Johnny Logan getting doubles, and Schoendienst a triple. Bauer's seventeen-game Series hitting streak came to an end. The Braves were up, three games to one, and on the brink of winning two straight World Championships.

But it was not to be. Turley dominated the rest of the Series, winning two games and saving the other as the Yankees wiped out their 3–1 deficit to dethrone Milwaukee. Burdette was pounded for six runs, all earned, in five and a third innings in Game Five. Gil McDougald clouted a solo home run in the third and lined a two-run double in New York's six-run sixth, and the Yanks won, 7–0. Turley pitched a five-hitter and struck out ten.

Spahn had a chance to be a three-game winner as his buddy, Burdette, had done the year before. He hooked up with Ford in Game Six at County Stadium, but the Yankee lefty lasted just one and a third innings. Bauer hit a two-out home run, his fourth of the Series, in the top of the first. The Braves tied it on Schoendienst's single, a sacrifice bunt by Logan, and Aaron's two-out RBI base hit. Milwaukee grabbed a 2–1 lead in the second, knocking out Ford in the process, with three singles. The third was a shot to right-center by Spahn that plated Covington. Ford was gone after walking Schoendienst to load the bases with one out. Art Ditmar came in to pitch, facing the prospect of seeing the Braves break the game wide open. Logan lifted a fly ball to left, Andy Pafko tagging in an attempt to score. But Elston Howard fired a strike to Yogi Berra for a double play that stopped the uprising and kept the Milwaukee lead at 2–1.

The Yankees tied the score in the sixth on singles by Mantle and Howard and a sacrifice fly by Berra. It remained 2–2 until the top of the tenth inning, when McDougald led off with his second Series home run. Spahn retired Bauer and Mantle, but Howard and Berra singled, and the great left-hander was out of gas. McMahon came in from the bullpen and allowed a run-scoring single by Skowron before fanning Ryne Duren.

The insurance run proved big when Aaron drove in Logan with a two-out single and went to third on Adcock's base hit. Duren had struck out eight in four and two-thirds innings, but Casey Stengel had seen enough of the hard-throwing right-hander with the thick glasses. In came Turley, who had just one day of rest after pitching a complete game. Frank Torre pinch-hit for Del Crandall and hit the ball right on the nose, but it was right at second baseman McDougald. Turley had a save, the Yankees had a 4–3 win, and the Series was going to the seventh game.

Larsen and Burdette squared off in Game Seven as they had in 1957. Just like the previous year, Larsen was finished after two and one-third innings, mainly because of wildness. The Braves scored a run on one hit and three walks in the first inning, leaving the bases loaded when Larsen struck out Crandall. New York scored twice in the second with help from first baseman Torre, who committed a pair of errors on tosses to Burdette covering first. Schoendienst and Billy Bruton rapped one-out singles in bottom half of the inning, and Stengel again waved Turley in from the bullpen. He walked Torre to load the bases, but worked out of the major jam without a run scoring. Milwaukee made it 2–2 in the sixth when Crandall clouted a solo home run.

Burdette pitched five shutout innings, but his magic evaporated in the eighth as the Yankees erupted for four runs. And it all started with two outs. Burdette got McDougald on a ground ball and fanned Mantle before Berra doubled into the right-field corner and scored on a single by Howard. Andy Carey also singled, and Skowron deflated the Braves by slamming a three-run homer.

Turley polished off Milwaukee, completing a two-hit relief job over six and two-thirds innings that earned him his second victory as well as the Series MVP award. The 6–2 triumph brought the Yankees their eighteenth World Series championship.

The Braves were shell-shocked. They had been within a single win of winning a second straight world title and had Burdette and Spahn on the mound, with three tries between them, to nail it down. Bruton made up for missing the 1957 Series, leading the Braves with a .412 batting average on seven hits in seventeen at-bats. Aaron hit .333, but did not manage a home run and drove in just two runs. Mathews set a World Series record by striking out eleven times, while batting .160. The Braves also established a record by whiffing fifty-six times. Schoendienst hit .300 and Spahn batted .333 with three RBI. The thirty-seven-year-old hurler drove in one more run than Aaron despite batting only twelve times. Adcock batted .304, but went to the plate only thirteen times. Torre hit .176 and Logan batted .120.

It was a huge disappointment for the Braves, who had been confident of repeating as World Champs. The fact that they came so close, that they had the Yankees in a 3–1 hole, made defeat more painful, harder to take.

Columnist Red Smith felt the Braves should have won the 1958 World Series and wrote, "New York won because Milwaukee wouldn't. The Braves had their second title wrapped up as far back as last Sunday night, but they tried to carry the bundle by the string. By mechanical bungling and sinful squandering of opportunities, they betrayed the admirable Lew Burdette today as they had betrayed the blameless Warren Spahn yesterday."[1]

The key players returned to Milwaukee in 1959, and the famous foursome of Aaron, Mathews, Spahn, and Burdette again turned out impressive numbers.

Hank Aaron had a monster season. He led the National League with 223 hits and in batting with a .355 average. He was also first in extra-base hits with ninety-two and with 400 total bases. Aaron blasted thirty-nine home runs, drove in 123 runs, and scored 116.

Mathews also enjoyed a tremendous season. He crushed forty-six home runs to lead the major leagues, while hitting .306 with 114 runs batted in and 118 runs scored. Mathews was second with 352 total bases and finished second in voting for the Most Valuable Player Award as the Cubs' Ernie Banks won it for the second straight year.

Joe Adcock belted twenty-five home runs and drove in seventy-six runs.

Del Crandall hit twenty-one homers and had seventy-two RBI. Johnny Logan batted .291 with thirteen homers and fifty RBI.

Spahn and Burdette both had 21–15 records, with the left-hander pitching twenty-one complete games and the right-hander twenty. Milwaukee again led the league, this time with sixty-nine complete games. The Big Three shared the National League lead in shutouts. Spahn and Burdette threw four as did Bob Buhl, who bounced back from arm trouble to go 15–9 with a 2.86 earned run average.

Mathews, Spahn, Aaron, Crandall, Logan, and Don McMahon were selected to the National League All-Star Team.

Red Schoendienst, though he had missed nearly a third of the 1958 season, was still considered a leader. So, the news that he had tuberculosis was devastating, as was the Redhead's loss, both in the clubhouse and on the field. The Braves tried eight different players at second base and never found anything close to a suitable replacement. Schoendienst had part of a lung removed, and although he returned to the Braves in 1960, he was never a full-time player again.

The Braves were in third place, two and a half games behind the San Francisco Giants, with the Los Angeles Dodgers in second, on September 1. On September 26, Spahn pitched a five-hitter in a 3–2 victory over Philadelphia. It was the 267th win of his career, moving him past Eppa Rixey to give him the most wins of any left-hander in major league history.

When the Dodgers swept a three-game series from the Giants with a week left in the season, Milwaukee and Los Angeles shared first place. The final weekend saw the Braves win two out of three at home from the Phillies, who were in last place. The Dodgers also took two of three from the Cubs in Chicago.

Milwaukee and Los Angeles both finished with 86–68 records, necessitating a best-of-three playoff for the National League pennant and a trip to the World Series. It marked the third time there was a playoff for the NL pennant, and the Dodgers were in all three. They lost to the St. Louis Cardinals in 1946 and to the New York Giants in 1951.

Playing the opener at home in front of a disappointing crowd of 18,297, the Braves owned a 2–1 lead after two innings, with Carlton Willey on the mound. The rookie right-hander pitched admirably, but was tagged with the loss when L.A. catcher Johnny Roseboro socked a home run in the sixth inning. Both Milwaukee runs came in the second. Billy Bruton singled in the first run, the other scoring on a bases-loaded ground out. Larry Sherry relieved Dodger starter Danny McDevitt in the inning and pitched brilliantly. Sherry allowed four hits in seven and two-thirds shutout innings to get the win.

An Indian Summer

Lew Burdette was given the task of keeping the Braves' season alive as he opposed Don Drysdale in the second playoff game, which was played in Los Angeles Memorial Coliseum. Frank Torre's two-run single gave Milwaukee a quick lead in the first inning. The Dodgers answered with a run, and the Braves got an unearned run in the second. In the sixth, Mathews belted a hooking line drive that stayed inside the foul pole for his forty-sixth home run. When Crandall tripled and came home on Mantilla's sacrifice fly in the eighth, it was looking like a deciding third playoff game would be needed.

Burdette carried a 5–2 lead into the bottom of the ninth inning. He could not retire a batter and left after surrendering singles to Wally Moon, Duke Snider, and Gil Hodges. McMahon came in with the bases loaded and no outs and gave up a two-run single to Norm Larker. Spahn was brought in to face the left-handed hitting Roseboro, but Carl Furillo batted instead and hit a fly to right that scored Hodges with the tying run. Joey Jay prevented further damage and went on to pitch two and one-third scoreless innings. Stan Williams was untouchable in three innings of relief for Los Angeles. He became the winning pitcher when the Dodgers scored a run in the twelfth inning off of Bob Rush.

With runners on first and second and no outs, Furillo smashed a hard grounder up the middle. Mantilla, who had moved from second base to shortstop when Johnny Logan was injured in the seventh inning, made a sparkling pickup. Mantilla's throw to first was too late. It was also wide of first, and when the ball got past Torre, Hodges scored with the pennant-winning run.

The loss was a bitter one for the Braves, who led by three runs and needed only three outs to force a third game. And they had a twenty-one game winner trying to protect that lead.

Things began to unravel after that. Five days after Milwaukee was eliminated, Fred Haney resigned as manager. The Braves offered him a one-year contract to return for the 1960 season, but Haney said he wanted to spend more time with his wife and family. He also insisted that there was no pressure to quit, saying the Braves' front office had given him strong support.[2]

Nearly three weeks after Haney's resignation, Milwaukee hired Dodgers coach Charlie Dressen as manager. They gave him a two-year contract. Dressen announced days later that changes would be made in the Braves' roster.[3] Things would never be the same.

Over the next four years, the Braves slid farther and farther down in the standings. In 1960, they finished in second place, seven games behind Pittsburgh. They fell into fourth place, ten games back of Cincinnati, in 1961. They dropped to fifth, fifteen and a half games behind San Francisco, in 1962. In 1963, they finished in sixth place, fifteen games back of Los Angeles.

In four seasons with Fred Haney as their manager, the Braves won 365 games, captured two National League pennants, and made their only trips to the World Series during the club's thirteen-year stay in Milwaukee.

The 1957 Braves made their mark by becoming the first Milwaukee team to win a pennant. This was a team, however, filled with the promise of more championships. And, following their World Series triumph over the Yankees, the Braves appeared to have the makings to be a National League powerhouse. They had confidence, young stars, proven veterans, and the start of an autumn winning tradition.

That it never panned out in terms of repeat World Series titles was disappointing to Milwaukee fans. But they will always have 1957, a year to relive and remember, the year their Braves won it all.

12

Breaking Up
the Old Gang

The 1957 World Champion Milwaukee Braves were, for the most part, a home-grown team that was built from within, by signing prospects and moving them up through the farm system. Fifteen of the twenty-five players on the Milwaukee World Series roster were originally signed by scouts from the organization. Most were signed when the team was in Boston.

By 1960, ten members of the World Series champs were no longer with the Braves. There were only seven players from the 1957 team on the 1962 roster. Hank Aaron, Eddie Mathews, and Warren Spahn were the only ones remaining in 1964. Two years later, when the franchise moved to Atlanta, Aaron and Mathews were the only holdovers from the team that won it all nine years earlier.

Two members of the '57 Braves would die before their fiftieth birthday, one before he turned forty. At the time of this printing, manager Fred Haney and thirteen players from the championship team were deceased. It is sadly ironic that Bob Buhl and Eddie Mathews, who roomed together more than nine years with the Braves, died within two days of each other.

It was hard to believe when the Braves pulled up roots and moved to Atlanta following the 1965 season. The club had a winning record each of its thirteen seasons in Milwaukee, yet the fans—as much as they loved their Braves—seemed to lose interest, and attendance had fallen off badly. The Braves led the National League standings as late as August 20, 1965, but went into a tailspin and never recovered, finishing fifth with an 86–76 record.

In the summer of 1964, the Braves' owners had asked the National League for permission to move, and the request was granted, but for the 1966 season and not 1965 because the league required the club to honor the final year of its County Stadium lease. Knowing that the Braves were on their way out of town, very few fans went through the turnstiles. After selling nearly 4,500 season tickets in 1964, the Braves had sold just thirty-six when the 1965 season opened. The Braves finished last in attendance in 1965 with a home figure of 555,584, an average of less than 7,000 paying customers per game.

The last time the Milwaukee Braves drew a million fans at home was in 1961, with 1964 the only season in the last four that County Stadium crowds averaged more than 10,000. It was a pathetic ending to such a beautiful romance, but the truth is that baseball and life are that way. Things change. Baseball players grow old and die. Sometimes, so do baseball teams.

But, no matter what, 1957 will always live in the hearts and memories of the people of Milwaukee, the ones who are baseball fans and the ones who are not, the ones who remember when the Braves were in town and the ones who do not. A championship team does that — it even creates old memories for those who were not around to watch the memories being made.

Major League Baseball Commissioner Bud Selig has never made a secret of his love for the Milwaukee Braves, particularly the 1957 edition. After following the Milwaukee Brewers minor league team (American Association, 1902–1952), he became a Braves fan when the team moved to Milwaukee. He later became the Milwaukee Braves' largest public stockholder, eventually selling his shares when the franchise moved to Atlanta. Following are Selig's thoughts about the '57 Braves:

"I saw many games and lived with every pitch and every out through the World Series," said Selig.

"I had a great feeling about this team when it arrived in Milwaukee. It was a thrill. Milwaukee loved the Braves and welcomed them with open arms like no baseball team had been received before. It was an incredible story.

"I have many memories of the 1957 Braves, none more important than the game that Hank Aaron hit the home run off of Billy Muffett in the eleventh inning to win the National League pennant. It was a great thrill and one that I'll never forget.

"Of course, Eddie Mathews' stop on Bill Skowron's ground ball over third to win the 1957 World Series is another indelible memory. The Braves' 1957 world championship is one of my favorite pieces of baseball history.

"Hank Aaron remains a great friend of mine to this day, certainly I believe the greatest player of our generation. Aaron had magnificent wrists and the ability to hit as well as any human being I have ever seen. He was also an outstanding right fielder with a great arm and a terrific base runner.

"Eddie Mathews was a remarkable player who was not only a great power hitter, but made himself into a great fielder. He was one of the toughest players on the field that I have ever seen.

"Warren Spahn, of course, arguably is the greatest left-handed pitcher of all time. He actually got better as he got older because he really made himself into a great pitcher in every way. Spahn was made special because he worked at his art. He was a very cerebral pitcher and, as I said, made himself into the greatest left-handed pitcher of all time.

"Lew Burdette was a tremendous competitor who knew how to win. Bob Buhl was a tough ex-paratrooper who knew how to pitch and, quite frankly, made himself into an outstanding pitcher. I had great admiration and affection for Bob Buhl.

"Del Crandall was a great catcher, mechanically perfect and extremely smart. Red Schoendienst was the glue that held the 1957 — and 1958 — Braves together after he came on June 15. He was not only a great player, but was an extraordinary presence in the clubhouse. Johnny Logan was a fine shortstop and a terrific clutch hitter with great instincts.

"1957 was an amazing year and one that will always rank as my greatest thrill in baseball."[1]

From the team that thrilled Selig and thousands of others across the country, four players are now in the Hall of Fame in Cooperstown. These, of course, are Aaron, Mathews, and Spahn, who were also the inauguural class of inductees for the Braves Hall of Fame, and Red Schoendienst. The Braves inducted Lew Burdette and Ernie Johnson in 2001, and Del Crandall entered in 2003.

Hank Aaron hit home run number 755 on July 20, 1976. It was his tenth homer of the season and his twenty-second over his last two years in the majors, when he batted .229 and .234 while playing for the Milwaukee Brewers. Just three years earlier, Aaron had hit .301 and belted forty home runs for the Atlanta Braves in what was his last big season. Of course, he still had enough in his tank to pass the Babe and add forty more homers for good measure. Aaron was forty-two years old when he retired from baseball. On September 7, 1982, a bronze statue of Aaron was dedicated. Located outside Turner Field, it depicts Hammerin' Hank hitting his 715th home run. In 1999, to commemorate the twenty-fifth anniversary of that record-setting homer, Major League Baseball began presenting the Hank Aaron Award to the best overall hitter in each league. There is also a statue of him at the entrance to Miller Park where the Milwaukee Brewers play. After his retirement as an active player in 1976, Hank Aaron returned to the Braves in the front office capacity of Vice President of Player Development. He is currently the Braves' Senior Vice President.[2]

Joe Adcock played his last three seasons with the Angels (Los Angeles and California) of the American League, retiring after batting .273 with eighteen home runs in 1966. The next year, he managed the Cleveland Indians, who finished in eighth place in the ten-team AL with a 75–87 record. Adcock died May 3, 1999 at his home in Coushatta, Louisiana, after suffering from Alzheimer's disease. He was seventy-one.[3]

After missing almost half of the 1957 season and all of the World Series, Billy Bruton returned in 1958 to play 100 games and then have an outstanding World Series. He batted .412 and hit a home run in the seven-game loss to the Yankees. His best all-around season was 1960, when he hit .286, scored 112 runs, had twenty-seven doubles, thirteen triples, twelve home runs, and stole twenty-two bases. Bruton was traded during the winter of 1960 to Detroit, and his first two years with the Tigers were outstanding. He hit thirty-three home runs, scored 189 runs, and drove in 137 runs in the 1961 and '62 seasons combined. He was released by Detroit after the 1964 season. In twelve years in the majors, he had a .273 batting average, with 102 triples, ninety-four homers, and 207 stolen bases. He died of a heart attack on December 5, 1995, in Marshalltown, Delaware, at the age of seventy.[4]

Bob Buhl won at least eleven games eleven times, totaling 166 victories in his fifteen-year career. He was an eighteen-game winner twice for the Braves, and he led the National League with four shutouts in 1959. Milwaukee fans will remember him for carrying the Braves during a period of the 1957 season when Warren Spahn was struggling and Lew Burdette was hurt. Buhl had a .720 winning percentage, fourteen complete games, and a 2.74 earned run average — all career bests — in 1957. His lifetime figures included twenty shutouts and a 3.66 ERA. He died at the age of seventy-two in Titusville, Florida, on February 16, 2001, two days after the death of Eddie Mathews, his long-time roommate with the Braves.[5]

Lew Burdette had a career earned run average of 3.66 while pitching over 3,067 innings and throwing thirty-three shutouts. He had 31 saves to go with 203 wins in 18 years in the majors, winning at least ten games 11 times, including 10 straight years from 1953 to 1962. He retired in 1967 at the age of 40, then scouted and coached for the Atlanta Braves. Burdette was a 20-game winner twice, with four World Series wins. He will always be synonymous with the 1957 Fall Classic when he pitched three complete-game victories, two of which were shutouts.[6] He died February 6, 2007, in Winter Garden, Florida, after a long battle with lung cancer.

Gene Conley spent six years with the Braves, two with the Philadelphia Phillies, and three with the Boston Red Sox. He had ninety-one career wins, forty-two with the Braves, twenty with the Phillies, and twenty-nine with the Red Sox. His lifetime earned run average was 3.82. A pretty fair hitter, he had five home runs and forty-five RBI with a .192 batting average in 548 at-bats. Conley will best be remembered by Braves fans for his outstanding stretch during the 1957 pennant drive when he won five of six starts, with all five wins coming on complete games. After experiencing arm problems that limited him to 40.2 innings, he retired following the 1963 season at the age of thirty-two.[7]

A huge contributor during the pennant drive of the 1957 campaign, Wes Covington followed up with his best season to help Milwaukee return to the World Series. He batted .330, bashed twenty-four home runs, and knocked in seventy-four runs — all career highs — in 1958. The Chicago White Sox picked him off the waiver list in May of 1961, and he also played with the Kansas City Athletics and Philadelphia Phillies before that season ended. Covington spent four years with the Phillies, putting together a fine 1963 season in which he hit seventeen home runs and batted .303 with sixty-four RBI. His final season was 1966, when he played for the Chicago Cubs and Los Angeles Dodgers, serving mostly as a pinch-hitter. His eleven-year career included 131 home runs, 499 RBI, and a .279 batting average.[8]

Del Crandall spent thirteen of his sixteen major league seasons with the Braves. The best was 1960, when he batted .294, while hitting nineteen home runs and driving in seventy-seven runs. He belted twenty-six homers in 1955 and had twenty-one in '54. Following the 1963 season, he was traded to the San Francisco Giants. He spent one year with the Giants, one with the Pittsburgh Pirates, and one with the Cleveland Indians, concluding his career in 1966. His lifetime numbers included a .254 batting average and 179 home runs. Although he was a clutch hitter with power, Crandall's defensive abilities and his leadership were his biggest assets. He returned to Milwaukee to manage the Brewers from 1972–75 and was the Seattle Mariners' skipper in 1983 and '84. His managerial record was 364–469. He served in the Los Angeles Dodgers' organization as a catching instructor for several years.[9]

Bob Hazle filled a huge void for the Braves, especially offensively, following their loss of Billy Bruton to injury in 1957. The next year, Hazle was batting .179 with no extra-base hits when Milwaukee sold him to Detroit in May. He batted .241 and hit two home runs for the Tigers. He was back in the minor leagues in 1959, playing for Charleston of the South Atlantic League, and then retired. Although he had only 261 major league at-bats, he finished with a fine .310 lifetime batting average and nine homers. He died in 1992 in Columbia, South Carolina. He was sixty-one.[10]

Aaron, Spahn, Mathews, and Burdette are the names most frequently associated with the Braves' success. But if a Mr. Braves Baseball were to be selected, it would have to be Ernie Johnson. He was a big part of the Braves franchise for over six decades, either on the field or in the broadcast booth. He served three years in the United States Marines. He spent eight years with the Braves, finishing out his career with the Baltimore Orioles in 1959. He pitched in 273 games, all but nineteen in relief, compiling a 40–23 record with nineteen saves, 119 games finished, and a 3.77 lifetime earned run average. For many years, there probably was not a better ambassador for the Atlanta Braves than Johnson. As a broadcaster for their radio and television games from 1962–99, he was the voice of optimism and experience. He worked on a part-time basis into the twenty-first century.[11]

Dave Jolly pitched in twenty-three games and had a 1–1 record with one save for the 1957 pennant-winners in what was his last year in baseball. Jolly's best season was 1954, when he posted an 11–6 record and had ten saves in forty-seven games, with a 2.43 earned run average, all but one of his appearances coming out of the bullpen. He pitched 111.1 innings that year and also enjoyed a big season at the plate, batting .290 and hitting a home run. In a career spanning five years, all spent with the Braves, Jolly had a lifetime 16–14 record, with nineteen saves and a 3.77 ERA. He died May 27, 1963, in his home state of North Carolina after undergoing surgery for a brain tumor. He was thirty-eight years old.[12]

Nippy Jones hit a couple of big home runs in his part-time role during the 1957 season, but the Shoe Polish Incident provided his biggest major league moment. It was also his last at-bat in the majors. His best season was 1948 when he smacked ten home runs, drove in eighty-one runs, and batted .254 for the St. Louis Cardinals. The next year, he batted .300 with sixty-two RBI for St. Louis. After playing in eight games with the Philadelphia Phillies in 1952, Jones was sent to the minors and did not return until Milwaukee called him up in 1957. Five days after the '57 Series concluded, he was assigned to Wichita in the American Association. He refused to report, was released, and played in the Pacific Coast League until the end of the 1960 season. He never played again for a major league team. In a career that covered eight seasons, he had a .267 batting average and twenty-five home runs. He worked in public relations and then became a fishing guide. He died October 3, 1995 in Sacramento, California, at the age of seventy.[13]

Johnny Logan will always be a Milwaukee Brave. In fact, he was living in Milwaukee and was active in the Milwaukee Braves Historical Association in his late seventies. A good bunter, he led the National League with thirty-one sacrifices in 1956 and had 125 for his career. He led the league with thirty-seven doubles in 1955 and had 216 in his career. He spent his last two and a half years with the Pittsburgh Pirates, retiring in 1963 at the age of thirty-six. Logan played thirteen seasons in the majors, finishing with 1,407 hits, ninety-three home runs, and a lifetime .268 batting average.[14]

In 1957, Felix Mantilla played seventy-one games for Milwaukee, seeing action at second base, shortstop, third base, and in the outfield. In 1958, he played the same positions for the Braves as they returned to the World Series. He spent six years with the Braves before being selected by the New York Mets in the expansion draft in October of 1961. He batted .275 with eleven home runs, then was traded to Boston. Mantilla enjoyed his finest years with the Red Sox. He hit .289 and belted thirty home runs in 1964, then made the American League All-Star team in 1965 when he hit eighteen homers and drove in ninety-two runs. He was traded to Houston in April of 1966 and played one year with the Astros. He was released by Houston, signed by the Chicago Cubs, and then released by them in July of 1967. At the age of thirty-two, his career was over. His lifetime statistics included eighty-nine home runs and a .261 batting average.[15]

Eddie Mathews played his last major league game when he was thirty-six years old. Four years later, he was a big league manager. He took over the Atlanta Braves with fifty games left in the 1972 season and was fired with sixty-three games remaining in the 1974 campaign. In his only full season as skipper of the Braves, they finished 76–85 and in fifth place in the six-team National League West Division in 1973. Mathews experienced numerous health problems in his latter years. After being hospitalized for several months with heart problems, he died of respiratory failure and complications from pneumonia in La Jolla, California, on February 18, 2001. He was sixty-nine.[16]

After not reaching the majors until he was twenty-seven years old, Don McMahon stayed until he was forty-four and had back-to-back seasons with sixty-one appearances when he was forty and forty-one. Pitching for seven teams, he compiled a career record of 90–68 with a 2.96 earned run average and 153 saves. He served as a pitching coach with San Francisco, Minnesota, and Cleveland. McMahon was working as an instructional coach and scout with the Los Angeles Dodgers, and he pitched batting practice before most home games. He suffered a heart attack while throwing batting practice and died July 22, 1987 in L.A. at the age of fifty-seven. He had undergone heart bypass surgery three and a half years before his death.[17]

Andy Pafko played his last seven years with the Braves, retiring after the 1959 season at the age of thirty-eight. He clouted twelve or more home runs nine times, including eight years in a row from 1947–54. He hit thirty-six homers for the Cubs in 1954, when he batted a career-high .304. He had thirty roundtrippers the next season, playing for the Cubs and the Brooklyn Dodgers. He had sixteen hits in four World Series, one each with the Cubs and Dodgers and two with Milwaukee. Pafko had a fine arm and recorded twenty-four outfield assists in 1944 with the Cubs. He was the Cubs' regular third baseman in 1948. In seventeen major league seasons, he slugged 213 home runs, drove in 976 runs, and had a .285 lifetime batting average.[18]

Taylor Phillips' best year was 1956, when he posted a 5–3 record with two saves and a 2.26 earned run average in 87.1 innings as a Milwaukee rookie. He won three games and saved two for the Braves in 1957, and after the season, he was traded to the Chicago Cubs. He was primarily a starter for the Cubs, going 7–10 with a 4.76 ERA in 1958. He would only win two more games in a career that ended in 1963 at the age of thirty. Phillips had a lifetime record of 16–22.[19]

Although he totaled eleven wins that helped the Braves win back-to-back pennants in 1957 and '58, Juan Pizarro never lived up to his potential while pitching for Milwaukee. He was involved in a three-team trade in December of 1960 that landed him with the Chicago White Sox. He pitched for the ChiSox for six years, winning sixty-one games over the first four, with a high of nineteen in 1964 when he worked 239 innings and posted a 2.56 earned run average. Pizarro also pitched for the Pittsburgh Pirates, Boston Red Sox, Kansas City Athletics, Cleveland Indians, and Chicago Cubs. He retired in 1974 at the age of thirty-seven, with a lifetime record of 131–105 and a 3.43 ERA.[20]

Del Rice played with the Braves through the 1959 season, when he batted just twenty-nine times. The next year, he wore uniforms of the Chicago Cubs, St. Louis Cardinals, and Baltimore Orioles, playing a total of twenty games. Rice joined the expansion Los Angeles Angels for their inaugural season in 1961 and hit four home runs in forty-four games. He retired after that season, having caught 1,249 games in the majors. He hit seventy-nine homers and had a .237 career batting average. He was named Minor League Manager of the Year by *The Sporting News* in 1971 after leading Salt Lake City to the Pacific Coast League title. He managed the (California) Angels in 1972 when they went 75–80 and finished fifth in the six-team American League West Division. He died at the age of sixty on January 26, 1983, in Buena Park, California, while attending a dinner in his honor. He had been suffering from cancer.[21]

Carl Sawatski was traded to Philadelphia early in the 1958 season and was dealt to St. Louis after the 1959 season. He spent his last four years with the Cardinals, serving as a back-up catcher and pinch-hitter. His best overall season was 1961, when he batted .299 with ten homers. He hit a career-high thirteen home runs in 1962. Sawatski concluded an 11-year career in 1963 with fifty-eight lifetime roundtrippers and a .242 batting average. He won four home run titles in the minor leagues, clouting forty-five in 1949 when he also led the Southern Association with 153 RBI. He was the general manager of the Arkansas Travelers and was the Texas League president from 1976 until he died on November 24, 1991 in Little Rock, Arkansas. He was sixty-four.[22]

Red Schoendienst helped the Braves return to the World Series in 1958, then missed almost all of the 1959 season while battling tuberculosis. Never a full-time player again, he was a standout pinch-hitter in the late stages of his career. His last full season was 1962, when he batted .301, while playing twenty-one games at second base. In nineteen big league seasons, the Redhead amassed 2,449 hits and had a lifetime batting average of .289. He played an important part in World Series championships won by the 1946 St. Louis Cardinals and the 1957 Milwaukee Braves. Schoendienst was a coach on the Cardinals team that won the 1964 World Series and managed St. Louis to the 1967 World Series title. His Cards also won the National League pennant in 1968. His twelve-year term, from 1965–76, as the Cardinals' manager is the longest in the franchise's history.[23]

Two months after being honored with the unveiling of his statue, which stands outside of Turner Field in Atlanta, Warren Spahn was dead. The winningest left-handed pitcher in major league history had earned 356 of 363 wins with the Braves. A war hero as well as a baseball star, he won a Purple Heart, a Bronze Star, and twenty or more games thirteen times. He died at the age of eighty-two on November 24, 2003, at his home in Broken Arrow, Oklahoma after experiencing poor health for several years. Spahn had no regrets. He made a career out of a game he truly loved, and he was exceptional at what he did. He was admired and liked by both teammates and opponents.[24] "If anybody asks me who my favorite pitcher of all-time is, I say Warren Spahn," said fellow Hall of Famer and New York Yankees pitching great Whitey Ford.[25]

Frank Torre was a smooth and graceful first baseman who was a terrific fielder, making only twenty-eight errors in 3,872 major league chances. He usually managed to get his bat on the ball and struck out just sixty-four times in 1,482 at-bats, or once every twenty-three trips to the plate. Torre's lifetime batting average was a respectable .273; his fielding percentage was .993. After playing his last two years with the Philadelphia Phillies, his career ended following the 1963 season when he was thirty-one. He had a heart transplant in

October of 1996, the day before the deciding sixth game of the World Series in which his brother, Joe, managed the New York Yankees past the Atlanta Braves.[26]

The best of Bob Trowbridge's five years in the majors was 1957, when he had a 7–5 record and a 3.64 earned run average to help the Braves win the National League pennant. The right-hander pitched his only career shutout that season and worked a career-high 126 innings. He pitched for Milwaukee four years, then played one year with the Kansas City Athletics. In 1961, he went down to the minors, where he finished his career. Trowbridge's lifetime statistics included a 13–13 record and 3.95 ERA. He died of a heart attack in 1980 at the age of forty-nine.[27]

Hired in June of 1956, Fred Haney managed the Braves through the 1959 season, leading the team to records of 68–40, 95–59, 92–62, and 86–68. The Braves finished second in the 1956 National League standings, first in 1957 and 1958, and tied for first in 1959, when they lost to the Dodgers in a best-of-three playoff series. Within a week, Haney resigned with a .598 winning percentage and three (outright or shared) first-place finishes in four years as the Braves' skipper. His World Series record was 7–7 as the Braves beat the Yankees in seven games in 1957 and lost to the Yankees in seven games in 1958. He was hired as general manager of the expansion Los Angeles Angels and served in that capacity from 1961–69. After retiring, he was a consultant for the Angels. He died of a heart attack at the age of seventy-nine in Beverly Hills, California, on November 9, 1977.[28]

Chapter Notes

Chapter 1

1. Geocities.com, "What Happened in 1957?" http://www.geocities.com/rodeodrive/9925.
2. David Pietrusza, Matthew Silverman, and Michael Gershman, *Baseball: The Biographical Encyclopedia* (Kingston, NY: Total Sports Publishing, 2000), p. 1011.
3. http://atlanta.braves.mlb.com/NASA pp/mlb/atl/history/story_of_the_braves.jsp.
4. Sportscyclopedia.com, "Milwaukee Braves," http://www.sportsecyclopedia.com/nl/milbraves/milbraves.html.
5. Atlanta.braves.mlb.com.
6. *Ibid.*
7. Pietrusza, *Baseball: The Biographical Encyclopedia*, p. 879.
8. Atlanta.braves.mlb.com.
9. *Ibid.*
10. *Ibid.*
11. Netshrine.com, "A Tale of Three Cities," http://www.netshrine.com/stroup.html.
12. *Ibid.*
13. Joseph M. Sheehan, "Haney Gains Vote of Confidence As Milwaukee Retains Manager," *New York Times*, September 12, 1956.

Chapter 2

1. "Braves' Burdette Beats Redlegs On Aaron's Home Run in 6th, 1–0," *New York Times*, April 19, 1957.
2. "League Umpires Concur, He Says," *New York Times*, April 24, 1957.
3. "Fred Haney Says, 'No El Foldo,'" *The Fayetteville (NC) Observer*, April 30, 1957.
4. Arthur Daley, "Sports of the Times," *New York Times*, May 7, 1957.
5. Mike Shatzkin, *The Ballplayers: Baseball's Ultimate Biographical Reference* (New York: Arbor House, 1990), p. 232.

Chapter 3

1. Danny Peary, *We Played the Game: 65 Players Remember Baseball's Greatest Era, 1947–1964* (New York: Hyperion, 1994), p. 320.
2. *Ibid.*, p. 461.
3. Canadianbaseballnews.com, "Claude Raymond," http://www.canadianbaseballnews.com/archives/ClaudeRay.html.
4. Mike Shatzkin, *The Ballplayers: Baseball's Ultimate Biographical Reference* (New York: Arbor House, 1990), p. 1062.
5. Al Silverman, *Warren Spahn: Immortal Southpaw* (New York: Bartholomew House), pp. 48–51.
6. Fay Vincent, The Only Game in Town (New York: Simon & Schuster, 2006), p. 143.
7. Roger Kahn, *The Head Game: Baseball Seen from the Pitcher's Mound* (New York: Harcourt, 2000), p. 170.
8. Lowell Reidenbaugh, *Cooperstown: Where*

the Legends Live Forever (New York: Crescent Books, 1997), p. 262.

9. Hank Aaron with Lonnie Wheeler, *I Had a Hammer: The Hank Aaron Story* (New York: HarperTorch, 1991), p. 220.

10. Shatzkin, *The Ballplayers*, p. 1,024.

11. *Ibid.*

12. Vincent, *The Only Game in Town*, pp. 169–170.

13. Reidenbaugh, *Cooperstown*, p. 263.

14. Joseph M. Sheehan, "Spahn Sure Age Won't Blackball 300-Club Bid," *New York Times*, August 27, 1957.

15. Jane Leavy, *Sandy Koufax: A Lefty's Legacy* (New York: HarperCollins, 2003), pp. 221–222.

16. Peary, *We Played the Game*, p. 354.

17. Kahn, *The Head Game*, p. 180.

18. Elliott Kalb, *Who's Better, Who's Best in Baseball?* (New York: McGraw-Hill, 2005), pp. 216–217.

19. Aaron, *I Had a Hammer*, p. 242.

20. David Pietrusza, Matthew Silverman, and Michael Gershman, *Baseball: The Biographical Encyclopedia* (Kingston, NY: Total Sports Publishing, 2000), p. 145.

21. Peary, *We Played the Game*, p. 425.

22. Baseball-reference.com, "Lew Burdette," http://www.baseball-reference.com/bullpen/Lew_Burdette.

23. Peary, *We Played the Game*, p. 501.

24. *Ibid.*, p. 321.

25. Shatzkin, *The Ballplayers*, p. 134.

26. Baseball-reference.com, "Lew Burdette."

27. Peary, *We Played the Game*, p. 319.

28. *Ibid.*, p. 215.

29. *Ibid.*, p. 214.

30. *Ibid.*, p. 385.

31. *Ibid.*, p. 501.

Chapter 4

1. Joseph M. Sheehan, "Milwaukee Wins, 8–5, Leads League," *New York Times*, June 14, 1957.

2. David Pietrusza, Matthew Silverman, and Michael Gershman, Baseball: The Biographical Encyclopedia (Kingston, NY: Total Sports Publishing, 2000), p. 669–670.

3. Schoendienst, Red, with Bob Rains, *Red: A Baseball Life* (Champaign, IL: 1998), p. 25.

4. Arthur Daley, "Sports of the Times," *New York Times*, August 20, 1957.

5. Schoendienst, *Red*, p. 93.

6. *Ibid.*, p. 95.

7. "Schoendienst Deal Rated Cheer That Made Milwaukee Famous," *New York Times*, September 24, 1957.

8. Bill James, *The New Bill James Historical Baseball Abstract* (New York: Free Press, 2001), p. 501.

9. John Drebinger, "Milwaukee Rallies for Six Runs in Eighth to Trip Brooks, 13–9," *New York Times*, June 27, 1957.

10. Pietrusza et al., *Baseball*, p. 761.

Chapter 5

1. Michael Strauss, "Frick Sidetracks Three Redlegs After Avalanche of Ohio Votes," *New York Times*, June 29, 1957.

2. *Ibid.*

3. "Logan Homer Helps Braves Triumph, 7–2," *New York Times*, July 12, 1957.

4. "2 Return to Milwaukee," *New York Times*, July 13, 1957.

5. "2 Braves Sent Home," *New York Times*, July 14, 1957.

6. "A Magical Whirlwind for Hurricane Hazle," *The (Columbia, SC) State*, July 26, 2004.

Chapter 6

1. Danny Peary, *We Played the Game: 65 Players Remember Baseball's Greatest Era, 1947–1964* (New York: Hyperion, 1994), p. 320.

2. Hank Aaron with Lonnie Wheeler, *I Had a Hammer: The Hank Aaron Story* (New York: HarperTorch, 1991), p. 167.

3. *Ibid.*, p. 168.

4. *Ibid.*, p. 169.

5. *Ibid.*, p. 241.

6. Fay Vincent, *The Only Game in Town* (New York: Simon & Schuster, 2006), pp. 168–169.

7. David Pietrusza, Matthew Silverman, and Michael Gershman, *Baseball: The Biographical Encyclopedia* (Kingston, NY: Total Sports Publishing, 2000), pp. 1–2.

8. Thad Mumau column, *The Fayetteville (NC) Observer*, April 9, 1974.

9. Aaron, *I Had a Hammer*, p. 326.

10. http://www.answers.com/topic/hand-aaron.

11. Geoffrey C. Ward and Ken Burns, *Baseball: An Illustrated History* (New York: Alfred A. Knopf, 1994), p. 429.

12. Atlanta Braves Media Relations Department, 2005 Braves Media Guide (Atlanta: ProGraphics), p. 11.

13. Elliott Kalb, *Who's Better, Who's Best in Baseball?* (New York: McGraw-Hill, 2005), p. 37.

14. Tom Haudricourt, "Fierce Competitor — Eddie Matthews Overlooked As One of the Game's Greats," *Baseball Digest*, June 2001, p. 74.

15. Pietrusza et al., *Baseball*, pp. 720–721.

16. Kalb, *Who's Better*, p. 273.

17. Pietrusza et al., *Baseball*, p. 720.

18. Mike Shatzkin, *The Ballplayers: Baseball's Ultimate Biographical Reference* (New York: Arbor House, 1990), pp. 680–681.

19. Haudricourt, "Fierce Competitor," p. 72.

20. *Ibid.*, p. 74.

21. *Ibid.*, p. 72.

22. *Ibid.*, p. 73.

23. *Ibid.*, p. 76.

24. *Ibid.*, p. 75.

25. *Ibid.*

Chapter 7

1. Tri-CityHerald.com, "Richland's Conley Set Standard Yet Unequaled for 2-Sport Athlete," http://richlandbombers.1948.tripod.com/Conley/1999–12–30TCHtop100.htm.

2. Baseball-almanac.com, "1955 All-Star Game," http://www.baseball-almanac.com/asgbox/yr1955as.shtml.

3. "Aaron Charges Card Pitchers Deliberately Throw at His Head," *New York Times*, August 18, 1957.

4. "Aaron Bean-Ball Charge Denied by St. Louisans," *New York Times*, August 19, 1957.

Chapter 8

1. Msnbc.com, "Stone Phillips' Interview with Joe Torre," http://www.msnbc.msn.com.

2. David Pietrusza, Matthew Silverman, and Michael Gershman, *Baseball: The Biographical Encyclopedia* (Kingston, NY: Total Sports Publishing, 2000), pp. 8–9.

3. *Ibid.*, pp. 554–555.

4. Hank Aaron with Lonnie Wheeler, *I Had a Hammer: The Hank Aaron Story* (New York: HarperTorch, 1991), p. 172.

5. *Ibid.*, p. 173.

Chapter 9

1. Danny Peary, *We Played the Game: 65 Players Remember Baseball's Greatest Era, 1947–1964* (New York: Hyperion, 1994), p. 319.

2. Hank Aaron with Lonnie Wheeler, *I Had a Hammer: The Hank Aaron Story* (New York: HarperTorch, 1991), pp. 164–165.

3. Roscoe McGowen, "Confident Haney Predicts Victory," *New York Times*, October 1, 1957.

Chapter 10

1. Roscoe McGowen, "Screwball Got Pitcher Out of Crucial Situation, Crandall of the Braves Says," *New York Times*, October 4, 1957.

2. Mickey Mantle and Herb Gluck, *The Mick* (New York: Doubleday, 1985), p. 173.

3. Roscoe McGowen, "Shoe Polish Mark on Ball Leads Umpire to Reverse Decision on Jones in 10th," *New York Times*, October 7, 1957.

4. Roscoe McGowen, "Happy Ending of 'Milwaukee Story' Celebrated Amid Dressing Room Bedlam," *New York Times*, October 11, 1957.

5. Elliott Kalb, *Who's Better, Who's Best in Baseball?* (New York: McGraw-Hill, 2005), p. 274.

6. "Pitcher with Last Laugh," *New York Times*, October 11, 1957.

7. Red Smith, *On Baseball: The Game's Greatest Writer on the Game's Greatest Years* (Chicago: Ivan R. Dee, 2000), p. 228.

8. Louis Effrat, "Yankees Pay Tribute to Pitching Artistry of Braves' Three-Game Winner," *New York Times*, October 11, 1957.

9. *Ibid.*

Chapter 11

1. Red Smith, *On Baseball: The Game's Greatest Writer on the Game's Greatest Years* (Chicago: Ivan R. Dee, 2000), p. 243.

2. "Haney Quits as Pilot of Braves to Have More Time for Family," *New York Times*, October 5, 1959.

3. "Dressen Signs 2-Year Contract to Manage Braves," *New York Times*, October 24, 1959.

Chapter 12

1. Letter from Bud Selig, June 13, 2006.

2. Atlanta Braves Media Relations Department, 2005 Braves Media Guide (Atlanta: ProGraphics), p. 11.

3. Mike Shatzkin, *The Ballplayers: Baseball's Ultimate Biographical Reference* (New York: Arbor House, 1990), p. 6.

4. David Pietrusza, Matthew Silverman, and Michael Gershman, *Baseball: The Biographical Encyclopedia* (Kingston, NY: Total Sports Publishing, 2000), p. 139.

5. *Ibid.*, p. 142.

6. *Ibid.*, p. 144.

7. *Ibid.*, p. 232.

8. Shatzkin, *The Ballplayers*, p. 229.

9. Pietrusza et al., *Baseball*, p. 244.

10. *Ibid.*, p. 480.

11. Baseball-reference.com, "Ernie Johnson," http://www.baseball-reference.com/bullpen/Ernie_Johnson.

12. Baseball-reference.com, "Dave Jolly," http://www.baseball-reference.com/bullpen/Dave_Jolly.

13. Pietrusza et al., *Baseball*, p. 574.

14. *Ibid.*, p. 669.

15. *Ibid.*, p. 703.

16. Shatzkin, *The Ballplayers*, pp. 680–681.

17. Pietrusza et al., *Baseball*, p. 761.

18. *Ibid.*, pp. 859–860.

19. Baseball-reference.com, "Taylor Phillips," http://www.baseball-reference.com/bullpen/Taylor_Phillips.

20. Pietrusza et al., *Baseball*, p. 893.

21. "Del Rie, a Former Manager and Baseball Player, Is Dead," *New York Times*, January 28, 1983.

22. Baseball-reference.com, "Carl Sawatski," http://www.baseball-reference.com/bullpen/Carl_Sawatski.

23. Pietrusza et al., *Baseball*, p. 1007.

24. Richard Goldstein, "Warren Spahn, 82, Dies; Left-Handed Craftsman of the Baseball Mound for 21 Seasons," *New York Times*, November 25, 2003.

25. *Ibid.*

26. Pietrusza et al., *Baseball*, p. 1137.

27. "Obituary, Bob Trowbridge," *New York Times*, April 5, 1980.

28. Pietrusza et al., *Baseball*, p. 464.

Bibliography

Periodicals

Baseball Digest 2001
The Fayetteville Observer (Fayetteville, NC) 1974
The State (Columbia, SC) 2004
The New York Times 1956–1959

Books

Aaron, Hank, and Lonnie Wheeler. *I Had a Hammer: The Hank Aaron Story*. New York: HarperTorch, 1992.

James, Bill. *The New Bill James Historical Baseball Abstract*. New York: Free Press, 2001.

Kahn, Roger. *The Head Game*. New York: Harcourt, 2000.

Kalb, Elliott. *Who's Better, Who's Best in Baseball?* New York: McGraw-Hill, 2005.

Leavy, Jane. *Sandy Koufax: A Lefty's Legacy*. New York: HarperCollins, 2003.

Mantle, Mickey, and Herb Gluck. *The Mick*. New York: Doubleday, 1985.

Peary, Danny (ed.). *We Played the Game: 65 Players Remember Baseball's Greatest Era, 1947–1964*. New York: Hyperion, 1994.

Pietrusza, David, Matthew Silverman, and Michael Gershman. *Baseball: The Biographical Encyclopedia*. Kingston, NY: Total Sports Publishing, 2000.

Reidenbaugh, Lowell. *Cooperstown, Where the Legends Live Forever*. New York: Crescent Books, 1997.

Schoendienst, Red, with Bob Rains. *Red: A Baseball Life*. Champaign, IL: SportsPublishing, 1998.

Shatzkin, Mike. *The Ballplayers*. New York: Arbor House, 1990.

Silverman, Al. *Warren Spahn: Immortal Southpaw*. New York: Bartholomew House, 1961.

Smith, Red. *On Baseball: The Game's Greatest Writer on the Game's Greatest Years*. Chicago: Ivan R. Dee, 2000.

Vincent, Fay. *The Only Game in Town*. New York: Simon & Schuster, 2006.

Ward, Geoffrey C., and Ken Burns. *Baseball: An Illustrated History*. Based on a documentary filmscript by Geoffrey C. Ward and Ken Burns. New York: Alfred A. Knopf, 1994.

Websites

http://www.answers.com/topic/hand-aaron
http://atlanta.braves.mlb.com/NASApp/mlb/atl/history/story_of_the_braves.jsp
Baseball-almanac.com
Baseball-reference.com
Canadianbaseballnews.com, "Claude Raymond," http://www.canadianbaseballnews.com/
    archives/ClaudeRay.html
Geocities.com
msnbc.msn.com
Netshrine.com
Sportsecyclopedia.com
Tri-CityHerald.com

Correspondence

Letter to author from Bud Selig, June 13, 2006

Index

213